Inflation, Stabilization, and Debt

Inflation, Stabilization, and Debt

Macroeconomic Experiments in Peru and Bolivia

Manuel Pastor, Jr.

Westview Press
BOULDER • SAN FRANCISCO • OXFORD

Westview Special Studies on Latin America and the Caribbean

This Westview softcover edition is printed on acid-free paper and bound in library-quality, coated covers that carry the highest rating of the National Association of State Textbook Administrators, in consultation with the Association of American Publishers and the Book Manufacturers' Institute.

All rights reserved. No part of this publication may be reproduced or transmitted in any form or by any means, electronic or mechanical, including photocopy, recording, or any information storage and retrieval system, without permission in writing from the publisher.

Copyright © 1992 by Westview Press, Inc.

Published in 1992 in the United States of America by Westview Press, Inc., 5500 Central Avenue, Boulder, Colorado 80301-2877, and in the United Kingdom by Westview Press, 36 Lonsdale Road, Summertown, Oxford OX2 7EW

Library of Congress Cataloging-in-Publication Data
Pastor, Manuel.
  Inflation, stabilization, and debt : macroeconomic experiments in
    Peru and Bolivia / Manuel Pastor, Jr.
      p. cm. — (Westview special studies on Latin America and the
  Caribbean)
  Includes bibliographical references and index.
  ISBN 0-8133-7765-X
  1. Peru—Economic policy. 2. Bolivia—Economic policy.
3. Structural adjustment (Economic policy)—Peru. 4. Structural
adjustment (Economic policy)—Bolivia. 5. Economic stabilization—
Peru. 6. Economic stabilization—Bolivia. I. Series.
  HC227.P37 1992
  338.985—dc20   92-18756
                                                                  CIP

Printed and bound in the United States of America

The paper used in this publication meets the requirements of the American National Standard for Permanence of Paper for Printed Library Materials Z39.48-1984.

10 9 8 7 6 5 4 3 2 1

In memory of Alex de Secada

Contents

List of Tables ix
List of Figures xi
Acknowledgments xiii

1 Macroeconomic Experiments in the 1980s 1

Introduction, 1
The Peruvian and Bolivian Experiments, 5
The Foci of Analysis, 6
Plan of the Book, 10
Notes, 13

**2 The Macroeconomics of Adjustment:
Orthodox Views** 15

Introduction, 15
Orthodox Stabilization and Adjustment, 16
Conclusion: Realism, Class, and Orthodoxy, 34
Notes, 36

**3 The Macroeconomics of Adjustment:
A Structuralist Model** 39

Introduction, 39
A Simple Model, 40
A Fuller Model, 48
Inflation Dynamics, Credibility, and Sequencing, 57
Conclusion: Heterodoxy and Class, 61
Notes, 62

4 Bolivia: Hyperinflation and Stabilization 67

Introduction, 67
Origins and Dynamics of the Bolivian Hyperinflation, 68
The New Economic Policy (NEP), 87

Conclusion, 99
Notes, 101

5 Peru: Stabilization and Hyperinflation — 107

Introduction, 107
Orthodox Strategy in Peru, 1980–1985, 108
The Rise and Fall of Peruvian Heterodoxy, 118
Conclusion: Requiem for Heterodoxy? 136
Notes, 138

6 Evaluating the Experiments — 143

Introduction, 143
Orthodoxy Versus Heterodoxy: Short-term Adjustment, 144
External Constraints and Debt, 149
Politics and Stabilization, 151
Toward the Long Run, 154
Conclusion, 156
Notes, 157

Bibliography — 159
Index — 169

Tables

1.1	Macroeconomic performance in Argentina and Brazil, 1982–1989	3
1.2	Macroeconomic performance in Mexico, 1982–1989	4
1.3	Inflation, growth, deficits, wages, and trade in Peru and Bolivia, 1982–1989	6
2.1	The effects of exchange rate targeting in Argentina	30
2.2	The effects of exchange rate targeting in Chile	31
2.3	The effects of exchange rate targeting in Uruguay	32
3.1	The structure of Peruvian trade, 1980–1985	45
3.2	Macroeconomic and other data for Peru, 1980–1985	46
3.3	Productive structure of the augmented model	50
3.4	Symbols and abbreviations in the augmented model	51
4.1	Macroeconomic data for Bolivia, 1980–1989	70
4.2	Tin prices, tin volume, and net capital flows to Bolivia, 1980–1989	76
4.3	Fiscal operations in Bolivia, 1980–1989	78
4.4	Monetary growth and its components, 1980–1989	83
4.5	Results for Granger-Sims causality tests on prices, money, and the exchange rate (Bolivia)	85
4.6	The determinants of hyperinflation in Bolivia	86
4.7	Real exchange rate indices for Bolivia, 1982–1988	93
4.8	Results for Granger-Sims causality tests on prices, money, and the exchange rate in the NEP period	95
4.9	The determinants of inflation in the NEP period	96
4.10	Real monetary aggregates and the composition of quasi-money	97
5.1	Sectoral composition of the Peruvian economy, 1980–1989	109
5.2	Investment in Peru, 1980–1989	112
5.3	Macroeconomic performance in Peru, 1980–1989	116

5.4	Trade, reserves, and debt service in Peru, 1980–1989	117
5.5	Real wages and distribution in Peru, 1980–1989	119
5.6	Public sector finances in Peru, 1980–1988	124
5.7	Results for Granger-Sims causality tests on prices, money, and the exchange rate (Peru)	131
5.8	The determinants of hyperinflation in Peru	134
6.1	Latin American economic performance, 1980–1989	146

Figures

2.1	Production possibilities frontier and social indifference curve for tradeables and non-tradeables	22
2.2	Excess absorption, trade deficit, and a shift in the composition of output	23
3.1	Macro equilibrium and trade deficit in a simple structuralist model	43
3.2	The effects of devaluation on equilibrium output and the trade deficit in a simple structuralist model	44
3.3	Net debt flows and payments balance in a simple structuralist model	47
3.4	Macro equilibrium and trade deficit in a fuller structuralist model	55
4.1	Macro equilibrium and payments balance in a Bolivian-style economy	73
4.2	The effects of falling export revenues in a Bolivian-style economy	74
4.3	The effects of a "capital shock" in a Bolivian-style economy	74
4.4	GDP and wages in Bolivia, 1982–1986	81
5.1	Monthly inflation in Peru, January 1985 to July 1990	129

Acknowledgments

All books take time and energy. This book seems to have taken inordinate amounts of each, reflecting the strong attachment I have developed over these years to the peoples of Peru and Bolivia and the concern I now share over their fate.

Both countries entered the 1980s already buffeted by debt problems and wracked by histories of social inequality and military rule. In the decade that ensued, political leaders whipsawed each nation through some of the most dramatic policy swings seen anywhere in Latin America. Through it all, the poor and working classes of these Andean neighbors struggled to make their lives bearable and their futures brighter. It is to these people—who played little role in the decision making over macroeconomic strategy but who most strongly felt its effects—that this book is dedicated.

The research presented here began as a comparative study supported by the Fulbright Commission in Lima, Peru; for their constant support over the last four years, I thank the director, Marcia Koth de Paredes, and the rest of the staff. In Peru, institutional support was provided by the Instituto de Estudios Peruanos and the Universidad del Pacífico, both in Lima; in Bolivia, by the Universidad Católica and the United States Information Service, both in La Paz. Subsequent funding and support for completion of the study in the United States came from the Guggenheim Foundation and Occidental College. I also acknowledge the able research assistance of Todd Clark, Carolina Lau, and Mark Marriott; special thanks on this front to Eric Hilt, who helped push the manuscript to completion while working on a grant from the Ford Foundation.

In each country, I had significant help in developing my analysis and obtaining data. In Bolivia, I especially thank Samuel Doria Medina, Arthur Mann, Juan Antonio Morales, and Herbert Müller. In Peru, I thank Luis Arreaga, Mercedes Inés Carazo, Daniel Carbonetto, Jorge Chavez Alvarez, Oscar Dancourt, Efraín Gonzales, César Herrera, Jenny Hoyle Cox, Esteban Hynilizca, Jürgen Schuldt, Julio Velarde, and many others who provided both insightful comments and moral support. In the United States, I thank Sam Bowles, Jeff Frieden, Keith Griffin, Robby Moore, Jeffrey Sachs, Woody Studenmund, Jim Whitney, and John Williamson as well as the anonymous referees who commented on parts of this work that went out early as articles.

As noted, some of the analysis in this book has appeared in modified form in earlier articles. The heterodox modeling of Chapter 3 was originally presented (in a more detailed exposition) in my article, "Ascenso y Caída de la Heterodoxia Peruana: Un Modelo Simple del Nuevo Estructuralismo," which was published in *Apuntes* (23, 2). Much of the analysis of Bolivia presented in Chapter 4 is taken from my article, "Bolivia: Hyperinflation, Stabilization, and Beyond," which appeared in the *Journal of Development Studies* (27, 2); the coverage in the book differs in that I include here a simple model of the Bolivian economy, a longer historical review, and a revision of the econometric results to reflect new data. The chapter on Peru draws upon my article (coauthored with Carol Wise) entitled "Peruvian Economic Policy in the 1980s: From Orthodoxy to Heterodoxy and Back," which appeared in *Latin American Research Review* (*LARR*) (27, 2); the review here differs substantially in that I am more focused on economic issues and include a variety of econometric exercises that were not appropriate for the *Review* readership. For allowing me the permission to draw upon the earlier work in this volume, I thank the editors associated with *Apuntes* and the Universidad del Pacífico; the editors of the *Journal of Development Studies* and Frank Cass Publishers; and the editors of *Latin American Research Review*.

Special thanks go to my sometime coauthor, Carol Wise, whom I first met in Lima in 1987. Over the last five years, she helped me understand that politics and state capacity really matter, an insight that sharpened my analysis in both this study and others. In addition, she was a sporting dinner partner during those less-than-exciting moments in Lima and has remained a good friend since. She graciously granted me permission to use material from our *LARR* article, and we continue to work together on a variety of research projects.

Finally, a word about my family. I have been sustained in my research by my father's pride and my mother's concern; the latter worries when I trek off to such "dangerous" countries but accepts the passion and curiosity that drive my travels. My wife, Betsy Hamilton, has been a constant source of support and love; my children, Joaquín Tomás and Anna Eliza, have brought me immeasurable joy even as they derailed my progress on this book and other academic projects. Ultimately, it seems, love matters more than science, family more than publication. To those who remind me of this daily, I offer my most profound appreciation.

Manuel Pastor, Jr.

1

Macroeconomic Experiments in the 1980s

Introduction

The 1980s have been an era of profound changes in macroeconomic policy in Latin America. Wracked by the economic and political stress produced by the need to service nearly half a trillion dollars of external debt, the region has become a laboratory for old and new cures to the problems of slow growth, high inflation, and an unequal distribution of income.

The initial years of the debt crisis brought a resurgence of monetarist and conservative strategies. This turn toward *orthodoxy*—a paradigm that celebrates market mechanisms and generally insists on budget tightening, monetary restraint, currency devaluation, and real wage declines—was not entirely voluntary. International bankers, nervous about the possibilities of debt moratoria and concerned about the consequences of Latin American domestic disequilibria, required that debtors adopt programs designed by the international institution most closely associated with orthodox thinking, the International Monetary Fund (IMF). Debtors had little choice: Needing both the short-term balance of payments support promised by the IMF and the private debt rescheduling that tended to follow in the wake of an IMF program, virtually all Latin American debtors signed formal agreements with the Fund.

By mid-decade, however, Fund-style orthodoxy seemed to have lost what little appeal it ever had in the region. Orthodox policies had been largely unsuccessful at restraining inflation even as output continued to stagnate. And despite domestic austerity, international banks offered little more than "involuntary" lending designed primarily to keep debtors current on old loans and thereby avoid the specter of default.

In summer and fall 1985, Latin American macroeconomic policy took a new direction. In Argentina and later in Brazil, new stabilization programs were launched without the initial blessing or guidance of the IMF. A new name—*heterodoxy*—was adopted to describe the unique features essential to the programs: incomes policies (i.e., wage-price controls), monetary reform (including the creation of new currencies), and a spoken (though often ignored) commitment to restrain demand through the reduction of government deficits.

The logic of the new heterodox programs challenged the orthodox analysis that the domestic inflation plaguing Latin America was largely the result of excess demand and could therefore be stopped by simply restraining monetary growth. Instead, argued the heterodox theorists, Latin American economies were characterized by *inertial* inflation: *Current* inflation was tied to *past* inflation through a system of formal and informal indexing. This phenomenon presented both dangers and opportunities. If inertial inflation was important, then the orthodox strategy was extremely costly, requiring a sustained recession that would convince economic agents to lower their expectations of inflation and rewrite wage and supplier contracts accordingly. In the meantime, the idling of capital and labor would generate inefficiencies and exacerbate social conflicts. On the other hand, the presence of inertial inflation and indexing presented a unique opportunity: If the government could simply freeze wages and prices, it could stop the spiral directly without incurring the recessionary costs. In addition, wage-price controls (or incomes policies) could make explicit the distributional burdens of adjustment and perhaps help to produce the political consensus necessary for stabilization. The other heterodox policies described above were important for making the basic incomes policy successful: A new currency would invalidate old contracts and allow the quick rewriting of noninflationary contracts while the promised fiscal restraint would lower demand to a level consistent with a lower rate of price increase. The new currency measures were viewed as especially important; indeed, the Argentine and Brazilian policy packages derived their popular names—the Austral and Cruzado programs—from the new currencies adopted.

The early results of heterodox economic policy were impressive in both Argentina and Brazil. Inflation was substantially reduced in both countries with little decrease in economic activity in Argentina and a significant improvement in both output and income distribution in Brazil (see Table 1.1). However, inflation soon resumed and output once again stagnated, particularly in Argentina. By 1989, hyperinflation was well under way in both countries, belying the promises of macroeconomic stability and tarnishing the image of heterodoxy.

The return of inflation did not resolve the debate between orthodox and heterodox approaches. Proponents of heterodoxy claimed that their policies had never really been tested, suggesting in particular that fiscal restraint had been promised but not pursued in either country. These critics pointed to Mexico, a country that reversed its accelerating inflation by adopting a unique brand of "quasi-heterodoxy": the coupling of heterodox incomes policies with tighter government budgets and freer external markets. This program halved inflation in 1988 with a surprisingly low reduction in growth, particularly given the concurrent slip in oil prices (see Table 1.2).[1] The Mexican case, however, simply muddied the analytical waters: Exponents of heterodoxy could claim that their half of the pro-

Table 1.1
Macroeconomic Performance in Argentina and Brazil, 1982-1989

	GDP Growth (annual % change)	Inflation (Dec. to Dec.)	Public Sector Deficit (as % of GDP)	Real Wage Index (1981=100)	Exports (FOB) (US$ mil.)	Imports (FOB) (US$ mil.)	External Debt (US$ mil.)	External Debt (% of GNP)
Argentina								
1982	-5.5	209.7	15.0	89.6	7,623	4,859	43,634	83.8
1983	2.9	433.7	14.5	112.4	7,835	7,119	45,920	77.3
1984	2.4	688.0	11.6	142.2	8,100	4,118	48,857	67.5
1985	-4.3	385.4	5.7	120.6	8,396	3,518	50,947	84.2
1986	5.6	81.9	4.9	122.5	6,852	4,406	54,374	70.4
1987	2.2	174.8	6.6	115.2	6,360	5,392	58,423	76.0
1988	-2.7	387.7	9.0	108.8	9,134	4,900	58,936	60.5
1989	-6.0	4,923.8	8.3	82.9	9,573	3,864	59,645	---
Brazil								
1982	0.7	100.3	6.6	112.1	20,173	19,395	62,221	35.8
1983	-3.4	178.0	3.0	103.9	21,898	15,429	97,496	50.1
1984	5.0	209.1	2.7	96.9	27,002	13,916	104,331	52.3
1985	8.3	239.1	4.3	103.9	25,634	13,168	104,593	48.2
1986	7.5	58.6	3.6	112.3	22,348	14,044	112,042	41.7
1987	3.6	396.0	5.5	94.4	26,210	15,052	123,865	39.4
1988	0.0	994.3	4.3	98.7	33,773	14,605	114,592	30.7
1989	3.6	1,910.6	12.4	98.8	34,392	18,281	114,572	---

Sources: For both countries, 1982-1983 GDP growth calculated from figures for real GDP at market prices; data taken from the data files of the World Bank as reported in *World Tables, 1989-90 Edition*. Argentina's 1984-1989 GDP growth from *The Economist Intelligence Unit, Country Profile 1990-91*, p. 10; Brazil's 1984-1989 GDP growth from *The Economist Intelligence Unit, Country Profile 1990-91*, p. 14. Inflation and the real wage index for both countries from the United Nation's *Estudio Económico de América Latina y El Caribe 1989*, pp. 64, 73, and 261; the Brazilian real wage series is for Rio de Janeiro. Argentina's public sector deficit is from the Inter-American Development Bank's *Economic and Social Progress in Latin America, 1990 Report*, p. 41. Brazil's 1981-1988 public sector deficit from the figures for the operational deficit in Cardoso and Dantas (1990:142), with the 1989 public sector deficit ratio from *Estudio Económico de América Latina y El Caribe 1989*, p. 281. Imports and exports from the International Monetary Fund's *International Financial Statistics Yearbook 1990* and *International Financial Statistics*, February 1991; Brazil's 1989 imports and exports from *The Economist Intelligence Unit, Country Profile 1990-91*, p. 42. Total external debt from *Economic and Social Progress in Latin America, 1990 Report*, pp. 41 and 147. Debt/GNP figures from the World Bank's *World Debt Tables, 1989-90*, Vol. 2, pp. 6 and 42. "---" indicates that the data were unavailable.

Table 1.2
Macroeconomic Performance in Mexico, 1982-1989

	GDP Growth (annual % change)	Inflation (Dec. to Dec.)	Public Sector Deficit (as % of GDP)	Real Wage Index (1981=100)	Exports (FOB) (US$ mil.)	Imports (FOB) (US$ mil.)	External Debt (US$ mil.)	External Debt (% of GNP)
1982	-0.6	98.8	16.9	98.7	21,230	14,435	86,019	52.5
1983	-4.2	80.8	8.6	78.0	22,312	8,550	92,964	66.4
1984	3.6	59.2	8.5	72.9	24,196	11,255	94,822	57.1
1985	2.6	63.7	9.6	74.0	21,663	13,212	96,875	54.9
1986	-3.7	105.7	16.0	69.9	16,031	11,432	100,876	82.3
1987	1.6	159.2	16.0	70.3	20,655	12,222	109,292	77.8
1988	1.4	51.7	12.3	69.7	20,657	18,905	101,566	58.0
1989	2.9	19.7	5.8	73.2	22,765	23,410	95,880	47.2

Sources: 1982-1983 GDP growth calculated from figures for real GDP at market prices; data taken from the data files of the World Bank as reported in *World Tables, 1989-90 Edition.* 1984-1989 GDP growth from *The Economist Intelligence Unit, Country Profile 1990-91*, p. 14. Inflation and the real wage index from United Nations' *Estudio Económico de América Latina y El Caribe 1989*, pp. 64 and 73. Public sector deficit figures from the Inter-American Development Bank's *Economic and Social Progress in Latin America, 1990 Report*, p. 147. Imports and exports from the International Monetary Fund's *International Financial Statistics Yearbook 1990* and *International Financial Statistics*, February 1991. Total external debt from *Economic and Social Progress in Latin America, 1990 Report*, p. 67. 1982-1988 debt/GNP figures from the World Bank's *World Debt Tables, 1989-90*, Vol. 2, p. 42; 1989 debt/GNP figure from *The Economist Intelligence Unit, Country Profile 1990-91*, p. 38.

gram delivered the telling blow to inflationary pressures, whereas orthodox economists could argue that their half worked the magic.

The Peruvian and Bolivian Experiments

Assessing the merits of orthodox and heterodox adjustment may be easier if we shift attention from the well-publicized large country cases to a set of macroeconomic experiments conducted in two smaller nations: Peru and Bolivia. In the same years that brought the Austral and Cruzado plans, both Peru and Bolivia inaugurated new presidents and new policy. Peru, suffering from economic dislocations under the relatively orthodox regime of Fernando Belaúnde Terry, elected Alan García to the presidency. The new president promptly adopted a particularly strong form of heterodoxy: Incomes policy was tilted toward increasing worker wages at the expense of profits, debt service was explicitly limited in order to relax external constraints, and fiscal deficits were applauded as a way to increase domestic demand. Bolivia, staggering from a hyperinflation produced during a leftist regime whose initial policies were vaguely heterodox, elected ex-President Victor Paz Estenssoro. Despite his involvement in the progressive and nationalist revolution of 1952, the new president adopted an economic program more orthodox than any seen in Latin America since the heyday of Chilean monetarism: Most significant government controls on the economy were lifted, fiscal deficits and monetary creation were dramatically reduced, and wages were allowed to plunge dramatically.

The results for each country were decidedly mixed. In 1986, the first full year of the heterodox program, Peru was able to post the highest growth rate in Latin America, cut inflation by half, and redistribute income in a progressive direction (see Table 1.3). In the subsequent two years, however, growth slowed, inflation reheated, and the distributional victories were reversed. By late 1988, Peru was isolated internationally, crumbling politically, and in the throes of a hyperinflation. Bolivia, on the other hand, had become a minor darling of both the international financial community and orthodox economic scholars. The so-called Miracle of La Paz had brought annual inflation below 20 percent (see Table 1.3), and Bolivian authorities sought and received significant new credit flows from official lenders. Yet the apparent success was tenuous: Growth remained stagnant, wages were perilously low, malnutrition and starvation were on the rise, and an overvalued currency, rising trade deficit, and renewed dependence on foreign credit seemed to threaten the future of the economic program.

What do the experiences of Peru and Bolivia tell us about small country adjustment in the era of debt crisis? What does each country's passage into hyperinflation tell us about the dynamics and determinants of this unfortunate economic phenomenon? And what does a comparison of the two cases tell us about the relative merits of heterodoxy and orthodoxy?

Table 1.3
Inflation, Growth, Deficits, Wages, and Trade in Peru and Bolivia, 1982-1989

	Inflation Rate (percent)	GDP Growth (percent)	Public Sector Deficit (% of GDP)	Real Wage Growth (percent)	Exports (FOB) (US$ mil.)	Imports (FOB) (US$ mil.)	Trade Balance (US$ mil.)
Peru							
1982	72.9	0.3	-7.3	0.0	3,293	3,722	-429
1983	125.1	-12.3	-9.8	-17.0	3,015	2,722	293
1984	111.4	4.8	-6.1	-14.7	3,147	2,140	1,007
1985	158.3	2.4	-2.4	-13.8	2,978	1,806	1,172
1986	62.9	9.5	-4.9	36.0	2,531	2,596	-65
1987	114.5	7.8	-6.5	8.8	2,661	3,182	-521
1988	1722.3	-8.8	-5.8	-35.2	2,695	2,750	-56
1989	2775.6	-10.4	---	-20.8	3,540	2,141	1,399
Bolivia							
1982	296.5	-4.4	14.2	-17.9	828	-578	250
1983	328.6	-4.5	17.0	-5.0	755	-589	166
1984	2177.2	-0.6	21.2	-3.6	720	-492	228
1985	8170.5	-1.0	8.1	-2.9	628	-691	-63
1986	66.0	-2.5	2.3	-6.1	588	-674	-87
1987	10.7	2.6	6.7	-11.9	519	-766	-248
1988	21.5	3.0	5.5	---	543	-700	-158
1989	16.6	2.7	4.5	---	724	-786	-63

Sources: For Peru, inflation rates, public finance, wages, and trade come from Cuánto (1990a); GDP growth is from the Instituto Nacional de Estadística (INE) (1988, 1989, 1990). For Bolivia, inflation rates for 1982 and 1983 from Müller (1988a), for 1984-1989 from Unidad de Análisis de Políticas Económicas (UDAPE) (1990:184). GDP growth, public sector deficit, and trade from UDAPE (1990); real wage growth for 1982 from R. Morales (1987), for 1983-1986 from UDAPE (1987), and for 1987 from Horton (1991). "---" indicates that the data were unavailable.

The Foci of Analysis

In what follows, I attempt to address the above questions as well as to offer some new insights into the processes of inflation and stabilization in the Latin American debt crisis. Throughout the analysis, four foci dominate the discussion: external flows, particularly those related to international debt; political considerations, including the distributional consequences and class basis of adjustment policies; the technical consistency and coherence of stabilization measures; and the relationship between short-run stabilization and the restructuring of a longer-run accumulation model.

Successful stabilization requires that governments address each of these issues. Programs may be technically elegant but politically unsustainable; they may build domestic coalitions but collapse due to a shortage of external resources; or they may end inflation while laying the groundwork for a future financial explosion and growth slowdown. Debt flows and class alliances are as central as any more technical measures involving budget deficits and monetary growth. Stabilization requires that small countries strike deals in international capital markets—be they to restrict payments or to attract credit flows—and form domestic coalitions—be they tilted toward the interests of popular classes or private capital. To understand policy "mistakes" such as excessive deficits or overvalued exchange rates, observers need to consider the backdrop of external and class pressures that make small country adjustment either possible or problematic.

The four foci detailed above—external flows, income distribution, technical consistency, and long-run viability—are therefore crucial to the analysis of each country's experience. The first, the external sector, was a critical determinant of the hyperinflation and stabilization in both Bolivia and Peru. Bolivia's passage into hyperinflation, for example, was related to the regional fall in external debt flows and the consequent shortage of foreign exchange. The Bolivian government, accustomed to external financing of government deficits, found itself forced to resort to domestic monetary creation even as falling international reserves required correctionary devaluations and thus added to the inflationary pressures. Ending the Bolivian hyperinflation necessitated the defense of the exchange rate, which in turn required actions to restore capital flows by raising domestic interest rates and adopting the sort of orthodox economic package that would attract the support of international institutions.

For Peru, the external sector was equally important. The attempt in the early 1980s to service the pressing external debt led the conservative government of President Belaúnde to pursue a course of inflation-inducing devaluation. The trade balance improved and the external debt was mostly serviced, but output and wages slumped even as inflation drifted upward. When Alan García swept into power in late 1985, he made the unilateral restriction of debt service the centerpiece of his economic policy. The rationale was straightforward: By slowing the external drain of resources, Peru could avoid devaluation even as it increased the importation of goods needed for economic growth. This debt strategy and the resulting reactivation of the economy brought new hope to the country, but the end result was a slide into hyperinflation. The unilateral debt restrictions angered international bankers, and Peru found itself cut off from new external finance even as the growth-driven import boom consumed the government's international reserves. The loss of reserves triggered fears of future devaluation and, hence, capital flight. The pressure on the exchange rate combined with large government deficits and pushed inflation upward.

The second focus of this analysis, the class character of each program, is especially important for an understanding of the dynamics of hyperinflation and stabilization in Peru and Bolivia. Bolivian politics in 1983–1985 were marked by a sort of class stalemate: Workers were able to persuade the government to mandate higher wages, but the government was unable to restrain capital from price hikes that soon eroded labor's gains. The government's fiscal deficit widened, reflecting its inability to saddle either class with the taxes required to finance state expenditures. When external finance was available, class and sectoral conflicts could be "papered over" with foreign funds, but as debt flows collapsed, the limited taxing capacity of the state became painfully obvious, and the resulting deficit-driven monetary growth combined with a wage-price spiral to bring about the hyperinflation. The clear anti-labor stance of the program that emerged in 1985—as illustrated by the government's arrest of labor leaders, the dramatic fall of real wages, and the regressive character of the tax program that quickly followed—appeared to resolve the conflict in favor of capital. This pro-business agenda was as important for restoring confidence and restraining inflation as any technical measure taken.

Peru's heterodox stabilization program is also best understood in light of class and distributional dynamics. Alan García essentially attempted to implement a sort of anti-imperialist social democracy in post-Belaúnde Peru. By limiting the outward flow of resources, his administration facilitated a boom in both worker and capitalist income, hoping that this would lay the foundation for a multiclass coalition. Workers were indeed pleased by rising wages, but labor representatives were given little voice in policy decisions. Capitalists, on the other hand, were directly courted by the García administration and were reassured that despite increasing government intervention and a rise in worker and peasant income, private investment would remain the motor of accumulation. This tenuous accommodation of local capital was termed *concertación*, and its death was signalled by the Peruvian government's July 1987 decision to nationalize the banking system. The resulting open war between the private sector and the García administration was a crucial factor in the subsequent hyperinflation: Business resisted new taxes, slashed investment, and engaged in a destabilizing capital flight that soon fed into a depreciation-inflation cycle.

The third focus in this study is the technical consistency and coherence of the stabilization programs. Analyses of the technical aspects of inflation and stabilization—the relationships between money, prices, and the exchange rate; the relative responsiveness of various producers to price signals; and the role of budget and trade balances—can sometimes obscure the fundamental determinants of the success or failure of an adjustment program. While it may be deficits, for example, that directly drive inflation, it is often class and distributional tension that drives deficits. Nonetheless, the technical matters, particularly the underlying vision of how the economy works, are crucial to understanding the logic of orthodox and heterodox stabilization efforts. In this work, I analyze the experiences and policies of Bolivia and Peru using some traditional mathematical and econometric tools; I attempt, however, to simplify the exposition and to place this analysis within the context of class and external dynamics.

Orthodoxy, as we will see, argues that socioeconomic structures are flexible, economic agents are price-responsive, and inflation is the result of government-induced excess demand. The appropriate short- and long-run policies follow directly: Devaluation should trigger a burst of exports, tight fiscal policy should counteract any resulting inflationary pressure, and a government retreat from the economy should gently shift the adjusting country to an optimal growth path.

Heterodoxy has its roots in what is now known as structuralist economics. The latter posits rigid economic, social, and political structures; focuses on the *lack* of price responsiveness in certain key sectors, particularly agriculture and primary commodity exports; and suggests the need for government intervention to push along the process of accumulation and growth. Industrial sector prices, in this view, are set by a markup on costs; as the economy expands, shortages of food drive up wages while shortages of imported intermediates (given a fixed level of export revenues from primary commodities) do the same to input costs. The older structuralist view seemed to suggest that advanced capitalist countries should provide their poorer neighbors with the resources to avoid import gaps while the developing countries themselves should learn to live with the inflationary consequences of growth. In the 1980s, with external finance in short supply and high inflation apparently threatening growth, the old, relatively passive policy prescription was inadequate. Structuralist-oriented economists then formulated their own set of policies to control inflation and termed this new view heterodoxy.

Heterodoxy argued directly against the orthodox policy package, suggesting that: Devaluation could do little to promote exports but much to promote inflation; recessionary policies designed to ease inflationary pressures were ill-considered in the context of a generalized economic slump; and mark-up pricing and formal or informal wage indexing in the industrial sector gave the economy an inertial inflationary impulse that would only be eliminated by wage and price controls. The Peruvian version of heterodoxy was especially radical: It insisted that the economy could grow as inflation subsided; it argued that private investment would not be deterred by raising real wages; it paid virtually no attention to monetary matters or the government's deficit; and it took an explicit position on limiting debt service in order to "create" new external flows and thus finance the imports required for growth.

Understanding the more technical aspects of orthodoxy and heterodoxy—that is, exactly how each perspective models developing country economies and provides a rationale for alternative policies—is, of course, not enough. Just because a framework views the economy a particular way does not mean the economy actually behaves that way; orthodoxy, for example, sometimes assumes away many of the institutional rigidities that do, in fact, characterize Latin American economies. Throughout the following analysis, I examine the logic of each framework, but also offer criticisms of how each view either ignores or downplays key issues or structural characteristics in its formal modeling. I also emphasize that even the most accurate technical specification may give an observer little insight about the international and class pressures that may dictate the choice of certain frameworks and policies. Indeed, I argue below that the Peruvian disaster was entirely predictable *within* the structuralist perspective itself; why the problem signs were ignored has less to do with algebra than with politics.

A final key focus in the analysis is the relationship between short-run stabilization efforts and long-run growth potential. The Bolivian and Peruvian shifts in policy in 1985 were not simply the result of short-term macroeconomic difficulties. Rather, each was born in the context of a larger crisis in the models of accumulation that had structured each country's growth over the previous decades.

Bolivia, for example, had pursued state-directed capitalism since its 1952 revolution, coupling a largely nationalized export sector with the import substitution efforts characteristic of many Latin American countries. The difficulties in the model had provoked earlier crises and shifts in development policy; throughout the 1970s, for example, the government rapidly accumulated debt to finance an expansion of agricultural and petroleum-related production in the eastern portion of its territory. The late 1970s and early 1980s were marked by profound political crisis, and the hyperinflation of 1983–1985 reflected this political conflict as well as the effects of falling export prices and collapsing debt flows. The orthodoxy initiated in 1985 essentially sought to both shift short-run macroeconomic policy *and* reshape the accumulation structure to one based more on private capital and market mechanisms.

The Peruvian crisis of the 1980s was also rooted in a failed model of long-term growth. Like Bolivia, Peru had attempted to combine its traditional reliance on primary exports with a heavily protected industrialization drive, particularly under the military regime of General Juan Velasco Alvarado between 1968 and 1975. This accumulation model was crumbling long before the global macroeconomic shocks of the 1980s; through the late 1970s, Peru foreshadowed the subsequent regional debt crisis with a series of debt reschedulings and adjustment difficulties. The initial solution was a brief and somewhat incoherent move toward orthodox liberalization; this attracted new loans but also produced an import surge that wasted precious international reserves. When Alan García took power in 1985, the economy was clearly in disarray and the new administration attempted to reshape not just short-run macroeconomic policy but, more importantly, the social and economic bases of long-term accumulation. Unfortunately, these more far-reaching efforts at restructuring were as mismanaged as macroeconomic policy. Hyperinflation arose from short-term problems, to be sure, but it also signaled a loss of faith in any possibility of a medium-term rekindling of Peruvian growth.

Plan of the Book

This book analyzes the Peruvian and Bolivian macroeconomic experiments with special emphasis on the four foci detailed above. Along the way, I contrast the logic of orthodox and heterodox policy, offer an account of the dynamics of hyperinflation and stabilization, explore the explicit and implicit class character of alternative adjustment schemes, and suggest some lessons for future policy.

Chapters 2 and 3 begin the analysis with a general review of the orthodox and heterodox paradigms. Chapter 2 sketches the general free market emphasis of orthodoxy, then offers a set of simple models that clarify the rationale behind orthodoxy's prescriptions of budget correction and devaluation; I also explain why orthodox theorists contend that such adjustment policies can be neutral in terms of the factor (or class) distribution of income. After covering issues such as the role of expectations, the sequencing of liberalization measures, and the exchange rate-fixing experiments of the Southern Cone, I criticize the orthodox perspective because it fails to effectively incorporate key structural characteristics of Latin American economies, and because the programs implemented in its name often exhibit a sharp class bias.

Chapter 3 presents the key elements of the heterodox paradigm. A simple set of models is developed to illustrate the structuralist critique of orthodoxy and the rationale for an alternative adjustment strategy. The first model presented is quite general and centers on the structural rigidities and external dependence typical of Third World economies, features that imply that orthodox policies such as devaluation may be stagflationary. The alternative policies usually proposed involve some degree of debt relief as well as direct controls to slow any built-in inflationary inertia. I then respecify the model to better fit the Peruvian economic structure and use the modified equations to illustrate the logic of the García administration's heterodox policy package; this analysis also illustrates the limits of heterodoxy and the need for a policy shift midway into the program, a need that was ignored by Peruvian policy makers due to political and other pressures. I then examine issues of credibility and policy sequencing and close with a general discussion of the class character of heterodox adjustment.

Chapter 4 begins the actual case studies with a look at hyperinflation and stabilization in Bolivia. After a brief review of the structural features and recent history of the Bolivian economy, I argue that the hyperinflation of the 1980s was fundamentally caused by external shocks and class conflict over bearing the burdens of those shocks. The more proximate causes of the hyperinflation, monetary growth and exchange depreciation, are also delineated and subjected to econometric tests. I then review the nature and performance of the 1985 New Economic Policy (NEP) of President Víctor Paz Estenssoro. Inflation was indeed dramatically reduced (after a brief resurgence early in 1986) using a combination of exchange rate stability, actual and expected budget corrections, measures to enhance capital flows, and the active repression of labor challenges. However, the stabilization outcomes of the NEP were quite problematic in terms of social costs and long-run viability. The conclusion to this chapter is a bit dismal: I argue that Bolivia in 1985 may have had little alternative but to implement the sort of program it did, especially in light of external pressures and the domestic disarray of the political actors likely to support an alternative policy. Nonetheless, growth remains quite slow and the current government finds its policy options limited by the country's dependence on foreign and domestic capital.

Chapter 5 focuses on Peru, beginning with a brief review of the economic structure and political history. I detail the failures of orthodox policy in the early 1980s and argue that this paved the way for the heterodox experiment of the García administration. I explain the economic reasoning and class character of the Peruvian program, arguing that both the particular policies followed and the accompanying process of government-business *concertación* illustrate the social democratic nature of García's project. I then explore why the program—which initially brought rapid growth, low inflation, and a significant redistribution of income toward the poorest sectors—eventually unraveled. Technical matters such as excessive budget deficits, negative real interest rates, currency overvaluation, and dwindling international reserves played a role, but the Peruvian collapse also reflects far more fundamental causes, including the well-intended but ultimately ill-fated debt service limits and the unsustainable nature of a multiclass coalition in a sharply divided society and poorly performing economy. The latter focus on class issues is especially important because the Peruvian passage into hyperinflation essentially dates from the nationalization of the banking system, a political event that triggered the resurrection of the right-wing and brought dramatic conflict between domestic capital and the García government. I detail the origins and nature of the Peruvian hyperinflation, conduct some econometric comparisons with the Bolivian case, and close by discussing the legacy of heterodoxy in Peru.

Chapter 6 completes the analysis by drawing some lessons that can be learned by other small countries in the age of debt crisis and adjustment. I return to the comparison of Bolivian orthodoxy and Peruvian heterodoxy, focusing on the policies of the two programs with respect to the key foci of external finance, class alignments, and technical coherence; the attempt here is not so much to pronounce one set of policies "better" as it is to explore the limits that face either strategy. I then consider some of the longer-run issues posed by each approach, a point particularly important given that the last ten years of macroeconomic crisis in Latin America has led to a perhaps excessive focus on short-run adjustment. I argue that both the state-driven, multiclass approach in Peru and the market-oriented, pro-capital strategy in Bolivia face problems in the current global economic context and suggest an alternative long-run vision that couples a concern for working people in Latin America with a pragmatic approach to both macroeconomic crises and the restructuring of Latin accumulation models.

The past decade has been a sad one for those observers concerned with economic development and social justice in Latin America. Pressed by debt service and confronted by an unfavorable global economy, Latin American output has stagnated even as inflation has risen. The poor, already living at marginal levels, have been especially hard-hit. In Peru, Bolivia, and elsewhere hyperinflation has eroded middle-class savings, damaged workers' real income, and forced governments to forego medium-term planning in order to address immediate financial emergencies. Unfortunately, ending these disastrous hyperinflations may, as in Bolivia (and as seems likely in Peru), involve high costs and leave the country vulnerable to a different set of shocks.

From these experiences, lessons can be learned and mistakes avoided. The people of Bolivia and Peru did not consent to the policies that caused their hardships; for the most part, a small group of elite owners and decision makers engaged in the borrowing that produced the current crises and transformed their economies into laboratories for orthodox and heterodox strategies. But the people of Peru and Bolivia would, I believe, agree to have their experience shared so that others may then be able to avoid the inflation, debt, and stabilization pitfalls of these two Andean neighbors. As gifts go, this may be all they can afford; it is, on the other hand, invaluable for both their own future and that of Latin America.

Notes

1. For an early analysis of the Mexican program, see Dornbusch (1988a).

2

The Macroeconomics of Adjustment: Orthodox Views

Introduction

Although the last decade in Latin America has been marked by particularly sharp shifts in adjustment strategies, the orthodox-heterodox debate that fueled these dramatic policy changes is rooted in an earlier set of disagreements between monetarists and structuralists (see Foxley 1983). Like monetarism, the orthodox paradigm celebrates market forces and generally ascribes inflation and trade problems to a government-induced level of excess demand; like structuralism, heterodoxy postulates imperfect markets and supply-side rigidities and argues that these features are primarily responsible for inflation and trade problems. Each paradigm offers distinct recommendations for policy: Orthodoxy favors monetary restraint and real devaluation, while heterodoxy emphasizes more direct inflation controls as well as long-run measures to reduce import dependence.

Although each framework may be characterized by its notions about the efficacy of markets and the rigidity of economic structure, they also differ in their analysis of what we might term class issues. Orthodoxy eschews class as a concept, postulating instead individual agents who exercise little power in the face of market forces. Despite this assumption, orthodox programs generally have important effects on the class structure of the adjusting economy: Capital is favored while labor suffers, particularly because unions and other workers' organizations are often seen as disruptive of a smoothly functioning market mechanism.

Heterodoxy often includes an explicit class analysis, particularly in its Latin American variants (see, for example, Bresser Pereira and Nakano 1987). Capitalists are viewed as *price-setters*, and not the relatively powerless *price-takers* of orthodox theory. Inflation is often analyzed as the result of a distributional struggle in which labor's attempt to increase its real wages is frustrated by capital's power to pass along cost increases. The government is thus buffeted by class tensions; monetary policy is viewed as passively responding to the need to "validate" or "sanction" capitalist price hikes and thus preserve profitability and accumulation. Despite the clear recognition of class issues and actors, heterodox economists generally have no radical agenda for redistributing income or altering the balance of class forces. They simply argue that the distributional struggle and capitalist monopoly power that drives inflation should be explicitly incorporated into both theory and policy. Stopping inflation, in this view, requires a new social compact that can ameliorate the underlying distributional pressures.

This chapter begins our consideration of the orthodox-heterodox debate by reviewing both the technical and class aspects of orthodox models; the following chapter covers much the same ground from the view of heterodoxy. I begin here with a simple exposition of the orthodox framework, coupling the underlying monetary balance of payments model that drives International Monetary Fund-style recommendations with a real sector approach that better illustrates the rationale for devaluation as well as the predicted distributive effects of such policy. This discussion leads into an examination of the roles of expectations and credibility in the adjustment process. I then turn to a discussion of sequencing issues, that is, which of the orthodox policies should be pursued first and why? I close with a discussion of the unspoken and often unanalyzed class character of orthodox stabilization.

Orthodox Stabilization and Adjustment

The orthodox perspective is essentially rooted in the neoclassical and monetarist visions of the economy. As such, it upholds the virtues of market liberalization and macroeconomic restraint. The support for market liberalization is based on fundamental assumptions that: (1) In the absence of government interventions, capitalist economies tend toward full employment and trade balance; (2) even if there exist institutional rigidities, such as historically low export responses to price signals or import-dependent industries, these can be broken down by the combination of maximizing behavior and the market; and (3) import competition from trade liberalization will force domestic producers to become more efficient.

These assumptions are also the basis for the orthodox view of macroeconomic dynamics. The central propositions in this area are that: (1) Both inflation and trade problems are symptoms of excess demand; (2) such excess demand is most often the result of government deficits and monetary creation; (3) currency devaluation is a productive strategy to increase the relative price of traded goods and thus close trade gaps; (4) devaluation will not necessarily be inflationary if reduced monetary growth simultaneously forces a decline in the prices of domestic goods; and (5) such a package need not have regressive distributional impacts given the low import content in workers' wage bundles. Newer variants of this policy vision also argue that the negative employment impacts of budget and monetary tightening will be small since agents have forward-looking (or "rational") expectations: Given "credible" policy, both business and labor will restrain

The Macroeconomics of Adjustment: Orthodox Views

price and wage hikes without needing a large dose of slack markets and unemployment to reinforce the message.

To illustrate these points more formally, it is useful to introduce the simple monetary model of the balance of payments that often serves as the basis for the International Monetary Fund's financial programming for adjusting countries. The initial version of the model assumes an economy producing a single good; a subsequent extension introduces tradeable and non-tradeable sectors in order to illustrate the reallocative effects of currency devaluation as well as the accompanying orthodox view that such devaluation will not necessarily reduce workers' real living standards.

A Monetary Approach to the Balance of Payments

Consider an economy that can be described by the following set of equations:

(2.1) $M^S = R + DC$

(2.2) $M^D = kPY$

(2.3) $\Delta M^S = \Delta M^D$

(2.4) $PY = PA + eNX^\$$

(2.5) $\Delta R^\$ = NX^\$$

(2.6) $R = eR^\$$

(2.7) $P = eP^\$$

where M^S refers to the money supply, R to international reserves in domestic currency, DC to domestic credit, M^D to money demand, P to the domestic price level, Y to real domestic income or output, A to real domestic absorption, NX to net exports, and e to the nominal exchange rate. The $ superscript denotes either dollar values (as in $NX^\$$) or a dollar price (as in $P^\$$), and Δ denotes the quantity of change in a particular variable.[1]

In order, the equations describe the following: (2.1) The money supply is composed of international reserves and domestic credit (which I will assume consists entirely of government bonds);[2] (2.2) money demand is a linear function, k, of the price level and real income (which implicitly assumes that velocity is constant); (2.3) the money market clears; (2.4) national income consists of domestic absorption and net exports; (2.5) the change in international reserves (that is, the balance of payments) is equal to the trade balance; (2.6) the domestic value of reserves is equal to the dollar value multiplied by the exchange rate; and (2.7) the domestic price level is equal to the exchange rate times the international price level. Note that this simple version of the model has no international capital flows other than reserve loss or gain due to the trade balance. Note further that (2.7) is a statement of the so-called "law of one price" in which, absent transport costs, the domestic price level conforms to that of foreign substitutes. This essentially assumes that there is no non-tradeable sector, a simplification that is dropped in a subsequent section.

It is straightforward to demonstrate that in this model, a government deficit (which produces an expansion of domestic credit) yields a corresponding trade deficit and reserve loss. Assume first that markets work such that the economy is always at full employment; this effectively fixes real domestic output at some level, Y_F. For ease, suppose that there is neither private investment nor private savings, a feature that simplifies the math by conveniently reducing leakages and injections to those emerging from the government and external sectors.[3] Real domestic absorption, A, then consists of the real level of government spending, G, and real consumption spending on domestic goods, C, where C is effectively fixed due to the stability of output, Y, and the lump-sum nature of the tax system. Dividing the macro balance equation, (2.4), by the price level and writing out the components yields:

(2.8) $\quad Y = C + G + e^r NX^\$$

where e^r is the real exchange rate, (e/P). Noting that $(Y - C)$ equals the real tax bill in this simple model, (2.8) can be rearranged as:

(2.9) $\quad GD = -e^r NX^\$$

that is, the mirror image of a government deficit, GD, is a trade deficit. It should be noted that little has been lost by assuming away the private investment-savings balance. If "excess" investment demand *also* contributed to the trade problem this would complicate the analysis but not remove the effect of the government deficit itself; moreover, because an abundance of investment opportunities would likely attract foreign funds, any investment-driven deficit would likely not cause a problematic reserve loss.[4]

An alternative (and more traditional) approach to this same notion of "twin" government and trade deficits is through the monetary equations. Noting that the fixity of k, P, and Y implies that money demand is constant, the change in the money supply must sum to zero to maintain monetary equilibrium. This, in turn, implies that:

(2.10) $\quad \Delta DC = \Delta R$

which can be restated in real terms by writing out R as $eR^\$$ and dividing both sides by P. The result is:

(2.11) $\quad \Delta DC^r = -e^r \Delta R^\$$

where ΔDC^r refers to the change in real domestic credit and is equivalent to the real domestic deficit (given the lack in this simple model of private investment and savings). The relation between (2.9) and (2.11) should be clear; once again, a government deficit (domestic monetary expansion) causes a trade deficit (reserve loss).[5]

The simple results above depend on the "law of one price": Excess demand in the economy from government spending consumes reserves without altering the exchange rate or the domestic price level. Suppose, however, that local producers can raise prices, perhaps because the government responds to the growing trade imbalance with protective tariffs. To see the effects, begin with the monetary equilibrium equation (2.3) and substitute as follows:

(2.12a) $\quad \Delta M^S = \Delta M_D$

(2.12b) $\quad e\Delta R^\$ + P\Delta DC^r + DC^r \Delta P = kY\Delta P$

where the exchange rate remains fixed but the price (and therefore money demand) can vary. Dividing (2.12) by P, letting a "hat," ^, above a variable denote a rate of change, and rearranging, yields:

(2.13) $\quad \Delta DC^r = -e^r \Delta R^\$ + (kY - DC^r)\hat{P}$

Because the demand for real balances (kY) must equal the real supply ($e^r R^\$ + DC^r$), (2.13) can be rewritten as:

(2.14) $\quad \Delta DC^r = e^r(R^\$ \hat{P} - \Delta R^\$)$

Note that for the same increase in real domestic credit, higher inflation, $\hat{P}$, means less reserve loss, reflecting the earlier argument that any ability to raise prices (and thus to absorb excess credit) must derive from protective measures against imports. Alternatively, one can view inflation as reducing the real effects of a nominal expansion in government expenditure and protecting reserves in that way.

However the story gets told, the punchline remains the same: Excessive government spending will yield both reserve loss and inflation. Moreover, since price increases lower the real exchange rate, e^r, maintaining the same real government deficits will, over time, create even higher levels of inflation and reserve loss (see (2.14). Eventually, the misbehaving government staggers to the Fund short on reserves, high on inflation, and a bit chagrined about its apparent inability to manage the economy.

The orthodox recommendations are straightforward: Reverse the policies that caused the troubles. Government budget surpluses (i.e., a negative GD) should yield corresponding trade surpluses and make room for the restoration of reserves. A liberalization of the trade account—i.e., removing the protective measures that allowed local producers to violate the "law of one price"—should help to restrain domestic price increases. A devaluation may be recommended as one way to avoid an actual price deflation in the face of the new competition; note that an increase in the exchange rate, e, will raise import prices up to the domestic level even through trade barriers have fallen. Both the devaluation and the increase in reserves have an expansionary impact on the domestic money supply, essentially taking up the slack produced by the reversal of domestic credit creation.

The story in equations is as follows. Assume that the price-reducing effects of a trade liberalization are exactly offset by devaluation; as a result, import prices shift up to the former ruling domestic price but no higher. Because P is unchanged and the demand for real balances, kY, is constant, the change in the money supply must total to zero. Starting from a similar condition stated in (2.10) but now allowing the exchange rate to vary, we can see that:

(2.15) $\Delta DC^r = -(e^r \Delta R^\$ + R^\$ \Delta e^r)$

That is, the decrease in the real level of domestic credit is driven by both an increase in the dollar level of reserves and by the revaluation of existing reserves (due to the new and higher exchange rate).[6] The revaluation effect implies that the initial boost in dollar reserves (due to government budget surpluses) is partly choked off; however, once the new exchange rate is stable, government surpluses will produce trade surplus counterparts in the context of no inflation and full employment. Our happy adjuster thanks Fund economists for their advice, then proceeds along until the nation's decision makers inexplicably forget the country's recent experience and commit another round of policy errors involving government deficits, trade protection, and inflation.

Structural Adjustment and Income Distribution

The above discussion clarifies some essential lessons of orthodoxy, particularly the negative effects of government deficits and the corresponding argument for domestic credit ceilings. It fails, however, to fully capture the orthodox rationale for devaluation policy. Orthodox packages, particularly those recommended by the IMF, tend to couple their domestic credit restrictions with an admonition to devalue in order to enhance net exports by shifting resources from the nontradeable to tradeable sectors. In this section, I explore both this allocative issue—that is, "structural adjustment"—and touch on the distributional impacts of such policy.

The alterations to the basic model are simple.[7] Let the "law of one price" be replaced with the following price equation:[8]

(2.16) $P = (P_N)^b (eP_M^\$)^{(1-b)}$

where b is the share of non-tradeables in the consumption bundle (and (1 − b) is the share of imports), P_N is the price of non-tradeables, and $P_M^\$$ is the dollar price of imports. For ease, assume that the dollar price of exports, $P_X^\$$, equals $P_M^\$$ and that both equal one; while this analytically eliminates the possibility of shocks in the terms of trade, it simplifies both the algebra and graphical presentation by allowing us to denote the price of both exports and imports with simply e, the nominal exchange rate.

Net exports depend on real income, Y, and the relative price of tradeables (e/P_N). Terming the latter the real exchange rate, e^r, net exports can be viewed as:

(2.17) $NX = f(Y, e^r)$

To avoid mathematical complications, let us now employ a graphical analysis. Figure 2.1 depicts a production possibilities frontier between non-tradeables (or domestic goods (N)) and export goods (X); the concave shape reflects decreasing returns to scale in both sectors. The convex line is a social indifference curve (ID) that agglomerates consumer preferences between non-tradeables and import goods (M); the assumed equality of export and import prices implies that one export buys one import and conveniently allows us to place both X and M on the same axis. Where the two curves are tangent, social welfare is maximized, the economy is at full employment, and trade is balanced. Note that there is only one budget line, B, consistent with this tangency; its slope, $-e^r$, gives us the real exchange rate that induces producers to produce N* and X* and consumers to consume N* and M*.[9]

Before proceeding it is worthwhile to return to the macroeconomic equilibrium equation:

(2.18) $PY = PA + eNX^\$$

Dividing through by the price index and making use of the fact that import and export prices are normalized at one, we obtain:

(2.19) $Y = A + (e^r)^b NX$

A trade deficit occurs when real absorption, A, exceeds real output, Y, a situation depicted in Figure 2.2.

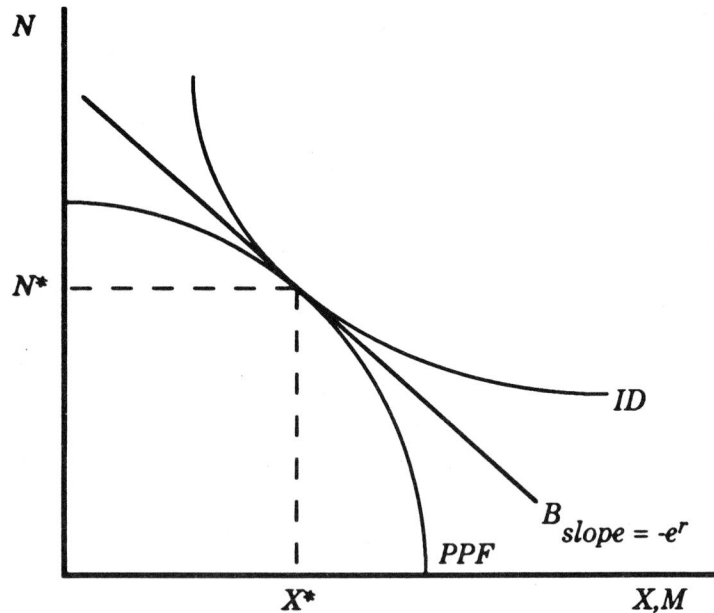

Figure 2.1 Production Possibilities Frontier and Social Indifference Curve for Tradeables and Non-Tradeables

The graphical story proceeds in two steps. The first panel of Figure 2.2 includes the full employment trade balance equilibrium from Figure 2.1, that is, (N*, X*). When absorption, A, increases, the budget line shifts to B' and the economy is able to achieve a higher level of social utility (associated with the higher social indifference curve, ID'). Note, however, that the level of non-tradeables demanded, N', exceeds that which would be produced, N*, given the original real exchange rate, e^r. With such excess demand, the price of non-tradeables, P_N, will rise and the real exchange rate will fall, moving the economy along both the production possibilities frontier and the social indifference curve until the relevant markets clear. The ultimate result is shown in the second panel of the figure: As compared to the initial position (N*, X*), there is a higher level of non-tradeables, N", a lower real exchange rate, e''', and a sizeable trade imbalance, (M" − X"). Note that nominal prices rose in the non-tradeable sector, implying domestic inflation.

The allocative and distributive impacts of orthodox policy may now be illustrated. The goal, of course, is to eliminate the reserve drain by restoring trade balance. This, in turn, necessitates both reducing domestic absorption, A (i.e., shifting back the budget line), and setting the real exchange rate (i.e., making the budget line steeper) such that it is consistent with (N*, X*). The latter shift away from non-tradeables toward tradeables (i.e., exports) is what the Fund and the World Bank now term "structural adjustment," and the requisite policies are tra-

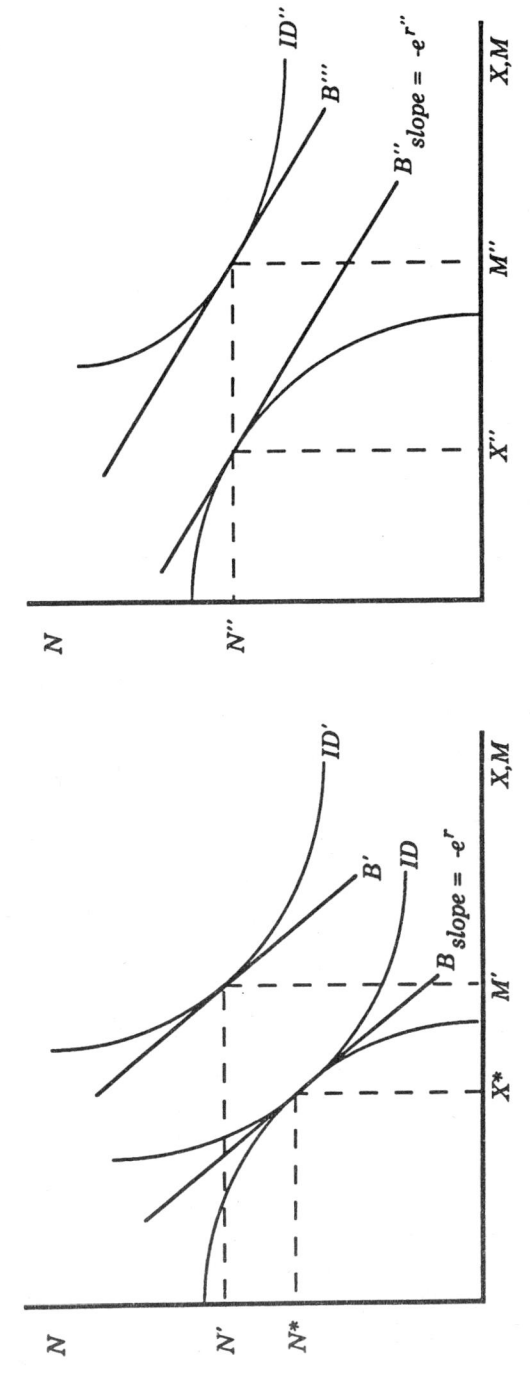

Figure 2.2 Excess Absorption, Trade Deficit, and a Shift in the Composition of Output

ditional orthodoxy: government deficit reduction and devaluation. This model is more realistic than the previous version in that the devaluation will likely trigger inflation by raising the price of consumer imports and can be made even more realistic by assuming that the sectoral shift will take some time, thus allowing for temporary unemployment effects.

What about distribution? Note that structural adjustment requires a decline in the real product wage in the tradeable sector in order to increase the profitability of export goods. The government must therefore ensure that nominal wages do not keep pace with the devaluation. It is, however, not necessary that nominal wages lag behind the increase in the non-tradeable price. Indeed, because along the production possibilities frontier the export increase *must* come at the expense of home goods production, a higher real product wage in the home goods sector is necessary to diminish the profitability of home goods (Cline 1983:180; Dornbusch 1980:77–78).

To see this more explicitly, divide the nominal wage, W, by the price index given in (2.16), and manipulate, obtaining:

(2.20) $\quad w^r = (w^X)(e^r)^b$

where w^r is the real consumption wage, (W/P), and w^X is the real product wage in the export sector, (W/e). Structural adjustment does require a fall in w^X but, as illustrated above, it also entails a rise in both the real exchange rate, e^r, and the share of expenditure devoted to non-tradeables, b.[10] The total effect on the real consumption wage is ambiguous and, with certain reasonable parameters, an improvement in workers' income is possible. Moreover, if the producers of home goods are, say, poor farmers, then the overall distributional effect may be quite favorable for low-income individuals.

Once again, a more realistic model of structural adjustment would acknowledge that it takes time to shift resources from one sector to another. If exporters, for example, respond slowly to price signals, the government might have to severely depress domestic absorption in order to bring imports in line with exports; imports could be subsequently expanded as export production itself picks up. In the meantime, of course, unemployment in the non-tradeable sector results, with negative effects on overall social welfare as well as the distribution of income.

The price responsiveness of producers is thus a critical determinant of the speed of structural adjustment. Also important is the degree of credibility of the government: If exporters suspect that the devaluation will not stick—that the government will subsequently expand the money supply and erode the real exchange rate through inflation—then no export resurgence takes place and the government is forced to balance trade through import austerity. This discussion suggests the importance of expectations, a topic explored below.

Expectations, Rational and Otherwise

Simple economic models generally rely on instantaneous time: Prices change and producers adjust in the same graph and seemingly in the same moment. Capitalist production, however, generally takes place in three phases: hiring labor and acquiring intermediate inputs, producing the actual good or service, and selling the produced item in the marketplace. To begin the process, firms must make predictions of future profitability based on likely wages, raw materials costs, ease of production, and selling price. Because workers may also make decisions on how much (or how hard) to work based on expected real consumption wages, they must gauge the nominal wage offered against the likely prices of the goods they wish to consume. In this sense, all economic agents are forward or future looking.

The real issue is how expectations are formed about that future. In macroeconomic theory, two approaches have been taken. The first, *adaptive expectations*, suggests that economic agents predict inflation (and other variables) by taking some weighted average of past inflation and extrapolating forward.[11] The alternative, *rational expectations*, criticizes this approach by suggesting that simple extrapolation may ignore important information: Even if a country has a history of zero inflation, an announcement that the central bank will soon double the money supply is likely to raise the public's expectations of future price levels. Rational expectations concludes that it is best (albeit difficult) to model expectations of prices by assuming that agents make use of all possible information about the future values of key variables (e.g., monetary policy, exchange rates, etc.).

For agents to consider more than simply past performance, they must employ some model of how the economy works. As a leading proponent of this view argues, "the hypothesis of rational expectations is that people understand these laws of motion [of the economy]" (Sargent 1986:3). Thus, the rational expectations or "new classical" macroeconomics essentially combines three key assumptions: first, that people use all available information in economic decisions; second, that they understand how the economy works; and third, that the economy *actually* works in the way described by the orthodox or "market-clearing" framework.

This is a bold combination of assumptions, particularly given that economists often disagree about which economic model is appropriate and that key markets, such as that for labor, often do not clear (particularly in Third World economies). Indeed, when taken to its logical extreme, the new classical perspective renders moot the problems orthodox economic policy is generally supposed to resolve. Consider, for example, the earlier scenario in which a government deficit created inflation, a trade deficit, and an overvalued exchange rate, all of which subsequently triggered a reserve loss and then a policy shift toward reduced government deficits and currency devaluation. If the economy really worked as the orthodox model assumes it does and expectations were "fully rational," none of this would happen! Actors would either reverse the expansionary effects of government spending by immediately raising savings (in order to pay for future taxes) or would fully anticipate the future devaluation and hence not adjust production along the production possibilities frontier.

How might the economy ever deviate from full employment and the production mix (N*,X*)? New classicals suggest that unannounced or unanticipated government actions are to blame. Suppose, for example, that the government quietly loosens the money supply. Private agents still "believe" markets are clearing: Unaware of the general price rise, workers and firms think there has been a shift in their own real price, and hence supply too much labor and output.[12] Once the inflation results are in, however, agents will realize that no such real increase has occurred and will quickly correct their predictions, decreasing labor supply and output. Repeated episodes along these lines will eventually erode the government's *credibility*.

Credibility is a crucial determinant of the speed of adjustment. If a government has a history of overspending, few agents may believe the authorities when they announce a new stabilization effort replete with deficit reduction and devaluation policies. Anticipating future inflation, workers may refuse to moderate their wage stance while exporters, unconvinced that a real devaluation will "stick," may be reluctant to enhance production; because these critical economic agents continue to demand prices above market-clearing levels, any return to full employment will be slow. Only after the government demonstrates its ability to tolerate a long period of unemployment and sustain a low real exchange rate will private agents adjust expectations downward, returning the economy to (N*,X*). In the rational expectations view, avoiding this costly disinflation process requires that the government make a *binding* and thus credible commitment to a new policy rule—say, a legislated limit on future monetary growth.

Such binding and credible commitments are more easily theorized than accomplished, particularly since high inflations usually arise after a series of failed stabilization efforts. The latter implies that inflationary expectations may only be altered after a clear change in *regime* and not just policy. Bolivia, for example, only arrested its hyperinflation after a new and very different government took power; as I argue below, it gained credibility not just through changing its monetary rules but also through a costly defense of its nominal exchange rate and a conscious effort to both lower wages and dismantle an historically strong labor movement.

Sequencing in Orthodox Adjustment

The above presentation of the orthodox perspective suggests a relatively rosy view of the adjustment process: With credible policy action by the government, markets quickly work to move the economy from a prereform disequilibrium to the ultimate equilibrium resting point pictured in Figure 2.1. Most economists, however, also warn policy makers to think through how the economy drifts toward equilibrium—that is, the *sequence* of policy changes made to push the economy to a desired outcome.

One central sequencing issue in orthodox adjustment involves the "correct" order of liberalizing trade and capital flows. Although orthodox theory would seem to celebrate an immediate surrender to free market imperatives and hence advise a rapid liberalization of both current and capital accounts, many economists worry that an excessively quick liberalization of the capital account may result in either: (1) a rapid outflow of capital because the economy has not yet stabilized, or (2) a rapid inflow of capital that will push down the real exchange rate and hence undermine the depreciation needed for trade adjustment. As a result, even many who share the orthodox goal of liberalizing both trade and capital flows warn that such liberalization should be sequential rather than simultaneous; Edwards, in a comprehensive study of the sequencing of external accounts, concludes that "the more *prudent* strategy is to liberalize the current account first" (Edwards 1984:19; emphasis in original) while a more recent study by Bruno (1989) arrives at exactly the same conclusion.

A related sequencing issue involves the correct timing of domestic financial liberalization. Many orthodox analysts point to "financial repression"—the maintenance of government control over credit allocation, interest rates, and external capital flows—as a major impediment to growth and adjustment (McKinnon 1973). Such repression, it is argued, produces artificially low domestic interest rates which in turn leads to low savings, poorly allocated investment, excessive self-financing by firms, an usurious parallel banking system, and a permanently underdeveloped formal financial structure. The remedy would seem to be clear: Let markets determine domestic rates and allow external capital flows to both supplement domestic savings and, through competition, force the domestic financial system to be more efficient.

But, as with the liberalization of international trade and capital flows, there are good reasons to be concerned about doing too much at the same time. Financial liberalization seems to often be followed by excessive real interest rates; in the Southern Cone experiments of Argentina, Chile, and Uruguay, real rates averaged 17 percent, 41 percent, and 15 percent during the postliberalization period.[13] Opening capital flows in this context means that domestic borrowers (sometimes including the government) will search abroad for funds. The result, particularly if trade liberalization has also allowed an increase in effective import demand, will be a rapid expansion of external debt. Thus, there may be a case for a sequential liberalization of external and domestic finance (see Bruno 1989:239).

A final sequencing issue is more general: the timing of inflation stabilization and liberalization. The orthodox view suggests that trade liberalization can constrain domestic price hikes and therefore aid in reducing inflation. However, liberalization in an economy not yet stabilized can actually derail the adjustment process. If producers doubt that a real devaluation will stick, they will refuse to either enhance export production or restrain domestic inflation; with open external markets, the result will be a reserve-draining import boom. Financial liberalization prior to a full stabilization can also be problematic. Dornbusch and Reynoso (1988) argue that allowing market interest rates to increase prior to budget correction will both raise government expenditures on domestic debt and reduce the government's ability to collect an "inflation tax" on money holdings (see also Bruno 1989); from both sides, then, the fiscal deficit is strained and this, in turn, may exacerbate inflation and wreck the stabilization process (Dornbusch and Reynoso 1988:22).

Moreover, as Sachs notes, "the instruments of stabilization may well compete with the instruments of liberalization" (Sachs 1987:305). For example, dampening inflationary expectations could require government intervention to stabilize the exchange rate rather than the sort of free currency float that might be associated with liberalized trade accounts. Ending inflation could require higher export taxes and import duties to reduce the government deficit while the liberalization imperative would seem to push trade tax policy in the other direction. Given these contradictions, the East Asian "success stories" of Korea, Taiwan, and even Japan all phased in liberalization measures only after macroeconomic stability had been achieved and maintained for a substantial period of time (Sachs 1987).[14] Thus, Sachs argues that "stabilization should precede any dramatic shift to liberalization" (Sachs 1987:322).

There may, however, be political reasons for complete and rapid liberalization. In his wide-ranging review of the Southern Cone experiences of the late 1970s, Foxley argues that the new military governments adopted dramatic orthodox packages "not only to bring the economy back to equilibrium but also to discipline the economic and social groups until they adhered to a new rationality" (Foxley 1983:30). Such discipline was not left to the market alone; the Southern Cone governments engaged in labor repression and other measures in order to convince agents to behave as orthodox theory predicted. Making credible its attempt to refashion the social order required that the government choose tough policies and stick with them. In short, the depth and rapidity of liberalization was at least partially a result of an ongoing attempt to disrupt and disorganize potential opposition to a new economic strategy; this political rationale for a quick liberalization also seems to have been important in post-1985 Bolivia.

The speed of liberalization may also reflect more general issues of credibility. Economic crises usually erode the public's faith in the current government. In this context, the announcement of a ten-year gradualist strategy complete with phased-in liberalization may cause few agents to alter behavior: Exporters will shake their heads in disbelief at the promises of maintaining a favorable exchange rate and low export duties while domestic financial interests, unconvinced that real interest rates will stay positive, will continue to park assets abroad. In the background, producers of import substitutes may tend their inefficient investments in the hopes of a return to high tariffs while workers' organizations maintain high wage demands in the belief that liberalized labor markets will not persist.[15] The government can gain credibility (and, as noted above, disorganize the opposition) by a rapid liberalization of all markets and external accounts: Such a strategy will dampen workers' wages, ruin import substituters, hurt favored borrowers benefiting from financial repression, and force the domestic financial system to compete with external lenders even as government authorities bask in their new image as stern, politically impervious leaders.

The picture is therefore complicated and contradictory. Economic considerations require caution in the sequencing of orthodox policies and goals: Stabilization should occur first, the current account and domestic financial system should be liberalized after the economy has adjusted, and external capital flows should be opened last. On the other hand, political considerations suggest that policy makers may wish to liberalize early in order to both gain credibility and beat back the potential opponents of freer markets. While it is not clear in orthodox theory which of these two imperatives should dominate policy making, Bolivian authorities, as we will see, opted for the latter strategy: a complete and rapid liberalization of all markets simultaneous with efforts to lower inflation. This did lend the program credibility but, as we will see, brought many of the economic problems outlined above.

Exchange Rate Targeting

Although the orthodox paradigm generally embraces the market determination of prices, there is a particular variant of orthodoxy that includes a "twist": the view that the government should fix one key price, the exchange rate, and allow all other prices to adjust freely. This strategy, it is argued, will eventually bring domestic inflation into line with international inflation, primarily because import competition will restrain domestic price hikes. Such an exchange rate targeting approach was an important part of the Southern Cone experiments of the late 1970s and a crucial element in the Bolivian stabilization program detailed in Chapter 4.

The logic of using the exchange rate to fight inflation can be discerned by transforming the "law of one price" used in the monetary balance of payments model into the following dynamic equation:

(2.21) $\quad \hat{P} = \hat{e} + \hat{P}^{\$}$

in which the rate of domestic inflation, $\hat{P}$, is equal to the rate of currency depreciation, $\hat{e}$, plus the world (or U.S.) inflation rate, $\hat{P}^{\$}$. The usual lesson drawn from such an equation is that countries must step up depreciation if domestic inflation begins to make their exports less competitive. The architects of orthodoxy in Chile, Argentina, and Uruguay in the 1970s, however, essentially reversed this logic, arguing that resistance to currency depreciation, if combined with a trade

Table 2.1
The Effects of Exchange Rate Targeting in Argentina

	GDP Growth	Inflation Rate	Real Effective Exchange Rate (1978=100)	Wage Share of Manufacturing Value-added (1978=100)	Exports (FOB) (millions of US$)	Imports (FOB) (millions of US$)	Merchandise Trade Balance (millions of US$)	Total External Debt (millions of US$)
Prereform								
1973	3.5	61.2	99.8	154.2	3,266	1,978	1,289	6,429
1974	5.5	23.3	85.3	169.4	3,930	3,216	714	6,789
1975	-0.5	182.5	130.4	153.4	2,961	3,510	-549	8,171
Monetarist stabilization								
1976	-0.2	443.2	86.0	97.2	3,918	2,765	1,153	9,880
1977	6.5	176.1	110.8	94.5	5,651	3,799	1,852	11,445
Exchange rate targeting								
1978	-3.4	175.5	100.0	100.0	6,401	3,488	2,913	13,276
1979	7.2	159.5	75.0	109.0	7,810	6,028	1,782	20,950
1980	1.9	100.8	67.2	125.7	8,021	9,394	-1,373	27,157
1981	-6.9	104.5	84.5	110.7	9,143	8,431	712	35,657
Aftermath								
1982	-5.5	164.8	109.7	77.4	7,623	4,859	2,764	43,634
1983	2.9	343.8	101.2	91.7	7,835	4,119	3,716	45,920

Sources: Figures on GDP growth, wage share (employee compensation as a percentage of value-added in manufacturing), exports, imports, and total external debt taken from World Bank, *World Tables, 1989-90*. Figures on inflation rate and real effective exchange rate from Ramos (1986). The dating into periods of prereform, monetarist stabilization (or traditional austerity), and exchange-rate targeting is also taken from Ramos (1986).

Table 2.2
The Effects of Exchange Rate Targeting in Chile

	GDP Growth	Inflation Rate	Real Effective Exchange Rate (1976=100)	Wage Share of Manufacturing Value-added (1976=100)	Exports (FOB) (millions of US$)	Imports (FOB) (millions of US$)	Merchandise Trade Balance (millions of US$)	Total External Debt (millions of US$)
Prereform								
1971	9.1	26.7	105.5	156.0	1,000	927	73	2,618
1972	-1.2	108.3	110.7	202.6	851	1,012	-161	3,050
1973	-5.5	441.0	123.1	111.9	1,316	1,329	-13	3,275
Monetarist stabilization								
1974	0.8	497.8	107.3	83.0	2,152	1,901	250	4,522
1975	-13.2	379.2	115.0	84.0	1,590	1,520	70	4,762
Exchange rate targeting								
1976	3.6	232.8	100.0	100.0	2,116	1,473	643	4,849
1977	9.8	113.8	96.9	119.7	2,186	2,151	35	5,884
1978	8.4	50.0	112.2	122.2	2,460	2,886	-426	7,374
1979	8.3	33.4	100.3	124.5	3,835	4,190	-355	9,361
1980	7.8	35.1	86.2	125.9	4,705	5,469	-764	12,081
1981	5.6	19.7	77.4	157.3	3,836	6,513	-2,677	15,664
Aftermath								
1982	-14.2	9.9	90.6	139.3	3,706	3,643	63	17,315
1983	-0.7	27.3	95.9	116.9	3,831	2,845	986	17,928

Sources: Figures on GDP growth, wage share (employee compensation as a percentage of value-added in manufacturing), exports, imports, and total external debt taken from World Bank, *World Tables, 1989-90*. Figures on inflation rate and real effective exchange rate from Ramos (1986). The dating into periods of prereform, monetarist stabilization (or traditional austerity), and exchange-rate targeting is also taken from Ramos (1986).

Table 2.3
The Effects of Exchange Rate Targeting in Uruguay

	GDP Growth	Inflation Rate	Real Effective Exchange Rate (1978=100)	Wage Share of Manufacturing Value-added (1978=100)	Exports (FOB) (millions of US$)	Imports (FOB) (millions of US$)	Merchandise Trade Balance (millions of US$)	Total External Debt (millions of US$)
Prereform								
1971	0.1	24.0	82.7	82.7	197	203	-6	352
1972	-1.5	76.4	102.2	102.2	282	179	103	402
1973	0.3	97.0	87.5	87.5	328	249	79	416
Monetarist stabilization								
1974	3.1	77.2	84.4	84.4	381	434	-52	715
1975	6.0	81.4	97.1	97.1	385	494	-109	787
1976	4.0	50.7	103.4	103.4	565	537	28	896
1977	1.3	58.2	102.6	102.6	612	687	-75	1,105
Exchange rate targeting								
1978	5.4	44.5	100.0	100.0	686	710	-24	998
1979	6.2	66.8	84.5	84.5	788	1,166	-378	1,323
1980	5.9	63.5	81.4	81.4	1,058	1,668	-610	1,660
1981	1.8	34.1	78.0	78.0	1,230	1,592	-362	2,174
Aftermath								
1982	-9.5	19.0	90.2	90.2	1,256	1,038	218	2,647
1983	-6.0	51.5	111.3	111.3	1,156	740	417	3,292

Sources: Figures on GDP growth, wage share (employee compensation as a percentage of value-added in manufacturing), exports, imports, and total external debt taken from World Bank, *World Tables, 1989-90*. Figures on inflation rate and real effective exchange rate from Ramos (1986). The dating into periods of prereform, monetarist stabilization (or traditional austerity), and exchange-rate targeting is also taken from Ramos (1986).

liberalization to allow in competitive imports, could *force* inflation down to world levels.

The results were disastrous—which leads one to wonder why the strategy was pursued with such vigor in 1980s Bolivia. Tables 2.1 through 2.3 track the experience in Argentina, Chile, and Uruguay. Following the periodization scheme given in Ramos (1986), each country's macroeconomic experience is broken up into a period of prereform crisis, initial monetarist stabilization, the period of exchange-rate targeting, and the aftermath. The problems caused by the exchange rate strategy differed slightly by country but nearly all experienced increasingly overvalued exchange rates, swelling imports, and rapid debt accumulation. The overvaluation stemmed from the stubborn refusal of inflation and inflationary expectations to head downward despite the relative stability of the nominal exchange rate. The competitiveness problem that resulted was aggravated in the Chilean case by the government's decision late in the program to index nominal wages to past inflation rates, a strategy that ensured that real wages would rise as the government successfully lowered the current inflation rate below previous levels.[16]

In all three cases, overvaluation and trade liberalization brought dramatic increases in imports. Supporting the exchange rate and the import boom required foreign borrowing, which in turn prompted a hasty opening of the capital accounts. In the Argentine case, the capital account was liberalized before a full tariff reform, which allowed jittery investors to react to the currency overvaluation with massive capital flight; my own estimates put Argentine capital flight between 1978 and 1982 at 76 percent of its debt accumulation over the same period.[17] Chile was more cautious, relieving first its restrictions on inflow and only later (and then just briefly) removing the controls that had made the exodus of Chilean private capital quite difficult. The result was massive debt accumulation in order to finance imports and avoid the usurious local interest rates triggered by domestic financial liberalization.

Each of the Southern Cone exchange rate experiments collapsed in the wake of internal inconsistencies and the world recession and debt crisis of 1982. The Chilean result is particularly disconcerting for the orthodox view because as McKinnon notes, Chile approximated "the correct order of liberalization" by opening the capital account only *after* tariffs had been restructured from the typically complicated Latin American arrangements to a uniformly low 10 percent (McKinnon 1982:159). Bolivia, which employed the same sort of exchange rate "fixing" coupled with liberalization of nearly every internal and external market, would seem to have either drawn few lessons from this experience—or perhaps simply calculated that history cannot repeat itself. The results, detailed in the Bolivian case study of Chapter 4, seem dangerously close to the fragility evidenced in the earlier Southern Cone experiments.

Conclusion: Realism, Class, and Orthodoxy

The next chapter outlines the heterodox alternative to orthodox analysis. That economists have spent time developing such an alternative implies the existence of doubts about the efficacy of the orthodox model and policies outlined above. This section concludes the chapter with a brief review of these doubts, particularly with respect to the realism of the orthodox model and the class biases of its policies.

The first question about orthodoxy concerns the relative realism of its models and approach. The balance of payments and structural adjustment models of this chapter are built on several key assumptions: (1) Markets clear and hence output is always (or nearly always) at the level associated with full employment; and (2) producers are price-responsive and will, for example, shift toward the production of tradeables after a credible devaluation. Throughout this framework, particularly its rational expectations variant, is the notion that adjustment processes can be relatively rapid; in the frictionless world of neoclassical economics, "doing the right thing" yields a quick return.

But is the world really as frictionless as the model? As elaborated in the following chapter, structuralist and heterodox critics argue that export and import responses are slow, domestic prices are determined by mark-up rather than markets, and expectations are nearly as rigid as the underlying economic structure. In this vision, inflation results from unresolved distributional conflict and is perpetuated by producers passing through wage and exchange rate pressures. Simple monetary restraint will not alter this process, and devaluation will actually accelerate inflation. The world, it is argued, is not the model; with sticky prices, rules, and expectations, direct government intervention is a must.

A second critique of orthodoxy centers on the class bias of orthodox-style stabilization policies. Such biases are difficult to detect from *within* the orthodox perspective itself: Individual workers and individual capitalists are viewed as striking individual deals, the sum total of which produces equilibrating markets. With classes essentially banished from the analysis, attention sometimes turns to a less political consideration of "distributional" issues. In this arena, it is argued that the orthodox economic adjustment need not reduce workers' real wages, particularly if the wage bundle does not include a high portion of newly expensive tradeable goods.

Ignoring class in the analysis, does not, however, cause it to disappear—and the notion that real consumption wages remain constant through orthodox adjustment is not supported empirically. My own study of the effects of IMF programs in Latin America between 1965 and 1981 indicates that the single most consistent and statistically significant impact of Fund programs was a reduction in labor share of income (Pastor 1987a, 1987b). The Southern Cone experiments detailed above are also associated with a reduction in real wages (except for the subsequent partial correction by the wage indexing experiment in Chile) and a general worsening of the distribution of income and wealth (see Ramos 1986:58–68 and Foxley 1981, 1983). While Edwards suggests that the devaluation episodes typical of orthodoxy do not consistently have negative impacts on wage share (see Edwards 1989), recent research has suggested a negative relation between the real exchange rate and the wage share (Pastor and Dymski 1990). Finally, a variety of studies have documented regressive redistribution during the years of the orthodox management of the debt crisis (Cardoso and Helwege 1989; Pastor and Dymski 1990; and Cornia et al. 1987).[18]

Some authors note that the distributional bias of orthodox policy is not simply a result but an intent. In his review of the Southern Cone experiences, for example, Foxley argues that "wage repression was a basic element of the orthodox policy package" (Foxley 1981:205; see also Ramos 1986:58–60 and Diaz-Alejandro 1981:135). I have suggested that the International Monetary Fund, a paragon of orthodoxy, favors elites both because this sector's cooperation in the stabilization process is essential to its success, and because one of the IMF's unspoken roles is to aid the reproduction of capitalist class relations in the various countries that it supervises (Pastor 1987a:28–35).

The class character of orthodoxy may also have important impacts on international relations and capital flows. Adjusting countries that adhere to orthodox policy and engage in domestic redistribution seem better able to attract loan flows from both official and commercial creditors. Previous research on the IMF has associated Fund programs not only with significant redistribution away from workers, but also with balance of payments improvement due to positive movements in the capital (and not the current) account (Pastor 1987a, 1987b). In a study examining the determinants of bank lending to Latin American countries, Dymski and Pastor find that loan flows responded not only to such traditionally important consideration such as current debt load and economic growth, but also to such country actions as enhanced trade openness and worsening income distribution (see Dymski and Pastor 1990). In short, coupling orthodox policy measures and regressive redistribution may be a strategy essentially forced upon a capital-short government. In the Bolivian case, orthodox economic policy and labor repression were indeed key to rekindling the capital flows that were necessary to support the exchange rate targeting central to Bolivia's stabilization program.

Policies that produce a more inequitable distribution of income might be less objectionable if in fact they actually enhanced some broadly defined measure of economic performance. But if the structuralist critique of the realism of the orthodox model is accurate, then the regressive character of orthodox stabilization may be both unnecessary *and* ill-considered, particularly because redistribution can contribute to the class conflicts driving inflation. It is just such a pessimistic view of orthodoxy—as well as political discontent with its distributional consequences—that led policy makers to cast about in the mid-1980s for a new stabilization alternative.

Notes

1. This is a simplified version of the model that Edwards presents as an authoritative version of the basic IMF framework (Edwards 1989). Edwards, in turn, uses as his source the models developed by IMF staff economists Khan, Montiel, and Haque (1986, 1988).

2. By setting the money supply equal to reserves and government bonds, I am also implicitly assuming that the money multiplier is one, that is, that the reserve requirement in the banking system is 100 percent and that there is no currency leakage from the system. This simplifies the math with no substantial effects on the analysis.

3. By removing savings and investment, we simplify the math and focus attention on the linkage between trade problems and government spending. Alternatively, one could argue that the effects of "excess" private investment on the trade balance are not problematic because if investment opportunities are in fact greater than domestic savings, foreign finance is likely to fill the gap and hence prevent reserve loss (see the expositions in Cline [1983:176] and Pastor [1987a:42]). This approach would require more algebra but not alter the central point that the government is the chief culprit behind trade problems, either because of excess spending or because state regulations prevent the free flow of compensatory financing.

4. See the discussion in Note 3.

5. As in Edwards (1989:9), equation (2.11) links domestic credit directly to reserves and thus "provides the intellectual rationale for using credit ceilings as a 'performance criterion'" in IMF programs (Edwards 1989:9). That such ceilings have long been preferred by the IMF and its orthodox practioners is evidenced in a study by IMF staff economists W. A. Beveridge and Margaret Kelly. The study is unusual in that it indicates what sort of performance clauses were incorporated in what are generally secretive Stand-by Arrangements with the Fund: Over the period 1969–1978, nearly 80 percent of upper-credit arrangements with the IMF had at least one fiscal performance clause and 86 percent of this subset included a specific limit on bank credit to the government (Beveridge and Kelly 1980:220–221).

6. Note that the change in the real exchange rate, Δe^r, is equal to the change in the nominal exchange rate because of the fixity of P.

7. A similar sort of approach to modeling structural adjustment is presented in Corden (1986:19–20).

8. This expression for the consumer price index is taken from Dornbusch (1980:70). Although the index appears unusual, its behavior is roughly the same as the more conventional additive index and it is simpler to manipulate in the equations that follow.

9. To see why this is the slope, note that along the budget line total nominal spending, Z, must equal the sum of $P_N N$ and eM. This implies that the equation for the budget line is $[N = (Z/P_N) - e^r M]$.

10. On the other hand, if the economy is devoted entirely to the production of tradeables, then b equals zero and the real consumption wage falls at the same rate as the export wage. In this sort of model, "real wage resistance" can straightforwardly derail adjustment. For a version of real wage resistance with a wage bundle composed of both traded and non-traded goods, see Dornbusch (1980:71–74).

11. More specifically, agents correct for past expectational errors by adjusting current inflation predictions by some percentage of previous errors. Mathematically, this amounts to taking a weighted average of past inflation levels (see Klamer 1983:13).

12. If, in fact, there was an increase in an individual domestic firm's or sector's real price, this would reflect a change in society's preferences. Such a shift could be represented graphically as a change in the shape of the aggregate indifference curve of Figure 2.1, and hence a new long-run equilibrium mix of tradeable and non-tradeable goods.

13. The averages are for the period from initial financial liberalizations until, in each case, maxidevaluations ended the exchange rate targeting characteristic of these Southern Cone experiments. The real interest rate is calculated by deflating the nominal rate by the wholesale price index; using the consumer price index would substantially lower the real interest figure for Argentina but leave the figures for the other two countries virtually unchanged. See Ramos (1986:147–148).

14. The East Asian industrializers had the further "benefit" of pursuing trade liberalization in a world with far less mobile capital. As a result, these countries "opened up on the real side long before it became relevant to open up the economy for capital flows" (Bruno 1989:225). Fate, in short, allowed the East Asian successes to unknowingly pursue the newly deemed "correct" sequence for liberalizing the external sector.

15. In reviewing the Argentine experience in the 1970s, for example, Rodriguez (1983) points to the continuation of investment in formerly protected industries by capitalists who seemed to believe that there would eventually be a reversal of the liberalization strategy.

16. Although the backward indexation of wages was partially in force earlier in the program, it was codified in the Labor Law of 1979 (Edwards 1985:230, and Edwards and Edwards 1987:147).

17. The percentage figure is calculated using external debt figures from the World Bank's *World Debt Tables* and yearly capital flight figures from the raw data used for both the regression exercises and the calculation of capital flight totals in Pastor (1990a). For the exact methodology used to estimate yearly flight, see that article.

18. Cornia directly argues that "prevailing adjustment programs tend to increase aggregate poverty" (Cornia 1987:66).

3

The Macroeconomics of Adjustment: A Structuralist Model

Introduction

Lance Taylor has argued that: "An economy has structure if its institutions and the behavior of its members make some patterns of resource allocation and evolution substantially more likely than others. Economic analysis is structuralist when it takes these factors as the foundation stones for its theories" (Taylor 1983:3). Orthodoxy, in this view, is not structuralist because it *assumes* that Third World economies can be understood using models of flexible prices and optimizing agents. The structuralist or heterodox approach instead views economic institutions, rules, and behavior as somewhat rigid and argues that models of stabilization in Latin America should incorporate mark-up pricing in industry, price inelasticities in the external sector, class conflict over wages, and other features characteristic of the region's economies.

In this chapter, I develop such a structuralist model. The first section uses a particularly simple version of the model to examine the relationships between debt service, inflation control, and economic growth, pointing out both the external restrictions on a developing economy and the possible negative consequences of orthodox policy. I then suggest the outlines of a heterodox policy alternative, but issue a few cautions about the possibility of "excess demand" and inflationary pressures when such an expansionary package is applied without sufficient attention to external sector constraints.

In the next section of the chapter, I develop the model so that it more closely resembles the Peruvian economy. This respecification is in keeping with the structuralist admonition that useful economic models ought to "fit" the particular economy being studied.[1] I use the augmented model to further explore the logic of heterodox reactivation as well as to point to some long-run constraints on the economy that went largely ignored by policy makers in Peru, but contributed significantly to the collapse of the program.

In the next section, I discuss inflation dynamics, policy credibility, and the sequencing problems associated with heterodox adjustment. I close the chapter by examining the class character of heterodox analysis and policy. I argue that while most variants of heterodoxy seek to ameliorate distributional inequalities, they are fundamentally pro-capitalist. The critical feature distinguishing orthodoxy from heterodoxy is not its class sympathies but rather its recognition that class and distributional conflicts are an important determinant of the inflationary process—and that therefore inflation control must involve an explicit attempt to arrive at a new consensus or *conciliation* between opposing social classes.

A Simple Model

This section offers a simplified version of a model developed in Krugman and Taylor (1978).[2] I begin by specifying the model's assumptions about production, pricing, and market-clearing, then go on to demonstrate how these economic characteristics can make orthodox policy both ineffective and distributionally regressive. I then explore the logic of heterodox policy, particularly the prescription for reducing debt service, and conclude by exploring the limits to heterodox reactivation of a structurally dependent economy.

Assume the economy being modeled has two basic sectors, primary commodity exports and formal industry. The latter produces a domestic consumption good, Q, under conditions of constant returns to scale using two inputs—labor and an imported intermediate—in fixed proportions. Exports are produced using labor alone, an assumption of convenience which is dropped in a subsequent section.

Let export and import prices be given by the world market. In industry, price is determined by a mark-up on unit labor and import costs. Formally:

(3.1) $\quad P_X = eP_X^\$$

(3.2) $\quad P_M = eP_M^\$$

(3.3) $\quad P_Q = (Wb^Q + eP_M^\$ m^Q)(1 + z)$

where P_X, P_M, and P_Q are export, import, and output prices respectively; the dollar (\$) superscript refers to world prices; W is the nominal wage; b^Q and m^Q are the labor-output and intermediate-output ratios in the Q sector; and z is the mark-up.[3]

There are three markets: exports, imports, and domestic goods. Export capitalists produce at full capacity and export volume is largely insensitive to short-run changes in the exchange rate or world prices.[4] Imports are composed entirely of intermediates and demand is derived from the level of output, Q. Domestic output, Q, is a function of domestic consumption spending and autonomous expenditures. Assume that workers spend all their income while capitalists spend only a portion, c. Assume further that both investment and government expenditures are autonomous; call the total of such spending G.

The Macroeconomics of Adjustment: A Structuralist Model

All three markets clear when:

(3.4) $P_X X = P_X X$

(3.5) $P_M M = P_M m^Q$

(3.6) $P_Q Q = c(P_X - Wb^X)X + Wb^X + c(P_Q - eP_M^\$ m - Wb^Q)Q + Wb^Q Q + P_Q G$

Note that domestic demand in (3.6) is composed of the spending of export sector capitalists and workers, domestic sector capitalists and workers, and the aforementioned autonomous spending.

Summing across the markets yields:

(3.7) $(P_M m^Q - P_X X) + (1-c)R^X X + (1-c)R^Q Q = P_Q G$

where R^i denotes the nominal unit profits from sector i (e.g., R^X equals $(P_X - Wb^X)$). Equation (3.7) is a standard "injection-leakage" equality: Foreign savings plus domestic savings from the export and industrial sectors must equal autonomous expenditures.

To simplify matters, set X equal to one (because it is fixed), let the capitalist saving propensity, s, equal $(1 - c)$, and let the profit share of output in each sector, r^i, equal nominal unit profits divided by the relevant price (R^i/P_i). Before manipulating any further, (3.7) can be expressed as:

(3.8) $(P_M m^Q - P_X) + sr^X P_X + sr^Q P_Q Q = P_Q G$

Arbitrarily normalizing $P_M^\$$ at one, and then dividing through by the output price, P_Q, we can restate (3.8) as:

(3.9) $e^r(m^Q Q - t) + sr^X t e^r + sr^Q Q = G$

where t is the price of exports relative to imports (or terms of trade) and e^r is the real exchange rate (e/P_Q). Solving for Q yields the relationship:

(3.10) $Q = \alpha[G + te^r(1 - sr^X)]$.

where α is the multiplier, $[1/(e^r m^Q + sr^Q)]$. Note that the profit share in industry is essentially fixed by the mark-up (i.e., r^Q equals $[z/(1+z)]$), a stability that implies that the multiplier, α, is unchanging over Q.[5]

Real foreign savings (i.e., the real trade deficit, TD) is the first term in (3.9), $e^r(m^Q Q - t)$. Trade is in balance when $Q = t/m^Q$; note that this level of Q, Q^{BOT}, is determined by "exogenous" factors, such as world prices and the technologically given import coefficient. The deficit rises along with output, Q, a relationship depicted in Figure 3.1; note that the intercept for the function is (-te^r), and the slope of the line is e^{r}m^Q.

We can determine the trade deficit associated with macroeconomic equilibrium, TD^{ME}, by rearranging (3.9) as:

(3.11) $\quad TD^{ME} = G - sr^X te^r - sr^Q Q$

where TD^{ME} falls as Q rises. The economic rationale is straightforward: Increases in output and income allow domestic savings to take the place of foreign savings. This relationship between the deficit (foreign savings) and equilibrium output is labeled ME in Figure 3.1; note that the intercept (for Q equals 0) is (G − sr^{X}te^r) and the slope is (-sr^Q). As usual, there is an answer where the lines cross: Here the actual trade deficit equals the trade deficit required for macro equilibrium and the associated Q is the equilibrium level of output, Q^E.[6] In the figure, the economy is incurring a trade deficit.

Suppose that the government tries to respond to the deficit with the typical orthodox policies of devaluation and absorption reduction. Devaluation naturally increases the profit share in export production, r^X, (because domestic wage costs are unchanged but local currency revenue has increased). As noted earlier, the profit share in industry, r^Q, is fixed by the mark-up and will therefore be unaffected by the devaluation-induced rise in import costs; essentially, the entire increase in the import bill is passed along to the output price. However, because nominal wages are fixed, the percentage increase in P$_Q$ will always be less than the percentage increase in the exchange rate; if, for example, import costs comprise 50 percent of all costs, a 10 percent increase in the exchange rate can be passed through with only a 5 percent increase in output price. This implies that devaluation will increase the real exchange rate (e^r or (e/P$_Q$)) even as r^X rises and r^Q remains the same. In our graphical apparatus, ME shifts down to ME', while the intercept of the TD line falls and its slope rises, giving us TD'. Determining the net effect is easy: because Q^{BOT} is structurally given as (t/m^Q), TD must rotate around the point labeled **A** in Figure 3.2. The result is that any devaluation when the economy is running a trade deficit will cause an output contraction—as well as the obvious increase in prices and erosion in the real wage.[7] Adding a reduction in absorption to this orthodox package (e.g., a cut in G) results in a further downward shift in ME, aggravating the stagflationary outcome.

The orthodox package of devaluation and spending cuts is therefore quite unattractive as an adjustment strategy: Short-run trade balance improvement will be driven by recession-induced import cutbacks and not job-creating export expansion. Inflation and class conflict over distribution will, in the meantime, surge. Gone are the rosy results predicted by the traditional models reviewed in Chapter 2. Gone too is the vision of excess demand inflation; here the inflation problem is due to the ability of capitalists to pass through cost increases.

43

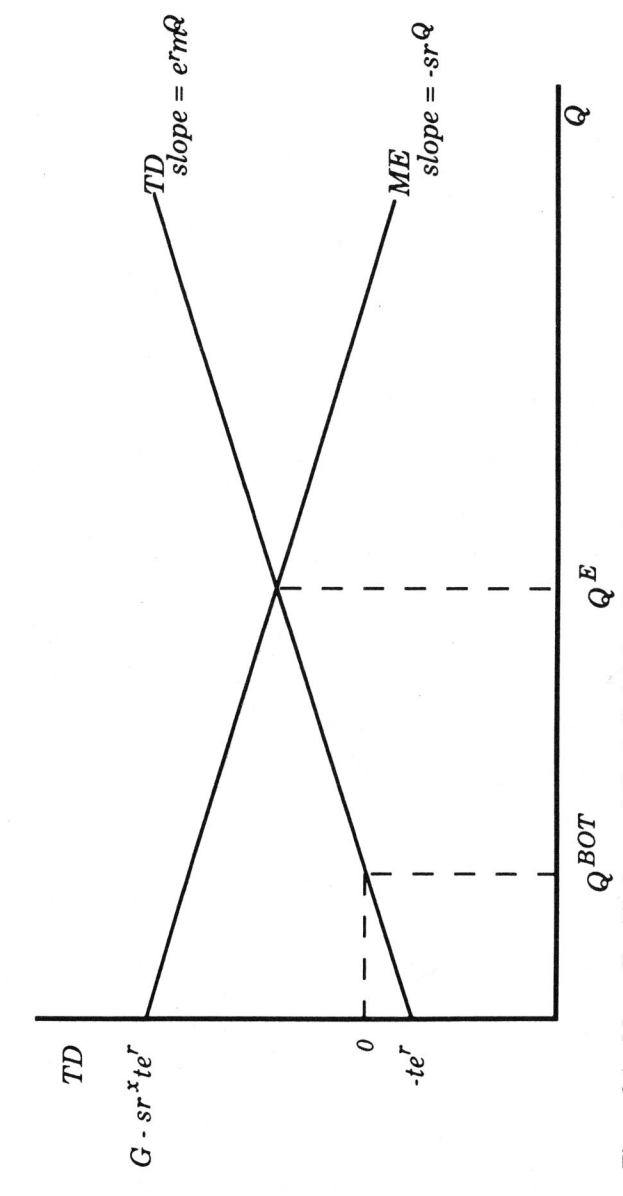

TD

$G - sr^x te^r$

TD
slope = $erm Q$

ME
slope = $-sr Q$

0

$-te^r$

Q^{BOT} Q^E Q

Figure 3.1   Macro Equilibrium and Trade Deficit in a Simple Structuralist Model

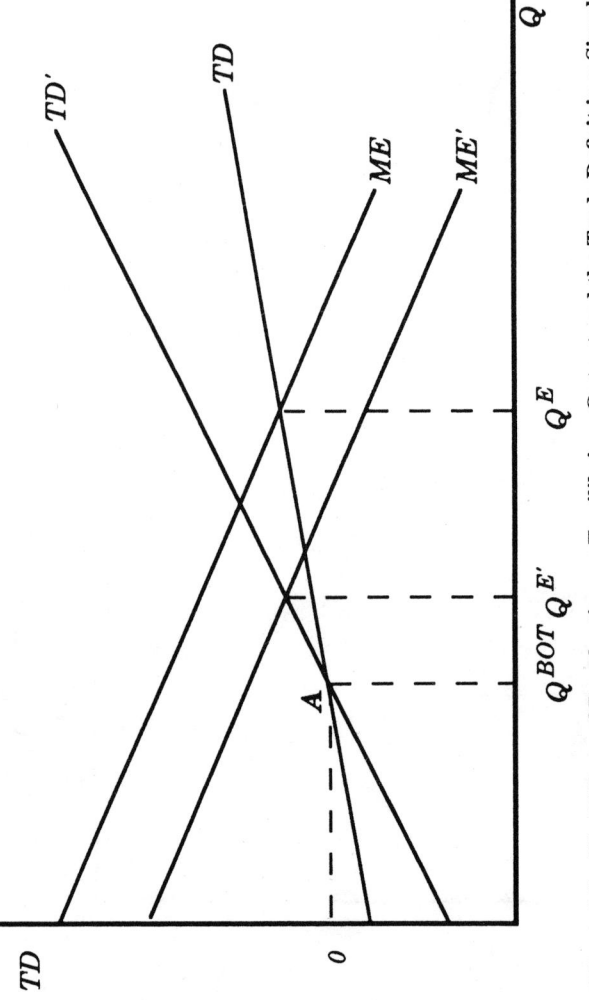

Figure 3.2 The Effects of Devaluation on Equilibrium Output and the Trade Deficit in a Simple Structuralist Model

Table 3.1
The Structure of Peruvian Trade, 1980-1985

	Traditional Exports (as % of exports)	Capital Goods and Intermediates (as % of imports)
1980	78.4	71.9
1981	78.4	73.7
1982	76.9	71.8
1983	81.6	69.4
1984	76.9	79.2
1985	76.0	76.5

Source: Calculated from figures in Cuánto (1990:838, 845).

How well does such a heterodox vision of sticky prices and even stickier supply responses match the reality of a developing country, particularly Peru? As it turns out, the simple structuralist description seems quite apt. In 1985, the year the heterodox team came to power, nearly 80 percent of Peruvian exports were of the price-insensitive "traditional" variety, while a similar percentage of imports were the sort of intermediate and capital goods used in relatively fixed proportions in domestic manufacturing (see Table 3.1). Pricing behavior was also quite sticky: Former Peruvian Central Bank President Richard Webb estimated that in 1980–1985, 33 percent of final domestic demand was in sectors where prices were determined by direct government control, 23 percent was in sectors where mark-up rules were the norm, 17 percent was in a "semi-flex" price sector (mostly tradeables or high import-content goods in which prices were largely determined by the government-set exchange rate), and only 27 percent of final demand was in the "flex-price" sector typical of orthodox theory.[8] In short, price-setting by capital or the government characterized most of the economy (Webb 1987b:14).

The results of orthodox medicine in Peru also fit the predictions of the simple structuralist model. After growth flattened in 1982 and fell by over 12 percent in 1983, the government, operating under an IMF arrangement through the Extended Fund Facility, implemented a policy of rapid depreciation and fiscal tightening (see Table 3.2). Exports barely budged upward in 1984, then fell in 1985. Adjustment came on the import side—a fall of nearly 50 percent in *nominal* terms between 1982 and 1985—and growth suffered as a result. Inflation doubled and, as feared by structuralists, the real wage declined by 30 to 40 percent (depending on the measure), prompting the profit share of income (net of interest payments to foreign creditors) to rise from around 35 percent in 1982 to 38.4 percent in 1985 (Cuánto 1990a:275).

Table 3.2
Macroeconomic and Other Data for Peru, 1980-1985

	1980	1981	1982	1983	1984	1985
GDP Growth	4.5	4.4	0.3	-12.3	4.8	2.4
Inflation rate (Dec.-Dec.)	60.8	72.7	72.9	125.1	111.4	158.3
Rate of depreciation (official rate, end of period)	36.6	48.4	95.2	129.5	150.8	144.9
Index of real wages (1980=100)	100.0	105.1	105.1	87.2	74.4	64.1
Public sector deficit (as % of GDP)	-3.9	-6.7	-7.3	-9.8	-6.1	-2.4
Exports (US$ mil.)	3,916	3,249	3,293	3,015	3,147	2,978
Imports (US$ mil.)	3,090	3,802	3,722	2,722	2,140	1,806
Trade balance (US$ mil.)	826	-553	-429	293	1,007	1,172

Sources: Growth of real GDP from statistics in Instituto Nacional de Estadística (INE) (1989:133); inflation from Cuánto (1990a:602); rate of depreciation from Cuánto (1990a:680) and *International Financial Statistics Yearbook, 1990*; real wage (for manual workers) from Cuánto (1990a:718); and exports, imports, and the trade balance from Cuánto (1990a:827).

If orthodox adjustment is so problematic, how then should inflation be fought? The structuralist view suggests that the government should avoid inflation-inducing devaluation and instead apply direct controls on wages and prices. Having forsaken the devaluation tool, the government must develop other ways of improving the payments and reserves position. To see the alternatives, assume for ease that net debt flows (NDF)—new debt minus amortization and interest payments—are entirely autonomous. When NDF is less than zero—during a time of crisis and repayment—the maximum attainable Q with payments balance, Q^{BOP}, is less than Q^{BOT}: The economy must restrain absorption (shift back ME) and run a trade surplus in order to pay creditors (see Fig. 3.3). Under these conditions, relief from debt payments (an increase in NDF) makes it possible to avoid devaluation and the inflationary consequences it may bring. Debt relief also creates the "space" for economic growth by allowing an increase in intermediate imports.

Debt service limits may therefore help to combat inflation and reactivate the economy. This policy is illustrated in Figure 3.3: NDF increases to NDF', shifting Q^{BOP} to $Q^{BOP'}$. This allows the possibility of output expansion but will not neces-

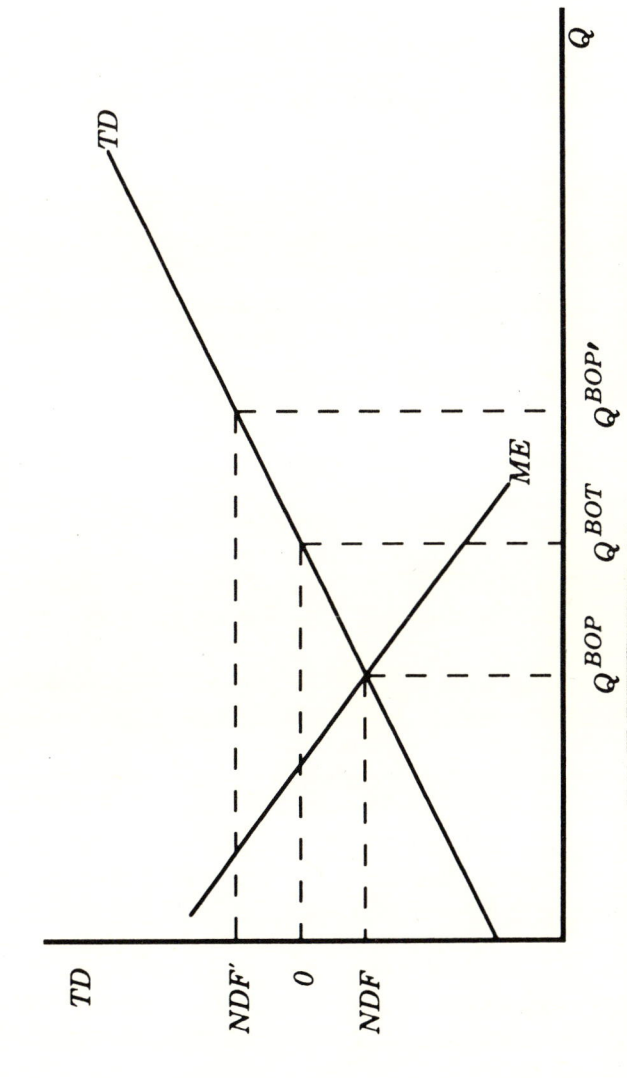

Figure 3.3 Net Debt Flows and Payments Balance in a Simple Structuralist Model

sarily induce it; that requires shifting ME up and/or rotating TD clockwise around $(0,Q^{BOT})$. In Peru, this was accomplished by a combination of short-term increases in wages and the fiscal deficit (both of which affect ME) and some degree of real currency appreciation (which affects both ME and TD). The tools of this demand boost are more fully specified and discussed in the expanded model of the next section.

What happens if ME is shifted so much that equilibrium output, Q^E, exceeds the new output level associated with payments balance, $Q^{BOP'}$? Reserves will drain, producing "excess demand" of a particular sort: a shortage of obtainable intermediate imports that prevents supply from rising to meet demand. Firms will respond by increasing the mark-up, creating a decline in e^r and an increase in r^Q. The graphical effects are complex: ME shifts up and becomes steeper while TD rotates clockwise around $(0,Q^{BOT})$. For all points to the right of Q^{BOT} (and some to the left), the net effect will be a reduction in the equilibrium level of Q. The economics are simple: the increase in the mark-up is redistributing income toward the higher-saving capitalist class, thereby reducing real aggregate demand and output.[9]

In short, operating above Q^{BOP} will yield stagflation—a result that would be exacerbated by the speculative attacks on local currency and collapse in investment that are likely to occur in the context of falling reserves. This possibility of "excess demand" arises *even if* the economy is far below full employment. Any rejection of demand-driven inflation should therefore be nuanced: What counts is not capacity constraints but import constraints.[10]

Although this inflation warning flows clearly from a structuralist model, it went largely ignored by the heterodox policy makers in García's administration. In Chapter 5, I explore the political and economic determinants of this and other policy errors; in the following section, I take on the more immediate task of augmenting the model to more closely fit the Peruvian case.

A Fuller Model

Structuralism admonishes the analyst to make models appropriate to the macroeconomy in question. To that end, I briefly augment the basic model above with features specific to both the Peruvian economy and the practice of Peruvian heterodoxy.

The augmented model includes a parastatal (or public enterprise) sector that produces goods (P) used as inputs in domestic production and priced at P_p; any losses in this sector essentially add to demand by subsidizing the private sector. The model also includes an agricultural sector in which output is generally insufficient to meet food demand (the per capita food requirement, f, multiplied by the number of workers) and so food imports are required.[11] Both domestic and foreign producers receive the "world price" for food, $eP_F^\$$, while consumers pay a government-set price that is less, $e'P_F^\$$; in essence, consumers receive a nominal

The Macroeconomics of Adjustment: A Structuralist Model

subsidy whose size is determined by the nominal exchange rate differential (e − e').[12] Finally, we now have a financial sector that receives income from interest charges on working capital. The gross profit share in either exports or domestic industry, $r^{i'}$, is now composed of that portion of value going to the relevant capitalist, r^Q or r^X, and that going to the financier; for ease, finance capitalists are assumed to have the same consumption propensities as their productive counterparts. Note that higher interest rates will, as in Taylor (1981), drive up prices because now P_Q equals $[(1+z)(1+i)(\text{unit costs})]$.

Investment is assumed to respond to lagged profitability and current business confidence: In the Q sector, it also responds positively, and in an increasing fashion, to utilized capacity (which can be proxied by lagged levels of Q). Investment plans are fixed in terms of real domestic expenditure (i.e., deflated by P_Q) but include the purchase of foreign capital goods, U, in a technologically set ratio, β, to domestic investment goods, I^Q. In sector i, then, total real investment, I^i, equals $I_Q^i(1+\beta^i e^r)$.

The productive structure of the model is summarized in Table 3.3 and a helpful list of symbols and abbreviations is offered in Table 3.4. The markets now include the industrial sector, exports, intermediate imports, parastatal goods, domestic food (as valued at producer prices with the state essentially serving as purchaser), food imports, total food at the subsidized prices (with the state as supplier and consumers as demanders), and imported capital goods. In notational form,

(3.12) $P_Q Q = cR^{Q'}Q + cR^{X'}X + (W - e'P_F^\$ f)(b^Q Q + b^X X + b^P P) + eP_F^\$ F^D + P_Q G + P_Q I_Q^Q + P_Q I_Q^X$

(3.13) $eP_X^\$ X = eP_X^\$ X$

(3.14) $eP_M^\$ M = eP_M^\$(m^Q Q + m^X X)$

(3.15) $P_p P = P_p p^Q Q$

(3.16) $eP_F^\$ F^D = eP_F^\$ f(b^Q Q + b^X X + b^P P + b^F F^D) - eP_F^\$ F^M$

(3.17) $eP_F^\$ F^M = eP_F^\$ f(b^Q Q + b^X X + b^P P + b^F F^D) - eP_F^\$ F^D$

(3.18) $e'P_F^\$ F = e'P_F^\$ f(b^Q Q + b^X X + b^P P + b^F F^D)$

(3.19) $eP_U^\$ U = eP_U^\$(U^Q + U^X)$

Macro-equilibrium can be determined, as before, by summing across markets. The result is:

(3.20) $[eP_M^\$ M + eP_F^\$ F^M + eP_U^\$ U^Q - eP_X^\$ X] + [sR^{Q'}Q + sR^{X'}X] = [P_Q I_Q^Q + P_Q I_Q^X + eP_U^\$(U^Q + U^X)] + [P_Q G + (Wb^P - P_p)P + (e - e')P_F^\$ F]$

Table 3.3
Productive Structure of the Augmented Model

Sectors	Classes	Productive Structure
Industry (Q)	Capitalists	$Q = f(L^Q, M^Q, P^Q)$
Exports (X)	Workers (L)	$X = f(L^X, M^X)$
Imports	Peasants	$F^D = f(L^F)$
Intermediates (M)		$P = f(L^P)$
Capital goods (U)		$L = L^Q + L^X + L^F + L^P$
Food (F^M)		
Parastatal (P)		
Food [domestically-produced] (F^D)		

Despite the abundance of symbols, the equation is straightforward: Macro-equilibrium is obtained when foreign savings and domestic savings equal investment and the budget deficit (which consists of government spending, parastatal losses, and food subsidies).[13]

To express macro-equilibrium in real terms, divide intermediate imports into those used in the production of Q and X, substitute the expression from (3.17) for food imports, substitute the expression from (3.15) for parastatal goods, divide the whole equation by P_Q, and solve for Q. Normalize *all* dollar import prices at one, which simplifies the math at the cost of temporarily assuming a stable structure of import prices. Solving for Q yields:

(3.21) $Q = \alpha\{G + (e^r - e^{r'})fb^f F^D + e^r X(t - sr^{X'}t - m^X - (e^{r'}/e^r)b^X f) + I^Q - e^r \beta^Q I_Q^Q + I^X - e^r \beta^X I_Q^X\}$

where the multiplier, α, equals $\{1/[e^r m^Q + e^{r'} f(b^Q + b^P p^Q) + sr^{Q'} - np^Q]\}$ and n equals the real per-unit loss in the parastatal sector, $[(Wb^P - P_p)/P_Q]$.

The effects of various variables on Q are as follows:

(3.22) $Q = f\{G(+), t(+), X(+), I(+), s(-), r(-), i(-), m(-), n(+), \beta(-), F^D(+), e^{r'}(-)\}$

where the signs following the variables indicate the direction of influence. Although most of the implied comparative statistics are straightforward, a few deserve special mention. First, an increase in the interest rate is stagflationary: It reduces demand by diverting income to high-savings financiers and raises prices as higher working capital costs are passed along to the final price of Q. Second, changes in the agricultural sector can have different effects: An increase in the price of food facing consumers, $e^{r'}$, is recessionary because it reduces government deficit spending while increases in domestic food production have a positive impact on output, mostly because they save foreign exchange. Third, the per-unit

Table 3.4
Symbols and Abbreviations in the Augmented Model

Input/output
- b^i: labor/output ratio in sector i
- m^i: intermediate import/output ratio in sector i
- p^i: parastatal input/output ratio in sector i

Prices
- P_i: price in sector i
- $P_i^\$$: U.S. dollar (world) price for product i
- e: exchange rate (locals/dollar)
- e': differential exchange rate for food imports
- z: mark-up in the Q sector on unit costs
- e^r: real exchange rate (e/P_Q)
- e'': real exchange rate for food imports or real relative price of food (e'/P_Q) with food import price set equal to one
- t: terms of trade ($P_X^\$/P_M^\$$)
- E: exchange rate subsidy ($e' - e''$)

Income
- W: nominal wage
- w: real industrial wage (W/P_Q)
- R^i: nominal unit profits in sector i
- r^i: profit share (R^i/P_i) in sector i
- n: real unit losses in parastatals (($Wb^P - P_P)/P_Q$)
- i: domestic interest rate
- $R^{i'}$: gross nominal unit profits in sector i (including interest on working capital)
- $r^{i'}$: gross profit share in sector i (including share to financial capital)

Capital Account
- $D^\$$: nominal debt in U.S. dollars
- D: real debt ($D^\$/P_M^\$$)
- g: growth rate of debt
- a: amortization rate of debt
- i^W: interest rate on debt
- $IR^\$$: stock of international reserves in U.S. dollars
- IR: real international reserves ($IR^\$/P_M^\$$)
- $CF^\$$: capital flight in U.S. dollars
- CF: real capital flight ($CF^\$/P_M^\$$)

Miscellaneous Symbols
- f: per capita food requirement
- c: consumption propensity (of capitalists)
- s: savings propensity (of capitalists)
- G: real government expenditure (deflated by P_Q)
- I^i: real investment expenditure in sector i (either Q or X) (deflated by P_Q)
- I_Q^i: real investment expenditures in sector i on good Q
- I_U^i: real investment expenditures in sector i on good U
- β^i: technically given ratio of imported to domestic capital goods in sector i
- F^S: domestic food surplus (above peasant requirements), i.e., $(1 - fb^F)F^D$
- H: business confidence

parastatal profit, $-np^Q$, is equivalent to a proportional tax rate on Q; if parastatals increase profitability, n falls and Q follows suit.[14]

Before exploring the effects of other policies, including devaluation, it is useful to specify the BOP$^\$$ (in dollars) as follows:

(3.23) $\quad BOP^\$ = BOT^\$ + (g - a - i^w)D^\$ - CF^\$ = \Delta IR^\$$

where BOT$^\$$ is the balance of commercial trade, D$^\$$ is the dollar level of debt, g is the growth rate of debt, a the amortization rate, i^W the world interest rate, CF$^\$$ the dollar level of capital flight, and $\Delta IR^\$$ denotes the change in international reserves. Given the productive structure, the balance of trade can be elaborated as:

(3.24) $\quad BOT^\$ = P_X^\$ X - P_M^\$(m^X X + m^Q Q) - P_F^\$[f(b^X X + b^Q Q + b^P p^Q Q + b^F F^D) - F^D] - P_U^\$(U^Q + U^X)$

Normalizing all import prices at one and solving for the output level associated with trade balance yields:

(3.25) $\quad Q = [X(t - m^X - fb^X) + F^S - (U^Q + U^X)] / [m^Q + f(b^Q + b^P p^Q)] = Q^{BOT}$

where F^S is domestic food production net of producer consumption, i.e., $F^D(1 - fb^F)$. The output level associated with payments balance, Q^{BOP}, (where ΔIR equals zero) is:

(3.26) $\quad Q^{BOP} = Q^{BOT} + \{[(g-a-i^w)D - CF] / [(m^Q + f(b^Q + b^P p^Q))]\}$

where D and CF are the real values of debt and capital flight (deflated by the average import price).[15] As usual, positive flows in the capital account can enhance potential output levels beyond those obtainable without such flows.

Now consider the effects of an adjustment package containing measures typically recommended by the IMF and orthodox economists: Cuts in food subsidies, reductions in parastatal losses, increases in domestic interest rates, and devaluation. This conventional package will, as in the earlier model, be stagflationary: Increases in $e^{r'}$ (the real consumer price of food) and reductions in n will decrease Q while the interest rate increases will raise both $r^{Q'}$ and the nominal price level.

Devaluation is likely to contribute to the other stagflationary outcome. Depreciation can have effects on e^r (the real exchange rate), $r^{X'}$ (the gross profit share in exports), and the levels of exports, domestic food production, and investment purchases. Assume that the resulting increase in r^X will not quickly increase exports (a traditional assumption for such traditional exports), that the devaluation-induced increase in food prices will not generate extra food production due to short-run supply constraints, and that all food subsidies are eliminated such that $e^{r'}$ equals e^r.[16] With these assumptions in mind, the derivative of Q with respect to

The Macroeconomics of Adjustment: A Structuralist Model

e^r can be determined by returning to the macro-equilibrium condition expressed in (3.21) and employing some straightforward substitutions for food and investment. The result is:

(3.27) $(dQ/de^r) = \alpha\{F^S + X[t - sr^Xt - m^X - fb^X - ste^r(dr^{X'}/de^r)] - U^Q - U^X + K\} - \alpha Q[m^Q + f(b^Q + b^Pp^Q)]$

where K equals $\{-e^r[(dU^Q/de^r) + (dU^X/de^r)]\}$ and is greater than zero.[17]

The derivative of $r^{X'}$, $[1 - (m^X/t) - (wb^X/e^rt)]$, with respect to e^r can be expressed as:

(3.28) $(dr^{X'}/de^r) = (wb^X/((e^r)^2t)) - (b^X/e^rt)(dw/de^r)$

where w, the real industrial wage (W/P_Q), falls as e^r rises. Substituting into (3.27) the expression for $r^{X'}$ and $(dr^{X'}/de^r)$ and manipulating yields:

(3.29) $(dQ/de^r) = \alpha\{F^S + X[t - st + sm^X - m^X - fb^X + sb^X(dw/de^r)] - U^Q - U^X + K\} - \alpha Q[m^Q + f(b^Q + b^Pp^Q)]$

This derivative falls as Q rises, equalling zero when:

(3.30) $Q = \{X[(t - m^X)(1 - s) - fb^X + sb^X(dw/de^r)] - (U^Q + U^X) + F^S + K\} / [m^Q + f(b^Q + b^Pp^Q)]$

which is generally less than Q^{BOT}.[18] Again, as long as the economy is operating with a trade deficit—or even with a moderate trade surplus—devaluation will be contractionary as well as inflationary.

Devaluation will also dent investment because for any level of real investment *expenditures*, less imported capital goods (and hence less complementary domestic investment goods) can be purchased. This negative impact will be worsened in subsequent periods because of recession and idle capacity in industry. On the distributional side, real wages will fall as a result of inflation, while agricultural incomes may rise *but only if* farmgate prices are actually raised to reflect the higher price of food imports.[19]

This is a picture even more dismal than in the simpler model. The previous section described the poor growth, inflation, and distributional performance of Peru's orthodox adjustment in the early 1980s. As suggested above, private investment also suffered, falling from 18 percent of GDP in 1980 to only 12 percent of GDP in 1985. On the sidelines, heterodox economists, using models similar to the one developed here, sharply criticized Peru's orthodox approach to adjustment (see Carbonetto 1987; Dancourt 1986a, 1986b; Herrera 1985; and Jiménez 1986). With the election of Alan García in 1985, the critics finally got their own chance to shape policy.

Heterodox strategy centers on reversing the pattern brought by orthodox-style adjustment: It shares the goal of inflation reduction but wishes to see this accompanied by output increases, a more progressive distribution of income, and some recovery of investment and agriculture. In Peru, the central policies used to pursue these seemingly contradictory goals included debt service reduction; increases in subsidies, parastatal deficits, and the real wage; reductions in nominal interest rates; freezes on prices and the exchange rate; and an attempt to protect industrial profitability.

The debt service reduction was intended to create "space" for economic growth by relieving the import constraint on domestic production; actually filling that space with new output required the other changes in macro policy outlined above. Figure 3.4, which adopts and modifies the earlier graphical apparatus to fit this more complex model, makes evident that the short-run targets for attaining more output are $r^{Q'}$, G, $e^{r'}$ (or the real exchange rate subsidy, E, which equals e^r minus $e^{r'}$), and n.[20] The Peruvian government was reluctant to expand its own investment or current spending because of concerns that capitalists would see this as an attempt to enlarge the state role and therefore hold back on their own investment spending. The fears of dampening private investment also precluded excessive reductions in r^Q, the postinterest profit share in industry. With government spending hikes and reductions in postinterest profits off the table, aggregate demand could only be expanded by: (1) reducing the gross profit margin, $r^{Q'}$, by reducing interest rates (which allowed an increase in the real wage while protecting the return on "productive" capital) and (2) increasing the government deficit through enhancing food subsidies and reducing the real price of parastatal inputs. To avoid the usual inflationary effects from such new demand, price controls were applied and the exchange rate was frozen.

The distributional impacts of the program were straightforward: With industrial prices fixed, the terms of trade shifted toward the unregulated agricultural and informal sectors. Real consumption wages for urban workers rose due to the food subsidy; reduced interest and parastatal costs even made possible an increase in the real product wage (W/P_Q) without significantly decreasing r^Q or triggering cost-push inflation. The real wage increases added to new demand and hence helped short-run growth. These distributional results, the Peruvian team argued, would not diminish investment, particularly in light of growing markets and the government commitment to protect the postinterest profit shares of productive capital.

The initial results of Peruvian heterodoxy were much as predicted: enhanced growth; lower inflation; improved distribution to workers, peasants, and the informal sector; and an eventual recuperation of private investment. Why then did the experiment eventually collapse into hyperinflation?

Although a complete explanation awaits the political and economic analysis of Chapter 5, the above model suggests several critical economic problems and limits. Consider, for example, the restrictions on debt service. Although such policies

TD

A

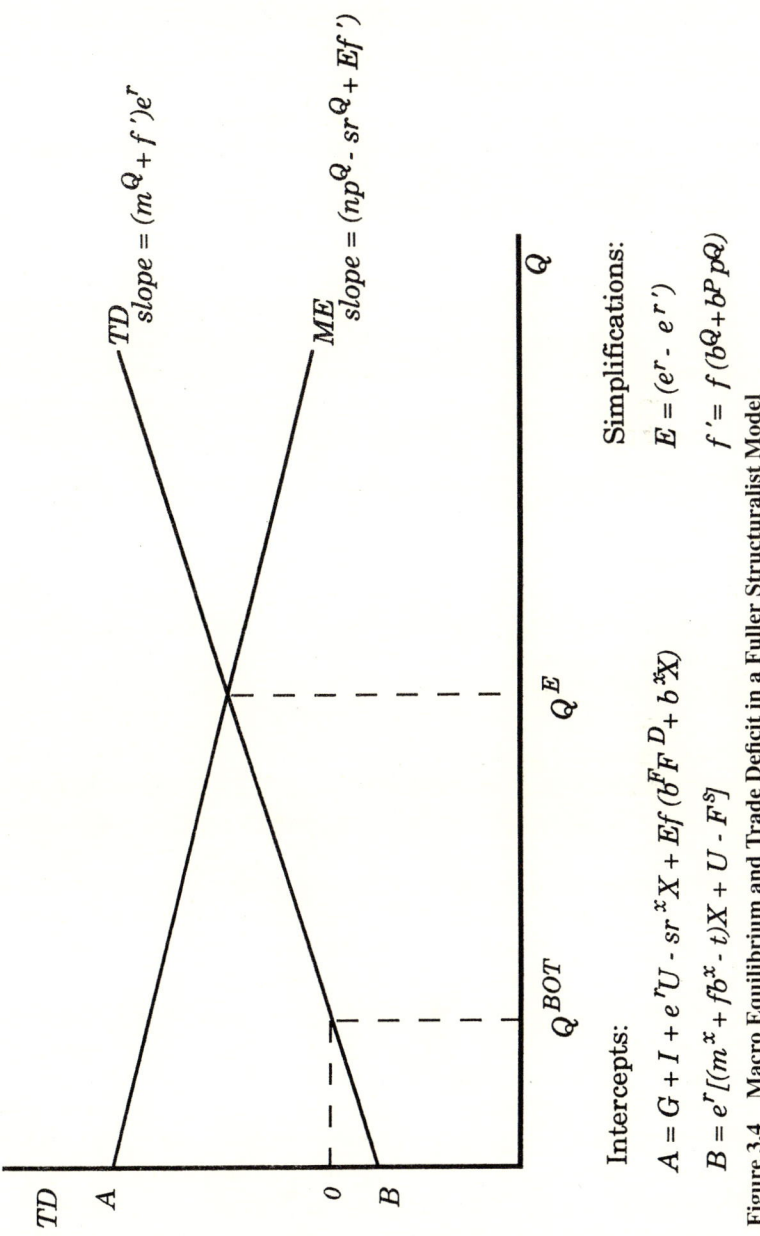

TD
slope = $(m^Q + f')e^r$

ME
slope = $(np^Q - sr^Q + Ef')$

0

B

Q^{BOT} Q^E *Q*

Intercepts:

$A = G + I + e^r U - sr^x X + Ef(b^F F^D + b^x X)$

$B = e^r[(m^x + fb^x - t)X + U - F^S]$

Simplifications:

$E = (e^r - e^{r'})$

$f' = f(b^Q + b^P p^Q)$

Figure 3.4   Macro Equilibrium and Trade Deficit in a Fuller Structuralist Model

may initially increase net debt flows, NDF, and hence the sustainable level of output, Q^{BOP}, international capital is likely to quickly reduce new loans and drag NDF downward again; the gains from restricting interest and amortization are, at best, temporary. It is thus critical to attack the structural barriers to growth and payments balance by lowering import requirements (for both intermediate and capital goods), expanding exports (to pay for necessary imports), and enhancing domestic agriculture (to save on food imports). If no progress is made toward these goals, the space gained by enhancing net debt flows will be depleted: Reactivation will simply drive up the importation of food and intermediates, and the economy will return to a position of external strangulation.

As for the exchange rate, a temporary freeze may help fight inflation but such a policy conflicts with the medium-term need to develop nontraditional exports (which may, in fact, be sensitive to devaluation-induced price changes) and can also encourage capital flight.[21] To see the latter effect, let capital flight ($CF^\$$) be specified as a function of business confidence, domestic interest rates, and the degree of perceived overvaluation (the expected exchange rate, e^{ex}, minus the ruling exchange rate), i.e.,

(3.31) $\quad CF^\$ = f(H, i, (e^{ex} - e))$

where exchange expectations are, in turn, a function of the change in dollar reserves, $\Delta IR^\$$, and the current exchange rate, e:

(3.32) $\quad e^{ex} = f(\Delta IR^\$, e)$

For any given exchange rate, a fall in reserves to support reactivation will lead economic agents to expect devaluation and hence a higher future exchange rate. This increases the perceived overvaluation problem and produces capital flight (or, more generally, any sort of retreat into dollars), a process that simply exacerbates the downward spiral in resources. Moreover, the expectation of a future devaluation and, hence, an increase in r^x, can cause investors to hold off on investment in export production until such devaluation occurs, a delay that will also worsen current reserve problems. Stemming flight and accelerating investment requires policies that slow (or reverse) the reserve loss and make the current exchange rate more "credible." Obviously, a devaluation could accomplish all these tasks; if policy reluctance continues, capital flight and reserve loss will as well.

Reactivation itself can also pose problems for inflation and distribution goals. As emphasized above, the relevant inflation barrier in a developing economy is not full capacity output (Q^F) but rather that level of output associated with trade and payments equilibrium (Q^{BOP}). As heterodox demand expansion pushes Q^E beyond Q^{BOP}, firms are tempted to increase the mark-up in order to ration demand to that level consistent with import constraints; the problem is worse if international capital reacts to debt limits by pushing NDF and Q^{BOP} down, and hence tightens the import/inflation constraint. Overexpansion, in short, may wind up triggering inflation as well as redistributing income away from those groups heterodoxy seeks to protect.

Deficit-widening is also a problem.[22] Even if accelerator effects dominate and investment is not "crowded out," rising deficits may contribute to instability by pushing output past that level consistent with payments balance. If this leads to expectations of inflation and future devaluation, there will be the aforementioned movement to hold wealth in dollars. The subsequent pressure on the exchange rate can trigger a cost-push inflation *even if* excess capacity exists in the economy.

In short, a successful heterodox strategy cannot long ignore the importance of orthodox concerns about exchange rates, the external sector, and budget deficits. Indeed, such external and internal bottlenecks are easily foreseeable *within* the structuralist framework.[23] As detailed in Chapter 5, euphoria about the initial growth and inflation-fighting successes of Peruvian heterodoxy seems to have led García's economic advisors to forget their structuralist roots; by the time the policy team recognized the need to change direction, political divisions and governmental weakness prevented implementation of a new package. The result was a macroeconomic disaster that tarnished heterodox economics and may prevent similar experiments for years to come.

Inflation Dynamics, Credibility, and Sequencing

Until now, I have analyzed inflation and growth with the tools of comparative statics. Such an approach is useful because it is simple and allows an easy incorporation of various structural features (including the rigidity of exports, import coefficients, and food supply). However, a full understanding of the heterodox anti-inflation program requires a discussion of the dynamics of inertial inflation and the questions of policy credibility and sequencing.

Consider a reduced expression for industrial output price, P_Q, as a function of the mark-up, z, on the costs of labor, imports, parastatal inputs, and credit:

(3.33) $P_Q = f(W, e, P_P, i, z)$

With nominal interest rates fixed by the government and the mark-up by capital, inflation is driven primarily by movements in wages, the exchange rate, and government-set prices:

(3.34) $\hat{P}_Q = f(\hat{W}, \hat{e}, \hat{P}_P)$

where the "hat," ^, above a variable indicates a rate of change.

If wages and the other right-hand side variables are themselves set in response to past inflation, perhaps because agents seek to maintain previous real incomes, then current inflation has an historical or *inertial* component. If such backward indexing is perfect, then *all* inflation is inertial and current inflation is *exactly* equal to previous inflation, i.e., $\hat{P}_Q$ equals $\hat{P}_Q^{-1}$.

In reality, both capital and labor's expectations about inflation and their respective abilities to "pass through" previous wage or price hikes is dependent on the current level of economic activity as well as the state of payments pressures (since, as noted in the model above, foreign exchange shortages allow a rise in the mark-up in order to ration demand). In addition, the government generally has sufficient discretion over the exchange rate and parastatal prices that it can increase these prices at rates either faster or slower than previous inflation. This suggests that (3.34) should be specified as:

$$(3.35) \quad \hat{P}_Q = \alpha_1(\beta P_Q^{-1}) + \alpha_2 \hat{e} + \alpha_3 \hat{P}_P + \alpha_4(Q/Q^F) + \alpha_5(Q/Q^{BOP})$$

where the first term accounts for wage behavior (set by its responsiveness, β, to past inflation), the second and third terms capture government price-setting, the fourth term indicates how close the economy is to full employment, the final term indicates how close the economy is to an inflation-triggering payments constraint, and the various α's indicate the effect of cost pressures on the current inflation rate.[24] These parameters (both β and the set of α's) may themselves vary with the level of economic activity—a sluggish economy, for example, makes it more difficult for firms to pass through wage hikes or exchange depreciation.

The orthodox approach to macroeconomic adjustment and inflation control essentially relies on curtailing demand while simultaneously devaluing in order to promote trade balance. Demand restriction produces declines in both the rate of capacity utilization (Q/Q^F) and utilization relative to payments balance (Q/Q^{BOP}). The slack economy reduces capital's ability to pass through exchange depreciation and parastatal costs (i.e., a decline in α_2 and α_3) and lowers both workers' capacity to adjust wages and capital's ability to pass on any wage increases (i.e., a decline in β and α_1). The positive effects on inflation, however, may be offset by more rapid depreciation (a higher $\hat{e}$) and attempts to close the fiscal gap by stemming losses in parastatals (a higher $\hat{P}_P$). In the orthodox view, devaluation's inflationary impact will be subdued by an increase in the level of output consistent with payments balance, Q^{BOP}. Structuralists are more pessimistic about export elasticities and see little dampening of devaluation's cost-push pressures. If the latter predictions are correct, the dynamic results are much like our comparative statics: Orthodox policy may produce recession, real wage declines, and perhaps even higher inflation.

The heterodox alternative is a wage and price freeze that essentially sets all α's (and β) equal to zero and thereby derails the propagation of inertial inflation. The government, in this view, can also help matters along by freezing its own prices, hence setting $\hat{e}$ and $\hat{P}_P$ to zero. Note that the elimination of inflation is achieved in this instance without reducing output; a crucial argument in favor of incomes policy is that inflation can be controlled without the output costs and real wage reductions associated with traditional adjustment.

Although a price freeze can quickly stop inflation, it does not necessarily eliminate any underlying pressure from demand and output levels in excess of production or import capacity. The government may therefore still need to recess the economy, although less than in the orthodox case. Such a conscious recessionary policy may prove difficult because, as Dornbusch and Simonsen conclude, "the temporary success of an incomes policy may lead policy makers to forget that price stability can only be sustained with aggregate demand discipline" (Dornbusch and Simonsen 1987:13). Nonetheless, credibility depends on whether the private price-forming agents, capitalists and workers, believe that the macroeconomic situation will in fact be sustainable if and when controls are lifted; in this light, demand restraint may be an important part of a heterodox package.

Credibility can also be enhanced or eroded by the sequencing of heterodox policies.[25] There are at least four critical issues: the relationship between wage-price controls and relative prices between economic sectors; the precise moment and method for lifting incomes policy; the correct degree (and timing) of remonetization; and the proper use of the political support that stabilization can bring.

To explore the relative price issue, consider an economy in which wage bargaining and price setting are firm- and industry-specific. With different adjustment periods in different contracts, one sector's real wages may be at a periodic peak while another sector's real wages are at a periodic low—even if each sector is adjusting to the general inflation rate by the same parameter β. Adopting a heterodox freeze would misalign relative prices and could also produce severe wage pressures in the "low-wage" sector. Brazil attempted to resolve this problem by determining period averages by sector and mandating an initial readjustment prior to the freeze (Dornbusch and Simonsen 1987:41–42). No such sophistication was employed in the Peruvian case, and this helped to perpetuate underlying inflationary pressure.

The relative price issue also enters into our second sequencing issue: when and how to free wages and prices. It is certainly possible to release too early—prior to altering the expectations and indexations that produced inertial inflation or reducing the demand and distributional pressures that give rise to initial price hikes. Releasing too late poses other problems, primarily because the longer controls exist, the more likely the misalignment of relative prices. Suppose, for example, that prices in noncontrolled sectors continue to rise while prices in sectors under government control remain constant. When the controls are released, producers will be strongly tempted to recover squeezed profits through an immediate inflationary burst. Such price hikes will trigger reaction from workers and the noncontrolled sector and lead to another round of price hikes. The new inflation makes the government's exchange rate and parastatal prices less credible and may raise fears of a large devaluation and increase in government charges; capitalists may seek to protect themselves from this contingency with ever-higher price hikes. In short, a one-shot release of all prices could lead firms to drive prices up as fast and high as possible, mostly to preempt attacks on their real earnings.[26]

A third sequencing issue concerns the money supply. If inflation is successfully stopped through price controls and other measures, monetary tightness will produce excessively high real interest rates. Although remonetization would seem to be the solution, too much new money could erode the credibility of the program, causing producers to evade price controls and wealth-holders to engage in capital flight. The balancing act between dampening interest rates and restraining expectations is likely to be difficult.

A final sequencing problem is political. Stabilization brings both an end to inflation and, because of this, a rise in social and political support for the government. The proper action at this point involves using the political "honeymoon" to push through medium-term corrections, such as the expansion of import capacity through export promotion and import substitution. Because many of these measures can involve reductions in immediate income, governments may be tempted to continue controls, reflation, and other popular measures. This was a severe problem in Peru; intoxicated by early macroeconomic success and pleased by the new support achieved by income redistribution, García and his policy makers failed to address the difficult task of fundamentally restructuring Peru's import-dependent economy.

Although any heterodox program faces a complex set of sequencing issues, the problems in the Peruvian case were even more acute. The explicit limits on debt service, after all, risked confrontation with international creditors; the increasing public sector deficit and misaligned relative prices courted domestic financial disaster; and the redistributive character of the program worried those domestic capitalists whose investment was deemed essential to the medium-term project of economic restructuring. The hope of the Peruvian heterodox team was that the growth resulting from price freezes, unilateral debt relief, and rising demand would produce an increase in private savings sufficient to "replace" the one-shot gain in foreign savings produced by debt service restrictions. Faster growth would also produce swelling tax revenues, shrinking deficits, and a more stable financial sector. Investment would rise once the government convinced capitalists that a new social democratic consensus based on limited redistribution would bring long-term stability.

Each of these hopes was a sort of "brinkmanship"—the economy would be brought to the edge and then rescued by a sudden rise in savings, a supply-side effect on taxes, and a rapid capitalist accommodation with the emerging structure of accumulation. This was sequencing, but of the riskiest sort. As detailed in Chapter 5, the gamble was lost, bringing hyperinflation and recession in its wake.

Conclusion: Heterodoxy and Class

Structuralist economists offer a telling critique of orthodoxy. Positing capitalist mark-up power, rigid exports, and limited price elasticities, structuralists demonstrate that the usual policies of devaluation and government deficit cutting are likely to induce recession, accelerate inflation, negatively affect the distribution of income, and even damage private investment. A heterodox alternative includes debt service limits to create space for growth and an exchange rate and parastatal price freeze to dampen inflationary impulses. In the Peruvian case, real wage increases were also pursued in order to add new demand to the economy as well as to satisfy pent-up social pressures.

Although such an alternative can immediately slow inflation and reactivate the economy, problems will arise along the way. If increases in demand create a foreign exchange shortage, firms will eventually raise their mark-up in order to ration demand. Restrictions on debt service can suspend but not eliminate this external constraint on noninflationary growth; in fact, the constraint will make it bind more tightly if international bankers respond to debt service limits by curtailing new capital flows. Relative prices are also a concern; if price controls are uneven and real prices become misaligned, those sectors suffering income losses are likely to respond to any relaxation of controls with an inflationary round of price hikes. Monetary policy also poses problems; excessive remonetization triggers inflationary expectations, but reining in monetary growth too much will elevate real interest rates and choke economic growth. Finally, the politics of heterodoxy are potentially contradictory: Although the political capital generated by new growth and redistributive incomes policies should be utilized to push through unpopular measures vital to the medium-term sustainability of the economy, this is an especially difficult task for a government basking in high approval ratings.

This last point suggests that politics and class pressures are as crucial to adjustment as any manipulations of exchange rates, government deficits, or the money supply. Structuralist economists generally include class pressures as important determinants of inflationary impulses and dynamics. This is not to say that structuralism, like Marxism, uses its recognition of class in order to argue for a revolutionary upheaval of the social order. Although many structuralists are sympathetic to the need for distributional improvement, their fundamental objective is to understand capitalist macroeconomies and prescribe policies that will improve their functioning.

In this sense, heterodoxy is fundamentally *conciliationist*, or social democratic. Incomes policies are espoused because they make evident distributional struggles and remove the destabilizing nominal adjustments that result from these struggles. Actual shifts in wage and profit shares depend on the particular political pressures facing the program—regressive in Argentina and Mexico and initially progressive in Brazil and Peru. Even if progressive distribution is pursued, it must be emphasized that state interventions associated with heterodox policies are not necessarily a precursor to socialism or even to an enhanced decision-making role for workers within an existing capitalist system.

This was particularly true in García's Peru. The incoming administration and economic team actively courted the support and investment of Peruvian business. Efforts were made to protect industrial profits even as wages rose; price controls may have squeezed profits but cost pressures were softened by reductions in interest rates, exchange rate stability, and declines in the real price of parastatal products. It was thought that such protection would induce private capital to participate in a new accommodation of class and political interests.

But someone clearly had to pay for the redistribution, particularly because government plans included not just a rising share for workers, but also improvements in agricultural and informal sector incomes. With reductions in domestic capitals income share ruled out because of the larger political project, the chosen target for new resources was foreign creditors, an "enemy" clearly consistent with the "anti-imperialist" line of the García administration. Unfortunately, this was a sector even more powerful than domestic capital. International bankers and financial institutions reacted by dramatically curtailing new resources, a phenomenon that threatened reserves and the exchange rate. Frightened by these developments and worried about capital flight, the García administration eventually attempted to nationalize the banking system, partly to secure more control over private sector outflows. For policy makers utilizing a framework cognizant of class dynamics and committed to social conciliation, the nationalization seems surprising. After all, the opposition of domestic capital and the consequent revival of the right wing was as easily foreseeable within the structuralist analysis as the external constraints that, once ignored, soon forced the economy into recession and hyperinflation.

Whether the heterodoxy outlined in this chapter was really tried in Peru is not debatable—it was. But the coherence of the Peruvian application and its consistency with structuralist insights seems to be seriously in doubt. External limits were ignored, class conflict was provoked, and a promising reactivation soon turned into economic chaos. Whether this indicts heterodox adjustment or simply the García experiment is an issue considered in the last two chapters of this book. Such subtle distinctions, however, were lost on the Peruvian populace and its policy makers; as the economy collapsed, a new government turned back to the orthodoxy that had created its own problems at the beginning of the decade. The heterodox alternative had failed and traditional austerity was once again the norm.

Notes

1. As Taylor notes, "plausible models of different economies will have different rules . . . lines of macroeconomic causality (or model "closures") run differently in accordance

with the relevant aggregations of sectors, periods, and economic classes, not to mention a country's politics, institutions, and recent history" (Taylor 1988:4, 26; although the quotes are from different pages, the topic he addresses is the same).

2. A similar model is presented, with slightly different assumptions and notation, in Pastor (1987a:44–51). Despite its simplicity (or perhaps because of it), this framework was the essential starting point for the Peruvian heterodox team.

3. This pricing behavior—cost increases passed through with the mark-up remaining constant—implicitly assumes monetary accommodation, either through a permissive central bank or increases in velocity. The money supply, in essence, is seen as passively responding to capital's need to "ratify" price hikes and valorize profits (Taylor 1988:12).

4. Alternatively, one could argue that export demand is determined by the income levels of advanced capitalist countries, is completely price-inelastic, and, because export capitalists have no incentive to produce unsold stocks, export volume adjusts to demand. The objective here is simply to fix the level of export volume. Such fixity is an assumption also used in the general structuralist model of Krugman and Taylor (1978) and in the Peruvian-specific model of Dancourt (1986b).

5. An alternative to this Kaleckian fixed mark-up approach would allow the profit share to fall (and hence the multiplier to rise) as workers' bargaining power increases near full employment. This sort of model "closure," in which class power and capacity utilization play a role in determining the size of the mark-up, could be labeled "Marxist"; it would also have the characteristic that profit rates (or shares, given the absence of fixed capital) would be equal across the domestic and export sectors. This latter feature implies that orthodox policy would be even more stagflationary, primarily because devaluation would now raise the domestic mark-up in line with increased profitability in export production; this would push prices upward at an even faster rate and choke off even more aggregate demand due to the redistribution of income to higher-savings capitalists. For a formal exposition of this approach, see the appendix in Pastor (1988a).

6. To see that such an equilibrium is stable, note that for any Q less than Q^E, the actual trade deficit (taken from the line, TD) is less than that required for macroeconomic equilibrium. This shortfall in actual foreign savings implies an excess of aggregate demand; Q therefore rises, producing both an increase in actual foreign savings (denoted by a movement up the TD line) and a rise in domestic savings (which is denoted by a movement down ME and implies a decrease in the level of foreign savings *required* for equilibrium). A simple reversal of this exercise for the other side of Q^E would also indicate stability.

7. To see the contractionary condition algebraically, take the derivative of equilibrium Q with respect to e^r. After some manipulation, the result is $dQ/de^r = \{\alpha[t(1-sr^X) - te^rs(dr^X/de^r)] - \alpha Qm^Q\}$. This term falls as Q rises, passing from positive to negative when Q equals $\{[t(1-sr^X) - te^rs(dr^X/de^r)]/m^Q\}$, a level of output that is always lower than Q^{BOT}.

8. Most of the flex-price behavior was in agriculture, a sector that had little short-term macroeconomic impact because price hikes there merely redistributed the source of the demand for manufactures from workers to peasants without generally diminishing the level of demand (see the discussion in Note 12 below). In the long-run, of course, price shifts toward agriculture could make an important contribution to the macroeconomy if supply responds and the government is able to stem any reserve drain prompted by food imports.

9. To see this algebraically, take the derivative of Q with respect to z, working through (de^r/dz) and (dr^Q/dz). The result is $\alpha(e^r/(1+z))[t(1-sr^X) - Q(m^Q + (s/e^r(1+z)))]$. Mark-up increases will therefore be contractionary for all Q greater than $t(1-sr^X)/[m^Q + (s/(1+z)e^r)]$; this level of Q is always less than Q^{BOT}.

10. For evidence of the relative strength of capacity and foreign exchange constraints, see Jiménez (1988). Jiménez's research indicates that the external "gap" is generally the key factor limiting output and growth.

11. The astute observer will notice that capitalists do not eat in this model, a feature that might make many Peruvian workers happy. Capitalists do, however, consume industrial goods. The assumption on capitalist food consumption simplifies the math involved in calculating a derived food demand with no significant loss in realism.

12. An alternative specification of the food sector would allow flexible prices. In this sort of model, producer prices would rise with demand, effecting a redistribution of income to the agricultural sector with increases in industrial production. Given the assumption that all net income in this sector is spent on domestic industrial goods, the direct macroeconomic effects of such a redistribution would be nil. There might be indirect effects if either: (1) the government seeks to lower food subsidy costs by replacing more expensive domestic foodstuffs with imports, thus raising foreign savings and reducing aggregate demand; or (2) food output responds to the price increase, lowering imports and raising aggregate demand. For mathematical simplicity, I stick with the behavior specified above; in the case study of Chapter 5, I recognize the flexibility of some prices and illustrate the redistribution toward agriculture (and the similarly flex-price informal sector) that occurred in the first year of the heterodox program.

13. Note that imported capital goods are on both sides of this equation; in accordance with an argument offered by Jiménez (1988), much of the macroeconomic impact of investment "leaks" abroad.

14. The dynamics of the model would thus gain little by the explicit introduction of taxes (although given the extent of tax evasion in Peru and elsewhere in Latin America, one cannot say the same about the economy).

15. A similar term for D is used by Cline (1984:2) and simply indicates the import capacity given by the debt.

16. Even if there was some export response, increased interest costs may dent into the devaluation-induced increase in r^X and stifle any export expansion. Note that real unit profitability in parastatals, n, may be affected by devaluation in complex ways: While the relative price of parastatal goods falls, so does the real wage (in terms of P_Q) paid to parastatal workers. For mathematical ease, I assume in the text that n does not change, i.e., that the government will seek to at least maintain real unit profitability in parastatal firms (and, in fact, may seek to increase it as part of a deficit reduction effort).

17. The term K captures the complex behavior of investment in this model. Recall that imported capital goods must be combined in fixed proportions with domestic investment purchases. Given fixed real investment expenditure, devaluation forces a reduction in real purchases of both imported and domestic capital goods. Although the cutback in local purchases is sure to dent overall demand, the reduction in leakages due to the curtailment of imported capital goods frees resources for intermediate imports and thus has a partially offsetting positive effect on output.

18. I say generally because while the first term in (3.30) is always less than the first term in (3.25), the presence of F^S and K in (3.30) will slightly increase the value of the numerator.

19. The macroeconomic impacts of this rise in agricultural income may be nil because purchasing power has essentially been transferred from workers to peasants.

20. To simplify the notation in the figure, I use f' to represent the direct and indirect food "embodied" through the labor of workers in one unit of Q (i.e., $f(b^Q + b^P p^Q)$) and, as noted in the text, denote the real exchange rate subsidy, $(e^r - e^{r'})$, with E. I also assume that the ratio of imported to domestic capital goods is the same across sectors (i.e., β^X equals β^Q), a feature that allows us to aggregate all real investment expenditures and denote them with I.

21. For evidence on the causes of capital flight, see Pastor (1990a).

22. Recall that the deficit in the model consists of government spending, parastatal losses, and food subsidies: $[P_Q G + (wb^P - P_p)P + (e - e')P_F^\$ F]$. The second term captures the total loss in the parastatal sector while the last term captures the so-called exchange deficit provided by a divergence between official export and import exchange rates, a subsidy that alone produced losses averaging above 2 percent of Peruvian GDP through 1986 and 1987 (Dornbusch and Edwards 1989:43).

23. This was a point emphasized by Rosemary Thorp, an economist quite sympathetic to Peruvian heterodoxy, when she visited the country in mid-1987 (Thorp 1987). One of the early heterodox theorists, Oscar Dancourt, also emphasized the external sector constraints early on in the program (Dancourt 1987:92; see also Herrera 1987).

24. This equation is similar to an expression in Dornbusch and Simonsen (1987:7). However, their "activity" terms refer to the state of the business cycle (proximity to full employment as in the fourth term of equation (3.35)) and supply shocks. Here, supply shocks would arise primarily from the external side and would be modeled as shifts in Q^{BOP} and changes in the rate of exchange depreciation. A further difference is that I separate the weighted effects of exchange depreciation and government price adjustments; this tactic and the notion of an inflation-triggering external constraint are also discussed in Taylor (1988:31–32, 41). Note that α_1, α_2, and α_3 are each less than one—even if a 10 percent rise in the exchange rate is perfectly passed through, output prices will rise less than 10 percent because such costs compose only a portion of unit costs.

25. This discussion draws on the exposition of heterodox sequencing in Mann and Pastor (1989:168–170).

26. In response to this, Dornbusch suggests "removing wage-price controls gradually, at successive sectoral steps" (Dornbusch 1988a:256); the trick is to do this in a way that allows the government to make the necessary relative price adjustments even as the program retains its anti-inflation credibility.

4

Bolivia: Hyperinflation and Stabilization

Introduction

By the middle of the 1980s, Latin America seemed to be making a dramatic change in economic paradigm. After years of rising inflation and stagnant growth, three important debtor countries—Argentina, Brazil, and Peru—rejected International Monetary Fund (IMF) advice and attempted the sort of heterodox strategies outlined in the previous chapter. Incomes policy and increased government intervention took hold and the new programs scored initial successes in controlling inflation and stimulating growth. The attention of policy makers and economists soon focused on these new experiments and some hastily predicted that a different road to macroeconomic stabilization had finally been created.

Against this backdrop, Bolivia stood out sharply. Staggering from an inflation rate of over 4,000 percent for just the first seven months of 1985, the country bucked the emerging heterodox trend and instead adopted a series of orthodox measures reminiscent of the Chilean and Argentine experiences of the late 1970s. Within weeks, the monthly inflation rate fell from over 50 percent to less than zero; discounting a brief inflationary blip in January, the annual inflation rate fell to slightly over 30 percent in 1986 and only 11 percent in 1987. The Miracle of La Paz was greeted with enthusiasm by the International Monetary Fund and mainstream economists: In the wilderness of the new heterodoxy, one nation had stuck to orthodoxy with what seemed to be tremendous success.

This chapter reviews the macroeconomic experience of Bolivia in the 1980s and seeks to discern both the causes of the hyperinflation and the reasons the turn to orthodoxy helped end it. I argue that the Bolivian hyperinflation had two fundamental determinants—the collapse of external finance and distributional conflict over burden-sharing—and two proximate determinants—a steadily depreciating peso and excessive monetary growth. The orthodox policy shift helped arrest the hyperinflation because it attracted the foreign financial support needed to stabilize the exchange rate and seemed to resolve the distributional conflicts in favor of capitalist interests.

The medium-term results were, however, similar to those achieved by Bolivia's orthodox precursors of the 1970s: an overvalued exchange rate and a swelling of imports, high real interest rates and increasing fragility in the financial system, an enhanced dependence on foreign capital flows and orthodox international institutions, and a regressive redistribution that sharpened social tensions and eventually eroded support for the government.

The chapter begins by using a simple model to analyze the inflationary impact of the external shocks of the early 1980s. I then offer a brief overview of the domestic class pressures that prevented any real adjustment to these shocks and ensured that the external inflationary impulses would be translated into a persistent high inflation. This political analysis is followed by econometric tests that explore the immediate determinants of the hyperinflation. The results suggest that as the hyperinflation progressed, monetary variables and past (or inertial) inflation ceased to play much of a causal role, giving way instead to movements in the parallel exchange rate. This "dollarization" of domestic prices is quite typical of hyperinflationary episodes and, as illustrated in Chapter 5, seems also to have occurred in a less dramatic form in Peru. Given the crucial roles of external finance, class conflict, and the exchange rate, Bolivia's immediate stabilization tasks centered on attracting new finance, controlling labor, and supporting the international value of the domestic currency.

The second section of the chapter analyzes how the New Economic Policy adopted in 1985 accomplished these tasks. This anti-inflation program included a set of technical measures, including the development of new mechanisms to stabilize the exchange rate and maintain fiscal discipline. Much of the success of the program, however, was due to the "credibility-gaining" political strategy of repressing the labor movement which, along with the more technical measures, helped Bolivian policy makers win the hearts and dollars of international financial institutions.

The chapter ends by considering whether Bolivia had any real alternative to the sort of distributionally regressive orthodox program it adopted in 1985. I conclude that it did not: The Bolivian left had exhausted itself politically and a shattered state was incapable of the elaborate interventions required by heterodox adjustment. The orthodox policy, however, eventually faltered, losing support among the Bolivian people and opening the way in recent years for a new regime and some possible modifications of macroeconomic and development policy. Unfortunately, financial fragility, social tension, and stark dependence on international finance constrain the country's options. Orthodoxy, in short, may be here to stay.

Origins and Dynamics of the Bolivian Hyperinflation

The Bolivian hyperinflation raged from early in 1984 until the implementation of the New Economic Policy in August 1985; the peak was reached in February 1985 when *monthly* inflation topped 180 percent.[1] Although such inflation levels are shocking, the 1984 slide into hyperinflation was predictable: Bolivia had been plagued by annual inflation rates of around 300 percent in the two preceding years, gross domestic product (GDP) had fallen by nearly 10 percent since 1981, the consolidated public sector deficit had reached nearly 20 percent of GDP, and the government had lost the support of almost every sector of Bolivian society (see Table 4.1 for macroeconomic trends).[2]

In his early and wide-ranging study of the Bolivian hyperinflation, Sachs remarks that "the Bolivian inflation is apparently unique in the annals of hyperinflations, in that it is the only hyperinflation in the twentieth century that did not come in the aftermath of a foreign war, a civil war, or a political revolution" (Sachs 1986:6). The hyperinflation was, however, less unique than Sachs contends. Like the German inflation following World War I, it was provoked by "reparations payments" in the form of debt service outflows. And although there was no civil war with open armed conflict, the inflation was partly a result of intense distributional conflict, and the New Economic Policy achieved its anti-inflation victory partly through suppressing working class demands and organizations. Below, I substantiate these assertions, beginning first with a simple sketch of the Bolivian economic structure and then moving into the class and distributional dynamics of the Bolivian economy in the early 1980s.

Economic Structure, External Shocks, and Inflation

With a 1987 per capita gross national product (GNP) below $600, Bolivia is one of the poorest and least developed countries in Latin America. Prior to the 1980s hyperinflation, the economy was characterized by three key economic sectors: (1) a domestically oriented sector, consisting of manufacturing (15 percent of GDP), agriculture (19 percent), and public administration (11 percent); (2) an export-oriented sector in which only two dominant activities (mining at 11 percent of GDP and petroleum at 6 percent) provided over 85 percent of export revenues and in which state enterprises played an overwhelming role; and (3) a service sector, including construction (4 percent), commerce (11 percent), and transport, financial, and personal services (24 percent).[3] The third sector is largely derivative of output and income in the first two sectors, suggesting that the main dynamism of the economy lay in exports, domestic manufactures, agriculture, and government services.

This structure can be modeled to show how the events of the early 1980s helped trigger a high inflation.[4] Consider an economy with several of the key sectors above: primary exports (X), manufacturing (Q), and government services (G^S); for the sake of simplicity, I omit agriculture.[5] Let production in X and G^S be a function of labor alone; Q, in contrast, requires both intermediate imports (M^Q) and labor. In the short run, demand for real exports, X, is fixed by world conditions. Demand for domestic output, Q, comes from the government and from

Table 4.1
Macroeconomic Data for Bolivia, 1980-1989

	1980	1981	1982	1983	1984	1985	1986	1987	1988	1989
Inflation rate (Dec.-Dec.)	23.9	25.1	296.5	328.6	2,177.2	8,170.5	66.0	10.7	21.5	16.6
Rate of growth of money (M1)	41.2	20.5	229.7	209.6	1,781.8	5,928.7	82.9	39.9	34.7	3.1
Rate of depreciation (official rate)	0.0	0.0	701.3	154.6	1,650.2	18,053.5	21.1	14.9	9.0	23.7
Rate of depreciation (parallel rate)	0.0	68.3	586.1	339.6	1,678.5	7,655.7	14.5	15.1	10.2	21.7
GDP growth	-0.5	0.9	-4.4	-4.5	-0.6	-1.0	-2.5	2.6	3.0	2.7
Public sector deficit (as % of GDP)	7.8	7.5	14.2	17.0	21.2	8.1	2.3	6.7	5.5	4.5

Private investment (as % of GDP)	7.2	6.1	2.8	4.7	5.4	7.2	6.2	---	---	---
Public investment (as % of GDP)	7.1	7.6	9.8	8.1	6.5	4.7	6.4	---	---	---
Exports (FOB) (US$ mil.)	942.2	912.4	827.7	755.1	719.5	628.4	587.5	518.7	542.5	723.5
Imports (CIF) (US$ mil.)	678.4	975.4	577.5	589.1	491.6	690.9	674.0	766.3	700.0	786.2
Trade balance (US$ mil.)	263.8	-63.0	250.2	166.0	227.9	-62.5	-86.5	-247.6	-157.5	-62.7
Total external debt (US$ mil.)	2,700	3,219	3,328	4,069	4,317	4,805	5,574	5,840	5,431	4,359
Total external debt (% of GNP)	93.3	104.3	106.4	147.7	178.0	184.9	167.6	156.8	134.1	103.1

Sources: Sources for various series reported in Note 2 of Chapter 4. The inflation rates, monetary growth, and depreciation are all end-of-period (i.e., from December of the previous year to December of the current year). "---" indicates that data were unavailable.

worker income in the export, manufacturing, and government service sectors. Export and domestic capitalists either save or consume imported luxury goods, M^B (i.e., Mercedes-Benzes).

The prices of exports and imports (intermediates and luxury goods) are determined in the world market and translated into domestic currency via the exchange rate, e. Manufacturing prices (P_Q) are set by a variable mark-up on labor and import costs; the mark-up varies such that profit rates in Q are always equivalent to their counterpart in X. For ease, I assume that there is no fixed capital, which implies that profit rates are equal to profit shares.

The model is represented graphically in Figure 4.1. Q^E depicts the combinations of Q and the real exchange rate, ($e^r = e/P_Q$), at which Q is in equilibrium. To understand its downward slope, note that a real devaluation implies an increase in the profit rate in X, which triggers an increase in the profit share in Q in addition to an increase in the Q-sector import bill. This redistribution toward domestic capital and foreign suppliers implies that workers' real wages and consumption capacities are reduced. Devaluation, in short, is contractionary and distributionally regressive.

The second line in the figure, BOP^E, represents the combination of the real exchange rate and industrial output levels at which foreign payments are in balance. To understand the slope, write out the balance of payments as:

(4.1) $BOP = P_X^\$ X - P_M^\$ M^Q - P_B^\$ M^B + K$

where $P_X^\$$ is the dollar price of traditional exports, $P_M^\$$ is the price of imported intermediates used in Q production, $P_B^\$$ is the price of luxury imports, and K is capital flows. Because imported intermediates, M^Q, are a fixed proportion, m^Q, of Q production and luxury imports, M^B, are a function of capitalist income, (4.1) can be expressed as:

(4.2) $BOP = tX - m^Q Q - \beta[(1-g^X)r^X tX + r^Q Q] + K$

where all import prices have been arbitrarily normalized at unity, t (or $P_X^\$$) now represents the terms of trade, β represents the propensity to consume luxury goods from profits, r^i represents the gross profit share in sector i,[6] and g^X represents the share of mining and petroleum profits captured through either taxes or direct ownership of export activities (i.e., Bolivia's government mining corporation, COMIBOL, and the government petroleum company, YPFB).

Note that a higher real exchange rate raises r^X and hence r^Q;[7] this income effect on luxury good demand may be partially offset by a fall in β due to the higher price of luxury goods. An optimistic scenario would suggest that devaluation could reduce β such that total luxury demand falls. In this case, the BOP^E line is upward sloping: Real devaluation reduces luxury spending, $P_B^\$ M^B$, enhancing the revenues available for M^Q and thereby allowing an increase in Q. The most pessi-

Bolivia: Hyperinflation and Stabilization

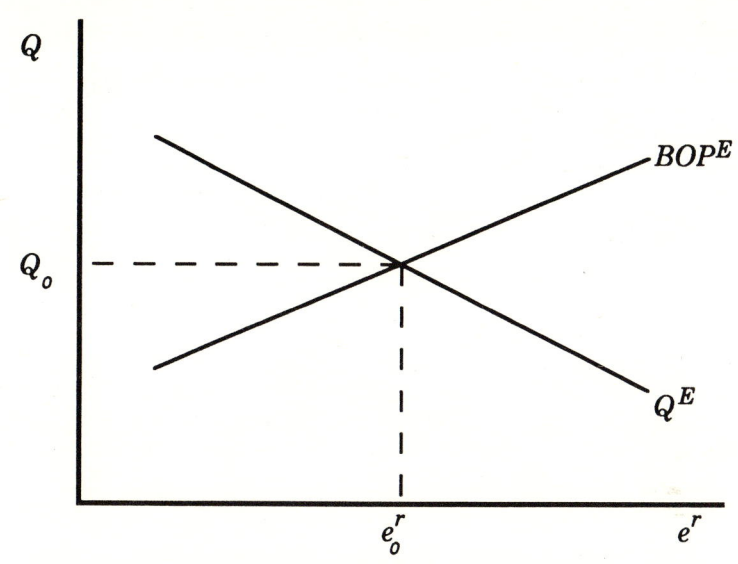

Figure 4.1 Macro Equilibrium and Payments Balance in a Bolivian-style Economy

mistic scenario would leave β untouched: In this case, the BOP^E line would slope downward (although less steeply than Q^E), because the devaluation-induced increase in capitalist income shares would actually swell luxury imports and cut off intermediates.[8] Figure 4. 1 depicts the optimistic scenario; the central dynamics of the comparative statics below apply even in the pessimistic case. Note that movements in BOP^E will be triggered by a variety of factors, including exogenous shifts in β, the propensity to import luxury items, and changes in the share of mining profits claimed by the government, i.e., g^X.

Two scenarios experienced by Bolivia in the early 1980s are explored here: a collapse in export revenues and a negative shift in capital flows. The first is pictured in Figure 4.2. Note that BOP^E shifts down (less revenue at any e^r to support intermediate imports and hence output) and Q^E shifts in (as unemployed export workers reduce demand). Q^E shifts less than BOP^E, resulting in a loss of reserves at the old real exchange rate which can be measured in domestic terms by the gap, $(Q_1 - Q_2)$.[9] Restoring external balance will now require a devaluation to reduce Q (and hence move along Q^E). The government could also adjust by reducing its own spending and shifting Q^E to the left; the result would be a more severe recession. Alternatively, it could move BOP^E up by restricting luxury imports (i.e., reducing β) or increasing the taxes on exporters, g^X, strategies that may be difficult if capitalists exercise significant influence over public policy. Meanwhile, the ongoing collapse of export revenues implies a decline in tax collection and parastatal earnings and hence an increase in the fiscal deficit. Both this and the highly probable devaluation will prompt inflation.

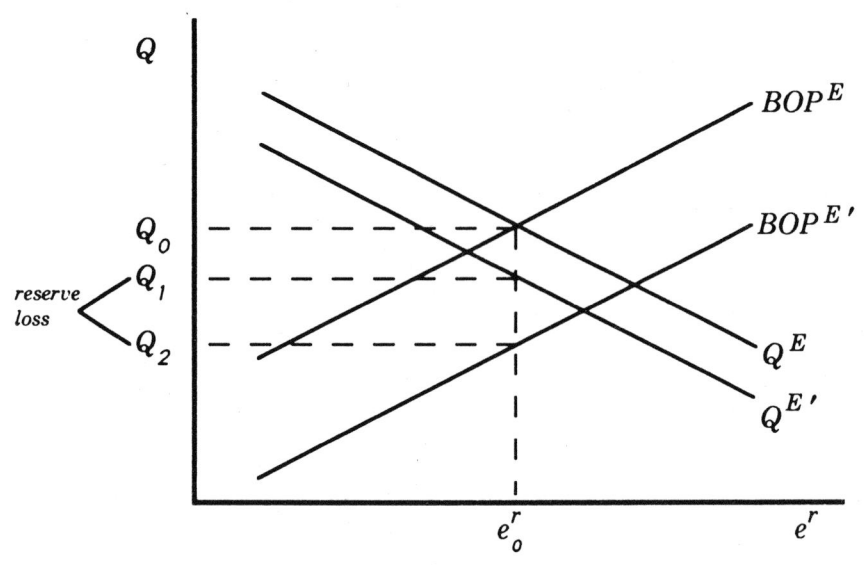

Figure 4.2 The Effects of Falling Export Revenues in a Bolivian-style Economy

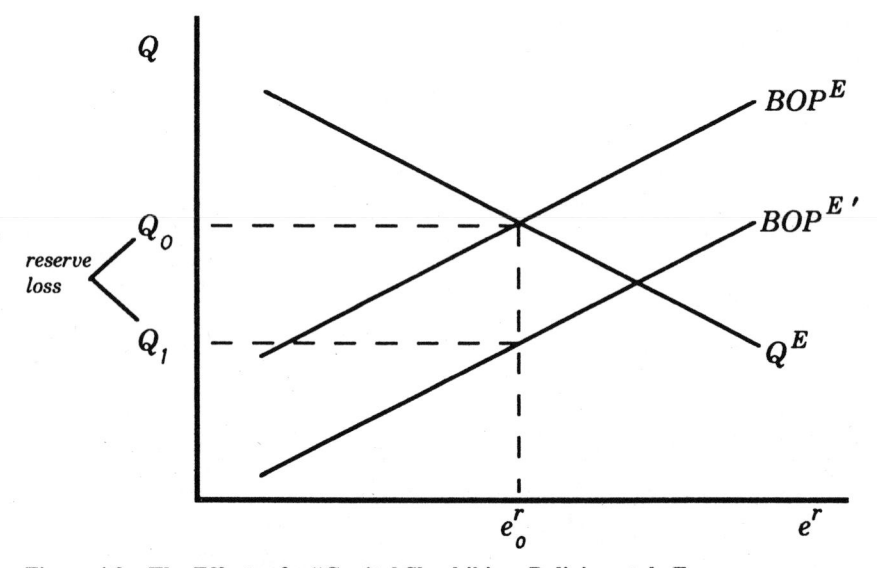

Figure 4.3 The Effects of a "Capital Shock" in a Bolivian-style Economy

However unappetizing the above scenario may seem, a "capital shock"—a sudden decline in net flows, K—may be even worse. As pictured in Figure 4.3, the BOP^E shifts down with no movements in the other curve. Initially, this seems less distressing because with no reduction in export worker demand, there has been no automatic reduction in Q. But this is precisely the problem: Because there has been no "natural" adjustment, however partial, the country must use discretionary policy to restore external balance or face losing reserves as measured by the gap, $(Q_0 - Q_1)$. Budget and exchange rate adjustments must therefore be large (compare, for example, the required change in the real exchange rate in Figures 4.2 and 4.3). If political or practical factors impede action on the budget *and* if the original capital flows were financing government deficits, monetization will result. In short, the difficulties of making such large policy changes and the implicit push toward monetization can lead a country toward both policy disorder and high inflation.

Such a combination of export difficulties, capital shortfalls, and policy paralysis seems to be what occurred in Bolivia in the early 1980s. As noted earlier, the country had a nearly monocultural export structure that also served as an important source of revenues to the public sector. Of particular importance to both dollar earnings and state coffers was tin; as Table 4.2 illustrates, both tin volume and tin exports slipped dramatically in the early 1980s, dragging GDP downward as well. The resulting reserve drain, depicted in Figure 4.2, generated pressure to devalue the exchange rate. Added to this inflationary impulse was the widening government deficit due to a decline in income from both government-owned mines and taxes on private exporters.

These difficulties were compounded by a "capital shock" due to both the regional debt crisis and a collapse in banker faith in Bolivia itself. The economy was especially vulnerable to such a shock because of its previous reliance on foreign funds to finance the public sector deficit. Over the period 1973–1981, Bolivia's public sector long-term external debt rose from $640.4 million to $2.7 billion. In the 1980s, the country's long-term net capital flows reversed sharply, becoming increasingly negative (see Table 4.2). The exchange rate quickly became unsustainable, and the government, unable to borrow and still facing amortization, was forced to turn to "internal finance," i.e., monetization of the government deficit. The "capital shock," in short, played the same role as reparation payments in the German case: Inflationary pressures emerged from the erosion in both international reserves and government finance.

Political Context and Policy Response

Although high inflation may be ultimately rooted in Bolivia's export structure and reliance on external finance, the take-off to a true hyperinflation also reflects both a long history of class conflict and the particular political tensions and policy paralysis of the administration of Hernán Siles Zuazo (1982–1985). The longer-run conflicts date back to at least the 1952 revolution in which labor and peasant forces coalesced with middle-class elements to depose the tin oligarchy (colorfully but appropriately nicknamed "the screw") and its military defenders. The first postrevolutionary government, headed by Víctor Paz Estenssoro, promptly passed a dramatic land reform and nationalized the large mines, placing control of the latter into a state corporation called COMIBOL. Despite these seemingly radi-

**Table 4.2
Tin Prices, Tin Volume, and Net Capital Flows
to Bolivia, 1980-1989**

	Tin Price (1985=100)	Tin Volume (1985=100)	Net Long-Term Capital Flows (US$ Mil.)
1980	141	140	79.6
1981	118	150	160.3
1982	107	136	-94.5
1983	109	99	-216.1
1984	103	126	-144.2
1985	100	100	-229.8
1986	48	104	-154.0
1987	57	62	-37.8
1988	59	67	85.6
1989	---	---	77.6

Sources: Tin price and volume indices and net long-term capital flows taken from the International Monetary Fund's *International Financial Statistics Yearbook*, 1990. Net capital flows figured as the sum of direct investment, portfolio investment, and other long-term capital. "---" indicates that data were unavailable.

cal moves, the government remained committed to capitalism, albeit with significant state ownership and control.

In the late 1950s, the fragility of the alliance between middle, worker, and peasant classes became evident when the second postrevolutionary government, headed by Hernán Siles Zuazo, became one of the first in the Third World to adopt and implement an IMF stabilization program. As adjustment dragged on into the 1960s, leftist and union forces broke off from the government party; eventually, a rebuilt military grew frustrated with civilian rule and took power in 1964. Even then politics were hardly stable: In 1969–1971, a left-wing faction of the military briefly held power, nationalizing more industries (including oil), freeing political prisoners, and generally promoting working class interests.

The 1970s brought General Hugo Banzer and a period of sharp political repression and debt-led growth. Although quiet at first, union resistance grew, particularly by the tin miners who had been the crucial vanguard of the 1952 revolution. In the context of intense domestic unrest, including a wave of hunger strikes in 1978 that was begun by a small group of miners' wives (Davila 1991:11), and facing international pressure from the new "human rights" policy of the U.S. Carter administration, Banzer decided to step down and call elections. Siles Zuazo was resurrected from his past service as a leader of the revolution and president in the late 1950s and became the titular head of a leftist coalition that captured a plurality in elections held in 1978, 1979, and 1980. After each victory, military coups or parliamentary maneuvers interceded and prevented Zuazo from taking the presidency. The final coup in 1980, one of the bloodiest in Bolivian history, brought to power a faction of the military with strong ties to the drug trade, which precluded support from the United States but not from the Interna-

Bolivia: Hyperinflation and Stabilization

tional Monetary Fund, international banks, and fellow dictators in Argentina. Finally embarrassed by having drug dealers run the country and chagrined by the economic collapse between 1980 and 1982, a new military regime restored the Congress elected in 1980. The Congress, in turn, awarded the Presidency to Siles Zuazo in October 1982.[10]

As in much of the rest of Latin America, the return to the barracks was preceded by a complete disorganization of the economy. In 1980–1981, government authorities had permitted capital flight of nearly $600 million.[11] Helped along by the drop in tin prices, 1982 alone brought a nearly 10 percent decline in export revenues and a close to 5 percent drop in GDP. With capital flows also collapsing, net international reserves declined to −$265.7 million by mid-1982 (Morales 1987a:22). The military responded to this reserve crisis with a dual exchange rate system that produced expectations of future devaluation and thus attacks on the Bolivia peso. As suggested by the model above, the external situation negatively affected government finance. The deficit for the consolidated public sector passed from 7.5 percent of GDP in 1981 to 14.2 percent in 1982 (see Table 4.3). Although net external flows had financed about two-thirds of the deficit in 1980 and 50 percent of the deficit in 1981, 1982 external financing was essentially zero, a shift that drove internal financing (or monetary emission) to nearly 14 percent of GDP (see Table 4.3). In the name of democracy, this economic mess was handed to the new president.

The model of the previous section suggests that adjustment to such a simultaneous export collapse, capital shock, and erosion of public finance requires that the government devalue the currency (with a negative impact on real wages) and reduce its own spending. Siles Zuazo initially leaned away from such orthodox policies and instead implemented a primitive heterodox program of real wage protection and government-mandated import restriction. The political reasons were clear—the new administration wanted to avoid measures that would hurt its constituency in the working and popular classes. Unfortunately, the policies failed economically and eventually forced an erosion in political support as well.

The new administration's first program, initiated in November 1982, specifically attempted to: (1) establish control over foreign exchange by requiring exporters to turn over 100 percent of dollar earnings (at the official exchange rate) and restricting imports directly or via differential tariffs and exchange rationing; (2) address the fiscal difficulties by raising export taxes; (3) protect real wages by instituting a trigger mechanism that would fully adjust the minimum wage after a 40 percent rise in the price level; and (4) "de-dollarize" the economy by converting all dollar-denominated contracts into peso terms. The program, in short, was heterodox in character: Market forces were eschewed in favor of government intervention and active redistribution.

The program slowed inflation for only a few months, partly because it could do little to reverse the external forces buffeting the economy. De-dollarization was especially problematic. Ostensibly designed to delink the economy from ex-

Table 4.3
Fiscal Operations in Bolivia, 1980-1989
(as percentage of GDP)

	1980	1981	1982	1983	1984	1985	1986	1987	1988	1989
Central administration										
Current revenue	9.4	8.7	4.9	3.1	1.7	2.4	5.0	6.3	5.9	---
Tax revenue	8.3	7.7	4.2	2.6	1.6	2.0	4.4	5.8	5.7	---
Current expenditures	18.7	16.2	13.2	12.6	14.2	13.0	13.5	13.8	13.7	---
Transfers	2.5	3.6	1.8	1.0	1.2	5.3	8.1	4.9	5.7	---
Current account	-6.7	-3.8	-6.6	-8.5	-11.3	-5.4	-0.4	-2.5	-2.0	---
Public firms										
Pretransfer current account	8.0	6.3	7.7	3.6	3.3	7.9	10.0	5.5	8.1	6.4
Net transfers to government	-2.8	-4.4	-3.7	-2.4	-2.8	-6.8	-9.3	-5.7	-6.4	-5.5
Current account	5.3	1.8	4.0	1.3	0.6	1.1	0.7	-0.3	1.8	0.9
Capital revenue	0.2	0.5	0.0	0.1	0.1	0.1	0.0	0.0	0.0	0.0
Capital expenditure	4.6	3.5	4.4	2.7	1.9	1.2	1.5	3.1	2.5	2.1
Overall surplus	1.2	-1.1	-1.4	-1.4	-3.6	-0.0	-0.8	-3.9	-0.8	-0.9
Consolidated public sector										
Current account	-0.8	-0.8	-0.9	-6.5	-9.9	-3.0	1.2	-1.6	1.0	0.9
Capital revenue	0.4	0.6	0.1	0.2	0.1	0.1	1.0	0.2	0.7	1.6
Capital expenditure	7.4	6.1	5.9	4.2	3.7	3.3	4.6	5.3	6.8	7.0
Overall surplus	-7.8	-7.5	-14.2	-17.0	-21.2	-8.1	-2.3	-6.7	-5.5	-4.5
Financing										
External	5.3	3.9	0.7	-1.3	2.2	3.6	5.5	2.2	4.0	1.7
Net capital flows	5.3	4.5	1.7	0.3	-0.3	0.1	2.0	1.8	2.1	1.4
Unpaid interest	0.0	-0.6	1.1	0.0	0.5	2.5	3.6	2.3	2.5	2.0
Sum of above	5.3	3.9	2.8	0.4	0.2	2.7	5.6	4.1	4.5	3.4
Internal	2.5	3.6	13.5	18.3	19.0	4.4	-3.2	4.5	1.5	2.9

Source: Unidad de Análisis de Políticas Económicas (1990). "---" indicates that data were not available.

change rate-driven inflation, it instead provoked a run away from the peso. This drove up the parallel market exchange rate and, in turn, inflationary expectations, adding to the existing inflationary impetus caused by the government's monetization of the widening deficit.

Exchange problems, government deficits, and inflation were further aggravated by the government's early efforts to partially meet its debt obligations. The government apparently believed that remaining current on debt payments would eventually produce a return to voluntary lending (and hence an upward shift in the BOP^E line in the graphical apparatus of the previous section). Unfortunately, new lending did not resume, leading to a net resource loss and a worsening of the fiscal situation.

In retrospect, it seems curious that a leftist government would honor international obligations at the cost of its own economy and working-class constituents. In 1982–1984, however, no Latin American government had yet attempted to openly (i.e., as a conscious policy rather than a temporary exigency) restrict debt service; as a result, the penalties for nonservice were perceived to be extremely high. Moreover, the new Bolivian leaders seemed to have believed that steering the country from a narcotics-ridden dictatorship to a fresh democracy would be sufficient to attract substantial aid from Western nations.[12] The advanced capitalist democracies instead responded to Latin democratization by insisting that the new regimes service debts contracted by their military predecessors.

Siles Zuazo thus inherited both a structural crisis of debt and export dependence and a social context in which workers and other popular forces had historically been strong enough to resist military governments *but* had proved too weak to hold power themselves and/or dominate middle-class elements with whom the 1952 revolution had been made. The more immediate past, through the late 1970s and early 1980s, involved political and economic disorder as well as dramatic policy errors by military managers (particularly the establishment of an unsustainable dual exchange rate system and the failure to correct budget problems). Stepping into this context, Zuazo's first moves simply deepened the crisis. De-dollarization led to a panicked shift toward and not away from the dollar and led to a sharp depreciation in the parallel exchange rate. The decision to continue servicing the debt allowed this source of reserve drain to play the same inflationary role that reparations payments played in the classic German hyperinflation. These problems might have been easier to overcome if the government had proved able to achieve a broad social consensus on how to distribute the costs of adjustment; as argued below, the "civil war" embodied in Bolivia's unequal social structure and unresolved social conflicts made such consensus impossible and therefore helped to maintain the inflationary dynamic.

Class Conflict and Inflation

Chapter 3 argued that social and class tensions may contribute to persistent inflation.[13] In particular, a wage-price spiral can occur if workers and capitalists are unable to arrive at an explicit agreement about the distribution of income and instead struggle for an increased income share by continually raising nominal claims. Rising government deficits and their monetization can also be understood in distributional terms: Generally, workers clamor for more social spending and government employment while capitalists resist surrendering the social surplus (in the form of tax revenues) that will fund these expenditures. If external financing is available, the inflationary impact of such social conflict can be dampened; if such financing is not available, monetization is required and inflation can result.

Bolivian inflation is certainly a candidate for such a conflict-driven explanation. The history above suggests a sort of class stalemate: Workers have historically had enough power to make demands but often lacked the power to enforce them.[14] Political control has alternated dramatically, with radical leftist forces dominating in the early 1950s, late 1960s, and early 1980s, and extremely conservative forces ruling through the middle of the 1960s and most of the 1970s. In light of this class and political seesaw, it is perhaps not surprising that outbursts of inflation have occurred several times in modern-day Bolivia.[15]

The hyperinflation of the Siles Zuazo era, although the most severe in Bolivian history, was therefore rooted in the unresolved class conflict lingering since the 1952 revolution. The wage-price spiral was quite evident and was, in fact, codified by government action. As noted earlier, Zuazo's early policies included a 100 percent indexation of the minimum wage, with adjustments scheduled to follow each 40 percent increase in the price level. This led better-off workers to demand similar treatment and by April 1984, the government promulgated a policy of 100 percent indexation for *all* wages; although adjustment was originally scheduled to occur every four months, the period between wage hikes was eventually reduced to a month. Union struggles to raise various sectors' wages gave a further impetus to the dynamic.

The pressure to maintain and even raise real wages was the legacy of wage stagnation in the 1970s and a dramatic decline in labor's share of income during 1980–1982.[16] The labor movement viewed Zuazo's presidency as their part of the policy cycle and therefore sought to make up for the previous decline. Labor's success at catch-up can be discerned from Figure 4.4 in which the movement of real wages and GDP on a quarterly basis are plotted from the beginning of 1982 to the middle of 1986; both indices are normalized at 100 for the first quarter of 1982. Note first the brief surge in real wages right after Zuazo took power in the fourth quarter of 1982, which reflects initial worker pressure to make up for lost ground. For most of the next two years, however, wages drifted downward; after the fourth quarter of 1984, there is a dramatic and short-lived increase in real wages that is subsequently eroded by the hyperinflation, then severely reduced by the 1985 adjustment program (with some recuperation in 1986).[17]

The pattern suggests several stylized facts. First, until late 1984, workers were not that successful at catch-up efforts and seem to have been fighting a mostly de-

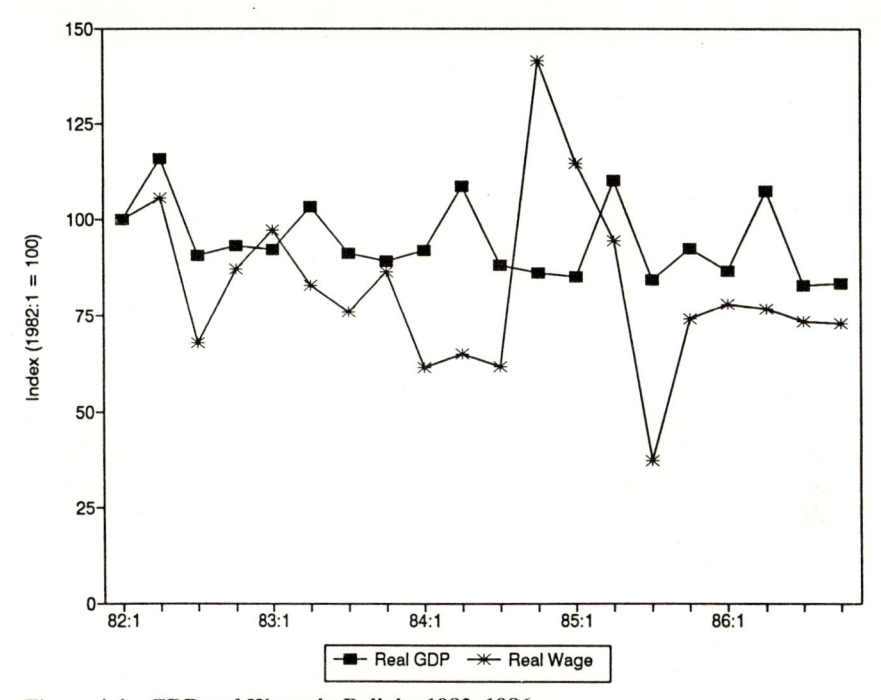

Figure 4.4 GDP and Wages in Bolivia, 1982–1986

Data sources for real GDP and real wages are reported in Note 17 of Chapter 4.

fensive battle against inflation. Second, after late 1984, unions resorted to demanding clearly unsustainable wage increases, which helped to push inflation to its highest level in the hyperinflationary period—a monthly rate averaging over 100 percent between December 1984 and February 1985.[18]

Late 1984 also marked a turning point in government-labor relations. Labor had initially been supportive of Zuazo and offered only moderate protest to early stabilization efforts. In April 1984, however, the major labor federation, the Central Obrero Boliviano (COB), staged a national strike to protest a new stabilization package that came on the heels of the visit of an IMF mission. The conflict produced one positive result: In May, the government met the COB's demand to finally stop servicing external debt, a move that unfortunately could not erase the damage that debt service had already done to public finances. Mostly, however, the results of this conflict between labor and the government were negative: The government was shown to have no control over its supposed allies in labor, the unions seized the opportunity to pursue unrealistic wage increases, capitalists began to step up their removal of wealth from the country, and the possibility of any sort of "social pact" to restrain inflation simply evaporated. With political support for his government virtually nonexistent, Siles Zuazo called for elections to be held in July 1985 rather than the previously scheduled date of July 1986; in the meantime, the government gave up any pretense of controlling the deficit, wages, or any other inflationary impulses.

Bolivia's profound distributional conflicts were also evident in the steady deterioration in the country's fiscal position between 1982 and 1985. Workers generally pressed for continued subsidies, other social expenditures, and increases in public employment and salaries;[19] in terms of the graphical apparatus of the previous section, this spending pressure prevented the downward shift in Q^E needed for macroeconomic adjustment. Meanwhile, inflation steadily eroded the value of nominal tax payments, and a relatively strong congressional right was able to prevent the implementation of new taxes to reduce the growing deficit. Table 4.3 illustrates the results: Tax revenues slipped from 7.7 percent of GDP in 1981 to less than 2 percent in 1984 while central government expenditures as a percentage of GDP fell only slightly over the whole period and actually rose in 1984. Whatever expenditure restraint existed came from cuts in government investment; capital expenditures for the consolidated public sector (including the central government, local government, and parastatals) fell steadily from 7.4 percent of GDP in 1980 to 3.3 percent in 1985. The future of the country was, in short, sacrificed to the distributional struggle.

Thus, the Bolivian experience of hyperinflation did indeed mirror other such inflationary experiences. On the one hand, "reparations payments" (in the form of debt service) strained the balance of payments and placed pressure on both the exchange rate and government finance. On the other, class and social conflict pushed the inflationary cycle along, partly through the wage-price dynamic and partly through the inability to either achieve consensus or saddle a particular group with the burden of financing government spending once international credit flows ceased.[20]

Intermediate Causes: Prices, Money, and the Exchange Rate

The above discussion suggests that there were two fundamental requirements for ending the hyperinflation: an improvement in net external flows and a resolution of the underlying social conflict driving both the wage-price spiral and the widening government deficit. There were also several intermediate causal factors—particularly monetary growth and exchange depreciation—that fed into the inflationary process and therefore had to be addressed by any stabilization effort.

Table 4.4 presents data on monetary behavior from 1980 to 1988 using December-to-December figures. The bottom half of the table documents the dramatic increases in the nominal monetary base between 1982 and 1985; on the right side of this data is the breakdown of the increase by the various components of the monetary base. Such "accounting" for monetary growth does *not* necessarily explain inflation: The "contribution" of net international reserves to changes in the monetary base reported in Table 4.4, for example, does not capture the fact

Table 4.4
Monetary Growth and Its Components, 1980-1989

(thousands of Bolivianos)

	Monetary Base	equals the sum of:	Net Int'l Reserves	Net Credit to Public Sector	Credit to Banks	Other Accounts
1980	13.7		-2.5	12.6	4.0	-0.3
1981	16.2		-6.4	16.1	4.8	1.8
1982	63.7		-67.2	81.5	21.0	28.4
1983	194.8		-35.4	275.8	54.1	-99.7
1984	3,344.5		649.6	2,926.5	981.1	-1,212.8
1985	201,194.0		151,560.0	-205,632.0	129,854.0	125,412.0
1986	384,165.0		474,406.0	-504,882.0	358,807.0	55,834.0
1987	533,473.0		418,169.0	-393,040.0	541,378.0	-33,034.0
1988	874,917.0		397,531.0	-138,470.0	827,075.0	-211,219.0
1989	1,142,979.0		55,283.0	376,823.0	1,296,045.0	-585,172.0

Percentage of Monetary Base Growth Attributable to Changes in:

	Percent Increase in Monetary Base	Net Int'l Reserves	Net Credit to Public Sector	Credit to Banks	Other Accounts
1981	17.8	-159.2	142.0	32.2	84.9
1982	293.6	-127.9	137.6	34.2	56.1
1983	205.7	24.3	148.2	25.2	-97.7
1984	1,616.5	21.7	84.2	29.4	-35.3
1985	5,915.7	76.3	-105.4	65.1	64.0
1986	90.9	176.4	-163.6	125.1	-38.0
1987	38.9	-37.7	74.9	122.3	-59.5
1988	64.0	-6.0	74.6	83.7	-52.2
1989	30.6	-127.7	192.2	174.9	-139.5

All reported figures are year-end; the components of the monetary base may not exactly add up to the reported base due to rounding. The contribution to monetary growth of a particular component is calculated by dividing the nominal increase in that component by the nominal increase in the base.

Source: Data taken from Unidad de Análisis de Políticas Económicas (1990).

that the general shortage of foreign exchange forced an exchange rate deterioration in the black market and hence domestic price adjustment regardless of what was occurring in the official monetary accounts. In addition, the December-to-December figures are slightly misleading, particularly for 1985 when domestic credit growth was curtailed midyear as part of the anti-inflation strategy. Despite these limitations, the data do suggest that credit expansion to finance the government deficit played an overwhelming role in monetary expansion throughout the early 1980s.

Did this monetary expansion play a causal role in the inflation? Although the immediate temptation is to conclude that it did, several studies have suggested that hyperinflations are accompanied by a reversal in the traditional causality from money to prices (see, for example, Sargent and Wallace [1981]). The specific mechanism by which money instead "chases" prices has been modeled in different ways, but one short explanation runs as follows: (1) Given political constraints, the government seeks to maintain some real level of spending; (2) as inflation proceeds, the real value of nominal tax payments declines; and (3) as a result, the government deficit widens and monetary growth accelerates. Sargent and Wallace (1981) offer formal tests supporting the notion that prices "led" money during the hyperinflationary experiences of post–World War I Europe. Morales (1987b) conducts such "causality" tests for the Bolivian experience and finds a similar pattern.

Sachs (1986) also points away from monetary growth *per se*, suggesting that the constantly depreciating parallel exchange rate may have been the true driving force behind the high inflation. Sachs argues that as inflation accelerated, economic agents sought to protect the value of both goods and assets in terms of dollars and adjusted domestic prices according to movements in the black market exchange rate; in this sense, the exchange rate "led" prices. Sachs presents evidence for this view by regressing inflation on changes in the exchange rate and finding a positive relation, a procedure that assumes causality, but does not directly test it.

These issues of causality can be explored further with Granger-Sims tests on inflation, monetary growth, and exchange depreciation. In such tests, prices, for example, are regressed on the lags and leads of a monetary variable. An F-test is then performed on the explanatory power of the leads (or future values) of money; if the F-value is significant, this indicates that the future predicts the past, a phenomenon likely only when the causality is actually running the other way, e.g., from prices to money.

The actual procedures of such causality tests are more complex and vary slightly between applications. This research follows the method of Sargent and Wallace (1981): The rate of change of the relevant variables, X and Y, is calculated by taking the natural log of the current value divided by its immediate lag; the resulting X' is regressed on Y' in order to obtain an estimate of the autoregressive parameter, $\hat{p}$; this parameter is used to "quasi-difference" both variables according to the formula, $(X'(1 - \hat{p}L))$ where L is the first order lag operator; and the resulting X" is regressed on Y" in order to obtain the relevant coefficient estimates and F-statistics (Sargent and Wallace 1981: 417–418).

In investigating the dynamics of the Bolivian hyperinflation, I conducted such causality tests using four lags, the current value and two leads of the independent that covered: (1) the longer period of both high and hyperinflation, and (2) the shorter period of "true" hyperinflation. The longer period begins in July 1982 because this is the first month for which a useable fourth lag could be calculated (the raw data begin in January 1982, giving a starting inflation rate in February, and a starting "quasi-differenced" rate in March). The shorter period begins in April 1984 because this is the first month identified by Morales (1987a:50) as involving "true" hyperinflation, i.e., monthly inflation in excess of 50 percent. The end for both tests is June 1985 because the last month of hyperinflation was August and the tests require two leads.

Table 4.5 reports the results of this exercise. For reasons of space, the table presents only the results of the F-test (and not all the coefficient estimates for lags

Table 4.5
Results for Granger-Sims Causality Tests on Prices, Money, and the Exchange Rate (Bolivia)

	P "leads" M	M "leads" P
July 1982– June 1985 (2,27)	3.265 *	9.856 ***
April 1984– June 1985 (2,6)	3.363 ⌗	7.474 **

	P "leads" E	E "leads" P
July 1982– June 1985 (2,27)	0.654	6.226 ***
April 1984– June 1985 (2,6)	0.239	3.597 *

*** Significant at 1%
** Significant at 5%
* Significant at 10%
⌗ Significant at 20%

All regressions include four lags, a current value, and two leads; the numbers in parantheses report the degrees of freedom used in calculating the significance of the reported F-values. The figures in the tables are F-values testing the explanatory power of the leads; the significance of each value is indicated below the reported F-value. As indicated in the text, all variables (X) are calculated as rates of change using the formula $\{\log(X^t/X^{t-1})\}$. Regressions are first "quasi-differenced" and include a time trend. P is taken from the consumer price index, M from the monetary base, and E from the parallel exchange rate.

Sources: Data from Morales (1987a) and Müller (1988b).

and leads); for simplicity, these results are listed under the alternative hypotheses (e. g., price leads money). For the money variable, I follow Morales in choosing the "monetary base" (bank reserves and currency in the public's hands) as the appropriate measure.[21] These results on money, however, are contrary to Morales's and suggest that monetary growth leads (or "causes") inflation, even during the period of "true" hyperinflation (after the monthly inflation rate topped 50 percent). The results for the exchange rate-price relationship do accord with the suppositions of both Morales and Sachs': The parallel or "free-market" exchange rate led prices through the whole period.

Why the difference with Morales on the role of money? Although Morales also follows the Sargent and Wallace method detailed above, he first deseasonalizes his data (Morales 1987b:21). Such a procedure is problematic for at least two reasons: (1) If seasonal peaks in inflation result from similarly seasonal increases in the monetary base, this relationship should not be eliminated in a causality determination, and (2) over the short two-and-a-half-year period tested here, a seemingly seasonal phenomena (occurring in, say, two of the three years)

Table 4.6
The Determinants of Hyperinflation in Bolivia

	Dependent = inflation			
	March 1982 to August 1985		April 1984 to August 1985	
Variables	(1)	(2)	(3)	(4)
Growth of monetary base	0.331 (2.132)**	0.381 (2.897)***	0.190 (0.680)	
Growth of lagged monetary base	-0.118 (-0.534)		-0.220 (-0.527)	
Change in parallel exchange rate	0.264 (2.398)**	0.221 (2.717)***	0.291 (1.221)	0.199 (1.394)#
Lagged change in parallel exchange rate	0.373 (4.242)***	0.421 (5.191)***	0.523 (2.947)**	0.553 (3.879)***
Lagged inflation	0.194 (1.442)#		0.074 (0.326)	
Constant	-0.010 (-0.284)	-0.001 (-0.038)	0.067 (0.481)	0.111 (1.458)#
Degrees of freedom	(36)	(38)	(11)	(14)
Adjusted R-squared	0.605	0.604	0.432	0.526
Durbin Watson	1.743	1.486	1.357	1.305
F-test	13.545***	21.835***	3.435**	9.876***

```
***  Significant at 1% (two-tail)
**   Significant at 5% (two-tail)
*    Significant at 10% (two-tail)
#    Significant at 20% (two-tail)
```

As indicated in the text, inflation is calculated as $\log(P^t/P^{t-1})$; the other variables (growth of monetary base and change in the parallel exchange rate) are calculated similarly. For each variable, the coefficient is reported; beneath it (in parentheses) is the t-statistic accompanied by a mark indicating the significance level.

Sources: Data taken from Morales (1987a) and Müller (1988a).

may simply be a random event and "correction" in this case would tend to produce inaccurate estimates. For these reasons, deseasonalization may be inappropriate and the causality results of Table 4.5 would be most relevant.[22]

Relying on these results, inflation was regressed on past inflation, monetary growth (and its lag), and changes in the exchange rate (and its lag). Once again, these rates of change are calculated as the log of the current variable divided by its immediate lag; in this set of regressions, "quasi-differencing" is not necessary. As before, tests were conducted for both the longer period of high inflation and hyperinflation and the shorter period of true hyperinflation; because the data are not "quasi-differenced" and there is only one lag, the starting and ending points for each regression are slightly different than those used in the Granger-Sims tests, even though they cover essentially the same time period. For both the long and short time spans, Table 4.6 presents results for the full model and for a reduced model that employs only the most significant variables. Starting in column (1) of the table, note the anemic performance of past inflation and monetary growth rates; dropping those two variables, as in the regression reported in column (2), does not reduce explanatory power (i.e., adjusted R^2). For the shorter time period of true hyperinflation, the results are especially interesting. For the full model (see column [3]), only the lagged exchange rate is significant at traditional levels with the current exchange rate next in order of significance. Dropping the monetary variables and the past inflation rate, as in the regression reported in column (4), actually yields a regression with greater explanatory power.

The general insignificance of past inflation (particularly in the shorter time period) indicates that structuralist-style inertial inflation—inflation resulting from the formal or informal indexation of wages or other prices to past inflation—ceased to play much of a role during the hyperinflationary period. Moreover, although monetary growth is significant over the longer time period, its effects are swamped by changes in the exchange rate during the era of "true" hyperinflation. In terms of immediate policy, then, inflation had to be cooled primarily (or at least initially) by stabilizing the "leading price"—the nominal exchange rate. Slowing monetary growth (i.e., reducing deficits) was also necessary but secondary in immediate importance to slowing the depreciation of the exchange rate.

With monetary restraint and exchange rate stability required, an orthodox adjustment package seemed to be a logical solution. Orthodoxy had the added "benefit" of being implicitly antilabor, which would help resolve the distributional conflicts, and was more likely to attract external support, which would help ameliorate the deterioration in fiscal revenues and hard currency reserves. Former dictator Hugo Banzer pulled together a group of economic technocrats and promised in the 1985 Presidential elections to implement a fairly conventional stabilization program. He won a plurality but not the majority, a fact that allowed Bolivia's newly elected Congress to select the president. The Congress promptly bypassed Banzer in favor of the runner-up, Víctor Paz Estenssoro, one of the heroes of the 1952 revolution. Most observers expected Paz Estenssoro to take a gradual approach to slowing inflation. Instead, he immediately contacted Banzer's orthodox technocrats, made them his own, and unveiled the New Economic Policy.

The New Economic Policy (NEP)

The New Economic Policy, initiated by Paz Estenssoro in August 1985, represented the most dramatic turn toward orthodoxy in modern Bolivian history and marked a clear break with the ineffective policies of the previous government.

Tighter fiscal discipline was embraced, as was a hard line against wage increases. Official creditors and international institutions were courted with promises and evidence of "good" behavior. Freer markets were adopted as both a short-term strategy and a long-term goal; the government, in fact, openly promised to abandon the state-led development model that had ruled in Bolivia since the 1952 revolution that Paz helped lead (Wilkie 1987). Indeed, the only significant state intervention—aside from soon-to-be examined antilabor actions—was in support of the official exchange rate. This policy, following an initial sharp devaluation, was reminiscent of the orthodox exchange targeting practiced in the Southern Cone experiments of the late 1970s (see Chapter 2).

The specific policies of the NEP included: (1) stabilization of the exchange rate through a "dirty" float; (2) liberalization of trade and capital accounts to constrain domestic price increases and attract home flight capital; (3) reduction of government deficits in order to curtail monetary emission; (4) labor market liberalization, real wage cuts in the public sector, and political suppression of the labor movement, all designed to stop at least one-half of the wage-price spiral; and (5) *rapprochement* with official creditors, in order to obtain the new external resources crucial to exchange rate stability. The program is examined in detail below.

The Policies of the NEP

The first goal of the NEP was exchange rate stability. The government began by dramatically devaluing the peso, taking the official rate from 75,000 pesos to the dollar to the parallel rate of 1,000,000 overnight. The government then adopted a "dirty float" system and attempted to meet most demand in order to prevent a recurrence of the sharp divergence between official and parallel rates. Three months of stability resulted, with only a slight depreciation of the peso between September and November 1985.

In December 1985 and January 1986, however, the exchange rate nearly doubled, reflecting both a shortage of dollar inflows due to the collapse of tin prices and increased inflationary expectations (and thus a flight to dollars) due to a 45 percent increase in monetary emission in December 1985 (Morales 1987a:84). The peso depreciation and a 33 percent monthly inflation in January 1985 led some analysts, including International Monetary Fund officials, to argue for more depreciation. Others, including U.S. economist and government advisor Jeffrey Sachs, contended that stabilizing the exchange rate was key to eliminating the vestiges of hyperinflation. The Paz Estenssoro administration followed Sachs and dumped international reserves into the market; the peso appreciated by around 10 percent and monthly inflation quickly fell to zero by March. The events of January and February 1985 mark a turning point in policy; from that date, Bolivian policy makers embraced the view that the exchange rate was the *key* instrument for controlling inflation and subsequently resisted any rapid depreciation to correct growing trade problems.[23]

The second component of the NEP was the liberalization of trade and capital accounts, including the elimination of import prohibitions and the adoption of a low uniform tariff.[24] Import competition, coupled with exchange rate stability, essentially played the role price controls served in the heterodox programs of Bolivia's Latin American neighbors: Domestic producers were constrained from raising prices beyond the exchange rate times the relevant dollar price. In addition, the uniformity of tariffs served as a signal of a commitment to orthodoxy, an image the Bolivians sought to project in order to attract support from international creditors and financial institutions.

The third major component of the NEP involved curtailing government deficits and monetary emission. The government immediately froze public sector salaries, spending, and investment; as a result, real wages of public employees fell, leading the way in the general reduction of worker income. New revenues were raised by increasing the price of gasoline to international levels and subsequently indexing it to movements in the exchange rate. This increased the *de facto* gasoline tax from 0.4 percent of GDP in 1984 to 5.6 percent in 1985 and 7.1 percent in 1986 (Morales 1987a: 79; Mann 1988:9).

These immediate measures were soon accompanied by a longer-term strategy to control expenditures and enhance tax revenues. The former was accomplished by reducing public sector employment, particularly in the government mining corporation, COMIBOL. COMIBOL's labor force fell by over 75 percent between 1985 and 1987, a trend that partially resulted from the collapsing tin market, but also reflected the government's goals of reducing public sector spending and weakening Bolivian labor by shrinking the size and power of its traditional vanguard, the miners' union. On the revenue side, the government struggled with Congress over a new tax system, eventually achieving a victory in the form of a regressive value-added tax.[25]

The regressive nature of the tax reform points to the fourth key aspect of the stabilization program: its political and class character. Paz Estenssoro struck a political truce with the major right-wing opposition party of former dictator and defeated presidential candidate Hugo Banzer and was therefore able to avoid the sharp party conflicts that had prevented Siles Zuazo from getting any serious legislation through Congress. More important than this direct political maneuvering, however, was the antiworker and antipopular agenda of the new government. Morales and Sachs are mild on this point: Morales describes the treatment of labor as "energetic" (Morales 1987a:80) while Sachs compares Paz's labor policies to Reagan's actions against PATCO, the air traffic controllers' union (Sachs 1986:30). The antilabor strategy was, however, more profound: When the government's freeze of public sector wages and elimination of wage indexation produced labor protest, the government detained thirty union leaders and confined 145 to remote river ports. As the program progressed, the government engaged in the wholesale sacking of tin miners, effectively destroying the country's most powerful labor union; instituted legislation that made it easier to fire workers and then allowed unemployment to rise from 15.5 percent in 1984 to 20 percent in

1986 (Müller 1988a:33); resolved the distributional conflict over government finance with a new regressive tax structure; and continued to harshly respond to workers' protests even several years after inflation had subsided.[26]

The effects of this antilabor program were reflected in a decline in real wages and an increase in the informalization of labor. The evidence for wage cuts is somewhat controversial. Government series collected by the Ministry of Labor acknowledge initial poststabilization declines in workers' pay, but show strong increases after 1986.[27] Horton (1991) points out, however, that after 1985, ministry officials included a wide range of previously excluded bonuses in the basic salary figure. As a result, "the Ministry series on real wages is highly suspect" (Horton 1991:11), and probably understates any real wage deterioration. The ministry series also reports only formal sector wages and thus misses the effects of the informalization of the labor force.[28] In the years of the NEP, the proportion of the workforce engaged in informal activities rose; along the way, informal-sector earnings deteriorated relative to formal-sector earnings (Horton 1991). Because of these problems, Horton relies on household survey information (which includes informal earnings) and finds sharp declines in the real wage in both 1987 and 1988.[29]

The distributional patterns wrought by the NEP cannot be subsumed under a general discussion of the "social costs of adjustment." Reducing labor's income and power was important symbolically, and the Paz Estenssoro government pursued its antilabor agenda not just through labor market liberalization, but also through direct measures against the union movement. Like the more technical policies involving exchange rates and monetary emission, the political and economic attack against labor demonstrated the commitment of the new government to orthodoxy and thus enhanced its "credibility" to both domestic capital and orthodox international institutions.[30]

The final key aspect of the New Economic Policy was an attempt to restore net capital flows to the country. Such flows were crucial for exchange rate stability, particularly given the twin pressures of falling export revenues and a liberalization-induced import boom. Capital flight repatriation was encouraged by the government's legalization of dollar deposits, the declaration of a tax amnesty for flight capital, and new regulations that allowed dollar deposits to be made without proof of origin, a thinly disguised ploy to draw coca dollars into the financial system. Moreover, the administration's failure to remonetize when the end of the hyperinflation raised the demand for local currency triggered a liquidity crisis that drove real interest rates to an average of 4.3 percent *monthly* (active or lending rate) between July 1986 and July 1987; these rates were sufficient to entice home flight capital but also tended to choke off domestic productive investment.[31]

The government also sought credit by reestablishing cordial relations with official international lenders, particularly the IMF, the World Bank, and the Club of Paris. In 1986, Bolivia signed its first Stand-by Arrangement with the Fund since

1980; an agreement on longer-term structural adjustment assistance and rescheduling with the Club of Paris was reached before the end of the same year. The new receptivity of the international financial institutions was demonstrated in several other ways. First, Bolivia was allowed to obtain new official loans even as it continued the previous regime's policy of refusing to make commercial debt payments; indeed, unpaid interest from the public sector to external creditors actually rose from 0.5 percent of GDP in 1984 to 3.6 percent of GDP in 1986 (see Table 4.3). What is more surprising than the specter of a supposedly orthodox regime paying less than its leftist predecessor was the reaction of international finance: Over the same period, net capital flows to the public sector rose from −0.3 percent of GDP to 2.0 percent of GDP. The support of international finance was also evidenced in 1987, when Bolivian authorities were allowed to indirectly enter into the secondary market for less-developed country (LDC) debt (using money deposited by friendly nations in an IMF escrow account) and repurchase their own loans at 11 cents on the dollar. Such repurchases are usually restricted by covenants in loan agreements for obvious reasons: The right to repurchase provides an incentive for debtors to intentionally restrict service in order to drive down the value of the debt and make it economically advantageous to buy back rather than repay the debt. That the usual restrictions against loan repurchases were dropped and that the action was coordinated through the IMF was unusual to say the least.

Why did Bolivia obtain such favorable treatment by international creditors and financial institutions? Although some of the external aid was surely "deserved" because of the NEP's inflation-fighting success, the timing, magnitude, and variety of types of support also reflected a desire by international institutions to reward Bolivia for sticking with orthodox measures. With Argentina, Brazil, and Peru turning to heterodox stabilization, Bolivia had become the "good boy" of an increasingly "bad" group of Latin American debtors. Rewarding the NEP's architects would, it was hoped, have a "demonstration effect" in steering other debtors away from the heterodox road.

The Results and Problems of the NEP

The NEP did manage to dramatically lower inflation, bringing the annual rate down to around 11 percent by 1987. Meanwhile GDP, basically stagnant during 1984 and 1985, fell by 2.5 percent in 1986 and then recuperated by a similar amount in 1987. Real investment, after rising (surprisingly) throughout the years of the hyperinflation, fell by around 16 percent in 1986, the first year of stabilization and the last year for which I have data. The trade balance slipped from a hard-earned surplus of $228 million in 1984 to a deficit of −$248 million by 1987, largely the result of liberalization, the export collapse, and Argentina's refusal to make timely payments on purchases of natural gas. Although net external capital flows rose to finance the growing deficit, these eventually proved insufficient and by 1987 net international reserves declined for the first time since 1982 (Müller 1988a:57).

Although the inflation victory was the most impressive feature of the program, this result should be placed in context. Hyperinflations may, in fact, be easier to end than the sort of high inflation that was experienced in Bolivia between 1982 and 1984 and in many other Latin American countries in the last half of the 1980s. The reasons for this apparent paradox are straightforward. First, hyperinflation destroys the sort of long-term contracts that embody inflationary expectations and might therefore continue to force prices up even after a change in policy regime (recall the extremely low significance of past inflation in the earlier regressions). Second, hyperinflation breeds a sort of social exhaustion that opens the way for an explicit or implicit consensus in favor of harsh macroeconomic measures (particularly if the measures are, as in Bolivia, accompanied by the repression of those labor leaders that might resist them).

Less impressive was the continuing stagnation of the Bolivian economy. GDP growth continued its downward trend through 1986, partly an outcome of falling prices but also a result of the fiscally tight adjustment program. By mid-1987, the government announced that it would respond to rising social frustration and political pressure with a "reactivation" program that included the establishment of a new working capital fund and a tax rebate for imported inputs used in exports (see Morales 1990:8). Despite the fanfare, economic growth remained constrained by the same problems experienced by Argentina and Chile during their own orthodox experiments in the late 1970s: an overvalued exchange rate that, coupled with liberalization, had produced a sharp rise in imports; high interest rates and financial fragility; and a slippage of the government's deficit-reduction success.

The overvaluation problem was made apparent to Bolivian policy makers by the import surge of the post-1985 period (see Table 4.1); 1988 saw a brief reversal of the trend, but in 1989, imports climbed above even 1987 levels. Although liberalization was clearly important in the trade deterioration, the import boom was also due to the appreciating peso (see Table 4.7). The NEP had produced a more rational exchange rate policy—as Table 4.7 makes clear, the large differential between official and parallel rates during the hyperinflation was nearly eliminated by 1987. This improvement, however, was accompanied by a falling real exchange rate (that is, an appreciation of the local currency, eventually renamed the "boliviano") as measured against the dollar and the U.S. wholesale price index (see Table 4.7). Although this pattern was reversed through 1988 and 1989, economists both in and out of the government agreed that the government's strategy of fighting inflation with a "strong" domestic currency had resulted in an overvaluation of at least 10 to 20 percent.[32]

The reason for this consensus on overvaluation can be seen by exploring a trade-weighted real exchange rate index; this measure may be more relevant because only 19.6 percent of Bolivia's trade in the 1986–1988 period was with the

Table 4.7
Real Exchange Rate Indices for Bolivia, 1982-1988

	Official Rate vis-à-vis U.S. WPI	Parallel Rate vis-à-vis U.S. WPI	Parallel/ Official
1982-85	84.3	192.3	2.28
1986	103.8	106.6	1.03
1987	100.0	101.0	1.01
1988	102.3	103.2	1.01
1989	106.6	107.5	1.01

	Trade-weighted Exchange Rate Using Official Bolivian Rate and Official Partner Rates	Trade-weighted Exchange Rate Using Parallel Bolivian Rate and Parallel Partner Rates
(October-December 1985=100)		
1982-85	67.7	155.5
1986	97.2	93.5
1987	95.3	73.0
1988	104.3	78.8
1989	97.7	75.2

In the first panel of the table, the real exchange rate, e^r, relative to the U.S. dollar according to the formula $[eP_{US}/P_{BOL}]$, where e is the peso/dollar period average exchange rate, P_{US} is the U.S. wholesale price index and P_{BOL} is the Bolivian price index. The official rate is normalized at 100 for 1987; the parallel rate is also normalized for 1987 but at a value reflecting the divergence between parallel and official rates for that year (note the third column), a procedure that allows us to more accurately assess the divergence between official and parallel rates in the 1982-1985 period of high and hyperinflation.

Sources: Period average prices and exchange rates taken from Unidad de Análisis de Polfticas Económicas (1990:48-50, 182) and the U.S. wholesale price index taken from the International Monetary Fund's *International Financial Statistics Yearbook 1990*. The trade-weighted rates use official and parallel partner rates and are taken from Unidad de Análisis de Polfticas Económicas (1990:58).

United States.[33] Two versions of this measure are presented in the second half of Table 4.7. The first rate, using the official rates of Bolivia and its trading partners, did rise (depreciate) in 1988 but quickly fell to near-1986 levels in 1989. This only moderately poor performance belies the increasingly unrealistic nature of the official rates of several of Bolivia's trading partners. In Peru, for example, the divergence between official and parallel rates was large, prompting trade between the two countries to be increasingly conducted outside official channels. To account for the effects of partner-country exchange rate differentials, the second measure in the second panel of Table 4.7 uses the parallel rates of Bolivia *and* its partners. This variable suggests some degree of overvaluation and helps to explain why the problem of contraband imports persisted even after Bolivia stabilized the economy, unified the exchange rate, and sharply reduced tariff duties.

The overvaluation outlined above conflicted with the longer-term need to shift resources toward the export sector, and gave new momentum to the shift away from domestic production and toward the commercialization of imported goods.[34] In fact, import levels and commercialization were surely higher than official data suggest, because the exchange rate differentials of Bolivia's neighbors generated thriving black markets. Besides these "real sector" problems, the government's strategy of controlling inflation through effectively "fixing" the exchange rate made it dependent on both official foreign finance and incoming "hot money."

Resisting depreciation to curtail inflation might have been a worthy strategy if in fact the exchange rate was still a significant determinant of price increases. To test this, I conducted causality tests for the NEP period similar to those conducted for the period of hyperinflation. As in the tests for the hyperinflationary period, the regressions include two leads, the current value, and four lags on the independent variable; the data are monthly and start after the January–February 1985 inflationary burst (when policy seemed to shift toward conscious support of the exchange rate). Given this starting point, the first appropriate lagged value is March; after "using up" an additional observation in the "quasi-differencing" procedure, the first month for a current observation is August 1986. The last month for a current observation is set at April 1989, implying that the last month for any leads is June 1989. This ending point coincides with the ending of the NEP, at least in its original incarnation under Paz Estenssoro. As discussed below, Gonzalo Sánchez de Losada, a primary architect of the NEP and planning minister in the Paz government, won a plurality in presidential elections in May 1989. By July, however, intense maneuvering by other parties to deny Sánchez de Losada the presidency seemed to be bearing fruit and in August, a coalition of groups in the Congress selected a moderate leftist candidate as the new president. Although August marks the formal shift in regime, July marks the realization of this upcoming fact by economic agents; June therefore seems to be a good ending point. The results below are not sensitive to other reasonable demarcations of the NEP period.

Table 4.8 reports on these causality tests for the variables explored earlier.[35] The evidence on either the money-price or the exchange rate-price relation is inconclusive. To pursue the issue further, I ran regressions on the determinants of inflation using the same general model employed for the hyperinflationary period; both a shorter period (for the first two years of the NEP) and a longer period (up till June 1989) were covered. In each case, I first ran a full model that included the current and lagged values of monetary growth, the current and lagged values of parallel market depreciation, and the lagged value of the infla-

Table 4.8
Results for Granger-Sims Causality Tests on Prices, Money, and the Exchange Rate in the NEP Period

	P "leads" M	M "leads" P
August 1986–April 1989 (2,24)	0.900	0.053
	P "leads" E	E "leads" P
August 1986–April 1989 (2,18)	0.385	0.055

*** Significant at 1%
** Significant at 5%
* Significant at 10%
# Significant at 20%

All regressions include four lags, a current value, and two leads; the numbers in parentheses report the degrees of freedom used in calculating the significance of the reported F-values. The figures in the tables are F-values testing the explanatory power of the leads; the significance of each value is indicated below the reported F-value. As indicated in the text, all variables (X) in all regressions are calculated as rates of change using the formula $\{\log(X^t/X^{t-1})\}$. The regressions are first "quasi-differenced" and include a time trend. P is taken from the consumer price index, M from the monetary base, and E from the parallel exchange rate.

Source: Data from Unidad de Análisis de Políticas Económicas (1990).

tion rate itself. I then dropped any variable with a t-statistic below one and ran the reduced model; if the t-statistic of any variable fell below one in this second run, I dropped the variable and ran a further reduced version. The results, reported in Table 4.9, are dismal: Explanatory power is low (as evidenced by the adjusted R^2s) and while the exchange rate variables are sometimes significant, signs here (and on the monetary variables) are sometimes the opposite of both expectations and the previous results. It seems clear that the model that worked relatively well in the hyperinflationary period does not accurately describe inflation behavior in the NEP period, a turn of events that casts some doubt on the NEP policy makers' insistence on holding the line on both depreciation and monetary growth.

Bolivian policy makers' fixation with the exchange rate can be revealed by using Granger-Sims techniques to further investigate chains of causation. There is mild evidence that authorities responded to rising inflation by slowing the rate of currency depreciation: The F-statistic for the hypothesis that prices led the *official* exchange rate over the entire NEP period is .774 (which is significant at the .472 two-tail level) and one of the leads is negative and significant at the .249 level. Authorities seem to have been setting the exchange rate in response to inflation worries (and the parallel rate closely followed its official counterpart, as evidenced by an F-statistic that was significant at the .069 level). As suggested

Table 4.9
The Determinants of Inflation
in the NEP Period

	Dependent = inflation			
	April 1986 to December 1987		April 1986 to June 1989	
Variables	(1)	(2)	(3)	(4)
Growth of monetary base	-0.054 (-1.195)		0.016 (0.332)	
Growth of lagged monetary base	-0.020 (-0.439)		0.006 (0.135)	
Change in parallel exchange rate	-0.685 (-3.702)***	-0.652 (-3.692)***	-0.433 (-1.978)*	-0.436 (-2.115)**
Lagged change in parallel exchange rate	0.289 (1.133)	0.181 (1.055)	0.288 (1.296)	0.222 (1.132)
Lagged inflation	0.219 (0.889)		0.117 (0.674)	
Constant	0.015 (2.236)**	0.014 (5.681)***	0.011 (2.029)*	0.013 (4.527)***
Degrees of freedom	(15)	(18)	(33)	(36)
Adjusted R-squared	0.387	0.240	0.028	0.093
Durbin-Watson	1.822	1.474	1.944	1.661
F-test	3.524**	8.075***	1.219	2.939*

*** Significant at 1% (two-tail)
** Significant at 5% (two-tail)
* Significant at 10% (two-tail)
# Significant at 20% (two-tail)

As indicated in the text, inflation is calculated as $\log(P^t/P^{t-1})$; the other variables (growth of monetary base and change in the parallel exchange rate) are calculated similarly. For each variable, the coefficient is reported; beneath it (in parentheses) is the t-statistic accompanied by a mark indicating the significance level.

Source: Unidad de Análisis de Políticas Económicas (1990).

above, however, there is little evidence that the exchange rate actually led prices as in the hyperinflationary era. In short, the exchange rate policy that worked to end the hyperinflation persisted throughout the poststabilization period, despite the possibility that it was increasingly inappropriate; by 1988, there was probably room for faster currency devaluation without a passage into accelerating inflation.

The government also stuck with its policy of monetary tightness throughout the NEP period. Table 4.10 reveals this by tracking the behavior of selected real monetary variables (the monetary base, M1 and M2). There is clearly a dramatic decrease in the real levels of money over the hyperinflationary period, a trend that reflects the efforts of economic agents to economize on cash assets; the most dramatic example of this is the decline of M1 *below* the monetary base (i.e., non–interest bearing deposits had actually fallen below bank reserves that are also used to "back" the time and savings deposits represented in M2). The end of the

Table 4.10
Real Monetary Aggregates
and the Composition of Quasi-Money

	Monetary Base	M1	M2 (includes quasi-money)	Money Multiplier (M2/base)
1980	100.0	103.6	169.1	1.7
1981	94.2	99.8	172.1	1.8
1982	93.5	83.0	144.6	1.5
1983	66.8	59.9	91.1	1.4
1984	50.3	49.6	59.9	1.2
1985	36.6	36.1	52.7	1.4
1986	42.1	39.8	86.3	2.0
1987	52.8	50.4	116.2	2.2
1988	71.3	55.8	137.1	1.9
1989	79.9	49.4	156.9	2.0

Quasi-money (time and savings deposits)

	Percentage of Deposits in National Currency	Percentage of Deposits in Foreign Currency
1980	67.7	32.2
1981	73.6	26.4
1982	96.6	3.4
1983	99.0	1.0
1984	98.5	1.5
1985	62.5	37.5
1986	39.8	60.2
1987	22.2	77.8
1988	21.1	78.9
1989	16.3	83.7

Sources: Real monetary variables are taken from Unidad de Análisis de Políticas Económicas (1990:160-162); the monetary base was normalized at 100 for 1980 and M1 and M2 were normalized for 1980 at values reflecting the relationship between their nominal values and that of the monetary base. M2 is defined as including both national and foreign currency time and savings deposits. The percentage of each as a share of quasi-money is calculated from data in Unidad de Análisis de Políticas Económicas (1990:157-159). This source offered no breakdown of quasi-money by national and local currency for 1980; for 1980, the breakdown is taken from figures in the International Monetary Fund's *International Financial Statistics*.

hyperinflation brought about an increase in the demand for suddenly useful and stable domestic currency. Fearful of reigniting inflation, the NEP's architects responded with only a modest expansion in the real money supply: Note that by 1987 the real levels of the monetary base and M1 were barely above their 1984 levels, while M2 had recovered only because of a dramatic increase in foreign currency deposits. This slow remonetization, combined with the government's conscious effort to attract and retain potentially mobile dollar deposits, produced extraordinarily high real interest rates: In 1987, the real interest rate on saving was around 20.1 percent (on an annual basis) while the real lending rate was 45.5

percent. In 1988, the real rate on saving fell to around 8 percent and the real lending rate to around 20 percent, an "improvement" that reflected some remonetization (see Table 4.10) but still constituted a significant obstacle to domestic investment. Figures for 1989 were virtually identical to 1988 figures, suggesting that monetary policy had still not eased years after stabilization had been achieved.[36]

The financial system, in fact, was quite fragile in a number of different ways. Bolivian bankers had profited from the hyperinflation by serving as channels for capital flight, acquiring fixed assets, and paying negative real interest rates on the few deposits they were able to attract (the collapse in deposits is reflected in the fall in M2 and the money multiplier indicated in Table 4.10). With the "success" of disinflation, fixed assets became less desirable and real interest rates skyrocketed. Both phenomena threatened the asset side of banks' balance sheets, the former directly and the latter by creating debt servicing difficulties for borrowers. By April 1988, 30 percent of bank portfolios were in arrears, which understates the problem by not taking into account banks' use of internal refinance to avoid declaring domestic borrowers out of compliance (Müller 1988b:29).[37]

Meanwhile, high interest rates and the legalization of dollar deposits had produced a domestic banking system quite dependent on dollar deposits: From a near-absence of foreign currency deposits in 1982–1984 (due to Siles Zuazo's ill-advised "de-dollarization" program), foreign currency deposits hovered at around 80 percent of total time and savings deposits ("quasi-money") between 1987 and 1989 (see Table 4.10). Moreover, nearly all of these deposits were short term, i.e., with a maturity of less than 90 days (Müller 1988b:7; Mercado 1988:58). Thus, the "success" at repatriating capital had also contributed to fragility: Any "bad news" and this capital would rapidly exit, shattering both the financial system and the exchange rate policy in its wake.

By 1988, government finance was also a source of concern. The NEP's initial efforts to reduce the central government's deficit had been largely focused on raising transfers from public enterprises to the central administration; such transfers increased from 2. 8 percent of GDP in 1984 to 9.3 percent in 1986 and around 6 percent in the following years (see Table 4. 3). This strategy starved public enterprises of new investment, especially the hard-hit state oil company, and threatened long-term growth.[38] Meanwhile, the deficit success seemed to be fading: The overall deficit for the consolidated public sector rose sharply from 2.3 percent of GDP to nearly 7 percent in 1987 (partly because of severance payments to displaced public enterprise employees [Morales 1990:6]) and eased only slightly in the following years. The continued budget shortfall delayed the implementation of a tax rebate for exporters on their purchases of imported inputs, derailing the government's plan to provide new incentives for nontraditional exports. Budget problems also triggered policy disagreements between the Bolivian government and the International Monetary Fund, particularly when the Fund's traditional insistence on austerity conflicted with the Bolivian government's desire to step up public investment, raise growth rates, and thus "preserve the economic model" by securing a victory in the 1989 presidential elections.[39]

The Fund won that battle but lost the war. The government scaled back its plans, reduced the 1988 overall public sector deficit to 5.5 percent of GDP, and went on to defeat in the Presidential elections. The government's candidate, Planning Minister Gonzalo Sánchez de Losada, managed to capture a slim plurality but the largest left- and right-wing parties in Congress struck a deal that awarded the presidency to the left's candidate, Jaime Paz Zamora, and most Cabinet positions, especially those involving economic policy, to technocrats and politicians of the right. The new government soon appeared to be as incoherent as the underlying alliance: While the administration stated that it would reactivate the economy and address the needs of the poor, it also pledged allegiance to the orthodox policies that had reduced working class income and power. These contradictions and the limits on government policy makers are explored below.

Conclusion

Bolivia's passage into hyperinflation and the subsequent efforts to stabilize the economy offer important lessons about both the dynamics of hyperinflation and the merits and limits of orthodox adjustment. Although there are some obvious conclusions, such as the need to control the government budget, monetary growth, and the exchange rate, the Bolivian experience also points to the need to consider more fundamental issues of foreign finance, external vulnerability, and class conflict.

Analysis of these fundamental issues may seem irrelevant when pressed with the immediate task of ending what seems to be a monetary phenomenon, a hyperinflation. But while hyperinflations take place in the monetary sphere, their ultimate causes are found in the economic and political disintegration of the real sector. The Bolivian experience seems to reflect such disintegration: On the one hand, external shocks to export revenues combined with the pressure of debt payments to shrink GDP and damage public finance; on the other, distributional conflict rooted in historic class tensions produced both a wage-price spiral and an inability to achieve a social consensus with regard to who should bear the costs of the fiscal adjustments required to close the public sector deficit.

The New Economic Policy (NEP) attacked the inflation problems by adopting an orthodoxy that attracted new funds and shifted the burden of adjustment onto lower income groups. The proximate causes of inflation—exchange rate deterioration, large public deficits, and excessive monetary growth—received equal attention: The exchange rate was supported by dumping scarce reserves, borrowing abroad, and raising real interest rates to attract previous flight capital home; deficits were reduced by raising gasoline prices and then installing a new regressive tax system; and monetary growth was curtailed dramatically, triggering a liquidity crisis that weakened the domestic financial system and limited investment possibilities. The strategy ended the hyperinflation but left a series of problems in its wake: an overvalued exchange rate, a significant trade deficit, high real interest rates, stagnant growth, weak private investment, dependence on short-term flight capital, and a regressive distribution of income that eventually provided the political ammunition for the ouster of the NEP's architects.

Was there an alternative to the NEP policies? Despite the apparent costs of the NEP, there may have been little else for Bolivia to do. Leftist parties and their labor union allies had squandered their political capital during the Siles Zuazo regime; thus, the main proponents of a distributionally progressive alternative lost their best chance to demonstrate that a more heterodox anti-inflation strategy was feasible. Heterodoxy, moreover, required two conditions sorely lacking in Bolivia: (1) a strong state able to implement price controls and other interventions, and (2) a degree of consensus between capital and labor over the burden-sharing implicit in an incomes policy. In 1985, Paz Estenssoro realized that a "withered" state had lost the capacity to influence a wide range of economic variables; meanwhile, consensus over distribution was impossible, and one side had to clearly "win" for the program to achieve credibility. As a result, the new administration focused its limited state power on a few key tasks: slashing the budget, reversing labor's power, and defending only one price, the exchange rate.

The NEP's austerity, tough as it was, provoked a remarkably low level of protest from working and popular sectors. Although this was partly a result of government repression, it also reflected a widespread rejection of both the left, which had seemed to mismanage the economy, and the union movement, which had seemed to pursue "salaryism" with little regard to the damage nominal wage hikes were causing to the macroeconomy. But while the populace may tolerate general austerity and regressive redistribution as long as the memory of hyperinflation is fresh, the relative complacency of the popular sectors seems to fade as recent history recedes (Mann and Pastor 1989). As Sachs (1987) notes in his study of "growth-oriented adjustment," the more equitable income distribution of East Asian LDCs allowed these countries the distributional "space" necessary to reduce real wages, consumption, and currency values in the face of macroeconomic difficulties. Given Bolivia's historically unequal class structure, the New Economic Policy had little such "space" and political support for the government soon waned.

The policy options for the incoming government of Jaime Paz Zamora were, however, limited by both the problems wrought by the NEP and the new government's politically unstable coalition. For example, Bolivia's financial fragility and dependence on local capital was made quite clear when uncertainty and fears of devaluation produced the withdrawal of one-fourth of local bank deposits prior to the 1989 elections; the new government finally assuaged depositors by promising to continue the previous administration's basic macroeconomic policy, a promise that seemed to contradict the simultaneous need to solidify the support of popular groups.[40] Deviations from the NEP's orthodoxy, in short, were constrained by the need for foreign exchange: Any distributionally progressive program could be short circuited by either capital flight or the loss of support from conservative international financial institutions such as the IMF. Meanwhile, the United States, involved in a general antidrug initiative, was pushing for coca eradication despite the damage this was likely to do to Bolivia's supply of foreign exchange as well as its ability to absorb those unemployed by the previous stabilization policy.[41] Against this backdrop, the government was tugged by rightists seeking further market liberalization and by a moderate left hoping to use interventionist policy to raise both wages and economic activity. For Bolivia, barely recovered from the hyperinflationary damage of the early 1980s, orthodox policy appeared to be the only constant in a distinctly uncertain future.

Notes

1. For lack of more precise definitions, most economists have adopted Cagan's classification of hyperinflation as beginning when the monthly inflation rate exceeds 50 percent (Cagan 1956). By this standard, Bolivia began its passage into hyperinflation in April 1984 despite a brief dip in June and July of that year into single-digit monthly inflation.

2. In Table 4.1, inflation rates for 1980–1983 are from Müller (1988a) and for 1984–1989 from Unidad de Análisis de Políticas Económicas (UDAPE) (1990:184); 1980 GDP growth is taken from Müller (1988a) and 1981–1989 GDP growth is taken from UDAPE (1990:2); and the breakdown of private and public investment comes from Müller (1988a). The growth rate of M1 for 1980–1986 is calculated from data in the International Monetary Fund's *International Financial Statistics* (*IFS*) and for 1987–1989 using data in UDAPE (1990:163). Yearly (end-year to end-year) depreciation rates for 1980–1987 is calculated using 1979–1981 data from UDAPE, "Annexo Estadístico," *Análisis Económico* (1986), and 1982–1987 data is from Müller (1988a); changes for 1988 and 1989 are calculated with data from UDAPE (1990:49–50). All export and import figures are from UDAPE (1990:115). External debt figures (and dollar GNP to calculate the ratio of debt to GNP) are from the World Bank's *World Debt Tables, 1990–1991*; the 1973 figure for total external debt in the text comes from the World Bank's *World Tables, 1987*. The fiscal figures in Table 4.1 are taken from the data in Table 4.3; the source, as noted there, is UDAPE (1990).

3. Data on the sectoral composition of GDP are taken from Unidad de Análisis de Políticas Económicos (hereafter referred to as UDAPE) (1990:1), and is for the year 1980. The figure for the percentage contribution of mining and petroleum to export revenue is the average for 1980–1985; the actual value ranged between 83.6 percent in 1980 and 94.3 percent in 1984.

4. The model, particularly its graphical representation, is inspired by Taylor's discussion of mining enclaves in Taylor (1983:48–56). The pricing behavior here in which the mark-up in Q varies to equilibrate profit rates across sectors is similar to the model "closure" explored in Note 5 of Chapter 3.

5. Agriculture could be incorporated as a "flex-price" sector in which demand varies against a more or less fixed supply. If agriculture producers are peasants and spend all in-

come on either food or industrial goods, this would, as in the augmented model of Chapter 3, vary none of the dynamics of model; an increase in price simply redistributes the source of industrial demand from workers to peasants. If agricultural commodities are produced under capitalist conditions (in which direct producers receive only a share of the sector's revenues and high-savings landowners pocket the rest), the math becomes complicated but the central implications about the inflationary impacts of export and capital "shocks" still hold.

6. The "profit share" in Q used in this equation, r^Q, is actually real unit profits in Q production, s^Q, deflated by the real exchange rate in order to obtain its overseas purchasing power, i.e., Q capitalist demand for luxury imports is $\beta(s^Q Q/e^r)$. For export capitalists, there is no need for such deflation, i.e., r^X equals s^X.

7. A devaluation will raise export profitability, r^X. Because profit shares equilibrate, the profit share in Q (or real unit profits), s^Q, will also rise; in fact, (ds^Q/de^r) will equal (dr^X/de^r). What does this imply about r^Q (which, as noted in Note 6, is actually (s^Q/e^r)? A sufficient condition for the positivity of (dr^Q/de^r) is that the elasticity of s^Q (or r^X) with respect to e^r exceed one. In such a case, devaluation will raise r^Q although by less than the increase in r^X.

To see whether this is true, note that r^X equals $[(eP_X^\$ X - WL^X)/WL^X]$, where W is the nominal wage and L^X is the total labor employed in the export sector. Setting the labor coefficient (L^X/X) equal to one, dividing both top and bottom by P_Q and then X, letting $P_X^\$$ equal t, and denoting the real wage with w^r, r^X can be reexpressed as $[(e^r t/w^r) - 1]$. Taking the derivative of this term with respect to e^r yields $[(t/w^r)(1 - E)]$, where E is the elasticity of the real wage with respect to the real exchange rate. Because (dr^X/de^r) is greater than zero, this wage elasticity must be greater than one.

Now obtain the elasticity of r^X (or s^Q) with respect to e^r by multiplying (dr^X/de^r) by (e^r/r^X). After some manipulation, the result is: $\{[e^r t/(e^r t - w^r)][1 - E]\}$. Both terms exceed one, suggesting that devaluation will raise the Q sector profit share even in the international terms captured by r^Q.

8. Even with β fixed, BOP^E would still lie above Q^E, a condition sufficient for the model's stability. To see this, note that along BOP^E, Q equals $[(tX - \beta(1 - g^X)r^X tX + K)/(m^Q + \beta r^Q)]$. Along Q^E, Q equals $[(tX - r^X tX + G/e^r + G^S/e^r)/(m^Q + r^Q)]$ where G is government spending on Q and G^S is the spending of government workers (recall that capitalists do not consume domestic output in this model). This latter macro-equilibrium condition is similar to that in the simple model of Chapter 3 although the dynamics are distinct due to the variability of the mark-up in the Q sector. Call the first condition, Q^{BOP}, and the second, Q^E. For all β between and including zero and one, increases in e^r (and hence r^X and r^Q) will produce a relatively smaller fall in the numerator and a relatively smaller rise in the denominator of Q^{BOP}. The Q^E line, in short, has a more negative slope. As for the BOP^E curve itself, higher values of β imply a more downward sloping line; as noted in the text, the line slopes upward if β is variable and falls by a sufficient amount in response to a devaluation. Note that the BOP^E line is not likely to be linear; it is drawn that way in the figures for convenience.

9. To see why Q^E shifts down less, note that for any given real exchange rate, the change in Q^{BOP} for a change in X equals $[(t - \beta(1-g^X) tr^X)/(m^Q + \beta r^Q)]$ while the change in equilibrium Q for a change in X equals $[(t - tr^X)/(m^Q + r^Q)]$. The latter is smaller for any possible value of β. An even stronger argument holds for a decrease in export prices, t.

Bolivia: Hyperinflation and Stabilization 103

In the extreme case where export capitalists pass on none of the decrease in the form of wage cuts, dQ^E/dt is actually positive (implying an upward shift in the Q^E line) because reduction in export profits does not affect aggregate demand while the accompanying decline in Q-sector profit share raises the multiplier; it is more likely, however, that wage cuts will be forced, leading to some downward shift in the Q^E line. In the Bolivian case, both export prices and quantities fell during the early 1980s, suggesting that the movement pictured in Figure 4.2 is a reasonable approximation.

10. This general history of Bolivian politics is drawn from Dunkerley and Morales (1986), Mayorga (1978), Burke (1979), and Wilkie (1987). Fascinating details have been necessarily glossed over, such as the unusually strong influence of Trotskyism on the Bolivian labor movement, a tendency that has surely contributed to the "permanent struggle" that has characterized modern Bolivian society.

11. This capital flight figure is taken from net errors and omissions as reported in the IMF's *International Financial Statistics Yearbook 1990* and likely understates the actual flight. For more on measuring capital flight, see Pastor (1990a) and Lessard and Williamson (1987).

12. This belief was conveyed to the author in a conversation with experts who had served as economic advisors to the Siles Zuazo government.

13. Rowthorn (1980) and Taylor (1983) offer especially good descriptions of the dynamics of such conflict-driven inflation.

14. The extent of worker power in modern Bolivia has been quite dramatic, albeit insufficient to force a socialist transition. Davila argues that "from its founding in the wake of the popular revolution, up to 1985, the COB (the main Bolivian labor federation) wielded greater influence over national political life than any other Latin American trade union movement" (Davila 1991:11).

15. The two sharp outbreaks of inflation in Bolivia (prior to the 1980s' episode) occurred in the immediate postrevolutionary era (with rates averaging over 100 percent in 1953–1957) and after the first oil shock (with rates averaging 50 percent). The first episode eventually brought the intervention of the International Monetary Fund (IMF) in 1956, giving Bolivia the dubious distinction of being one of the first Latin American countries to adopt an official IMF program; the first was Peru, an interesting fact given the comparative study of this text (see Gold 1970: Appendix A). Data on inflation is from Wilkie (1987: 915).

16. Between 1973 and 1979, real wages fell by nearly 7 percent even while GDP per capita rose by nearly 10 percent; the divergence suggests a distributional shift away from workers. Over the years 1980–1982, real wages dropped nearly 40 percent (from the 1979 level) while GDP declined by only 12 percent, also suggesting a shift away from workers. More direct evidence of this distributional pattern is offered in Lupo and Larrazabal (1986:95): By one of their measures, the wage share of national output fell from 43 percent in 1980 to 26 percent in 1982. This last datum likely overstates the shift but other evidence corroborates the view that the magnitudes of redistribution were large. The data on real wage behavior during 1973–1982 used above are taken from Delons and Bour (1988).

17. The quarterly real wage from 1982–1986 is taken from UDAPE (1987) and is quite similar to the real wage series offered in Morales (1987a). Like other sorts of data in the Bolivian case, real wage series are of relatively poor quality and different series report slightly different trends; the quarterly real wage series after mid-1986 is most problematic

for reasons discussed later in the text. The reported series reflects a compromise between several other series and likely overstates wage improvement in the second half of 1986. Data on quarterly GDP are taken from UDAPE (1990:9).

18. It would be interesting to submit the wage-price relationship to causality tests similar to those used below in testing the money-price and exchange rate-price relationships. Unfortunately, consistent wage series for the inflationary period are available only on a quarterly basis, which does not offer sufficient observations for the econometric techniques used with the other variables.

19. Central government wages and salaries, for example, actually rose from 5.6 percent of GDP in 1982 to 7.3 percent in 1985 (Morales 1987a:76).

20. The apparent partial recuperation of external finance in 1985 (to 3.6 percent of GDP, about 45 percent of that year's total financing needs) mostly stems from the moratorium on debt service and thus represents accumulating arrears and not new external credit. Note in Table 4.3 the dramatic increase in 1985 in unpaid interest as a percentage of GDP.

21. Morales (1987b:21-22) suggests that M1 could also be appropriate but dismisses M2 as "unsuitable" because of the presence of dollar-denominated deposits in the latter measure. Both the causality tests detailed below and the subsequent analysis of inflation would yield quite similar results if we used M1 instead of the monetary base, suggesting that the results are robust to the choice of a monetary variable.

22. On a more practical level, Morales's results are nearly impossible to replicate because his method of deseasonalization—"a ratio-to-moving average method with geometric weights"—is noted without any further comment as to how many observations are "averaged" or what weights are employed (Morales 1987b). Employing more standard methods to deseasonalize the raw data (an exponential smoothing technique and a detrending procedure that uses standard OLS and monthly dummies), I discovered that causality tests with such deseasonalized data do indeed reverse the monetary causality—prices lead money as in Morales—while leaving the "causal" role of the exchange rate unchanged. Because of the theoretical problems mentioned in the text, however, these results are problematic and my exercise in deseasonalization was mostly an investigation of *how* Morales obtained his results.

23. Morales contends that "exchange stability was a *result* and not the principal *instrument* of the anti-inflation fight . . . " [emphasis in original] (Morales 1987a:80). My opposing view is given in the text and seems to be supported by the history, the econometric evidence, and Bolivian policy makers' continual reluctance to allow any sizeable real depreciation throughout the 1985-1989 period.

24. Tariffs were immediately set at 10 percent plus 10 percent of the previous tariff; in August 1986, tariffs were set at a flat 20 percent on all imports (Mann 1988:8). In March 1988, this strictly uniform approach was altered slightly with a halving of the tariffs of capital goods. The policy shift was a response to sagging investment and reflected the government's effort to encourage some reactivation of economic growth.

25. The new tax system was enacted into legislation in mid-1986 but did not become operational until a year later.

26. In July 1987, for example, the government reacted to the threat of a petroleum workers' strike by arresting the leaders of the relevant union and declaring the oil fields a military zone, an action that implied that strikers would be arrested for being "absent without leave" ("Conflicto petrolero sin vía de solucion," *Ultima Hora*, July 31, 1987, p. 32;

Bolivia: Hyperinflation and Stabilization

"Trabajadores y empleados de YPFB se encuentran bajo leyes militares," *Ultima Hora,* July 27, 1988, p. 16.)

27. UDAPE (1990:210) relies on the Ministry data for its series on quarterly averages for the real wage in the private sector. Year averages for these figures suggest a 7 percent deterioration in the real wage from 1985 to 1986 followed by improvements of 31.3 percent, 26.6 percent, and 5.3 percent in the subsequent years. This pattern does not seem to square with the observed poverty in Bolivia in those years and is of dubious reliability for reasons detailed in the text.

28. The post-1985 ministry series also covers only real wages in the private sector. This misses the effects on the economy-wide average due to the post-1985 shrinkage in public sector employment and the 23.2 percent decline in public sector real wages between 1982–1985 and 1986–1989 (UDAPE 1991: 221).

29. The real wage declines are on the order of 11.9 percent in 1987 and 25.3 percent in 1988 (Horton 1991: Table 8). However, the 1988 real wage figure used in figuring the decline seems somewhat understated and is generated using a method slightly different than that used for the 1986 and 1987 figures; for both these reasons, the decrease in real wages reported for 1987 is much more reliable than that reported for 1988. Given this, I report only the 1987 decline from Horton in the Bolivian real wage growth series of Table 1.3.

30. The government did try to soften the impact of austerity on the poor with the creation of an Emergency Social Fund in late 1986, well after the antilabor tone had been made clear to both the populace and international creditors. The fund provided short-term employment on selected infrastructural projects as well as some free or subsidized social services. For a review of the modest impact of the program and a view of how it could be part of a longer-term development strategy, see Griffin (1991).

31. The real interest rate figures come from UDAPE (1990:176–178) and seem to be lower than a series that could be constructed by using nominal rates from sources such as Mercado (1988:84) and Doria Medina (1987:67) and the inflation rate from UDAPE (1990). I use the more conservative figures here, suggesting that the degree of the liquidity crisis may, in fact, be underestimated.

32. This assessment was offered during conversations with government and academic economists and foreign advisors in June 1988.

33. The percent of trade with the United States is calculated using both imports and exports, with partner country and total trade figures taken from UDAPE (1990:80–84). The average is reported only for the 1986–1988 period, because UDAPE did not report import figures on a partner country basis for 1989.

34. Despite the apparent overvaluation in the poststabilization period, nontraditional exports did grow. This pattern, however, may reflect the thinness of domestic markets caused by stagnant domestic growth and low real wages. As for the shifting balance of goods and services, goods output as a percentage of GDP fell during the hyperinflation from its 1980–1982 level of 53 percent to around 51 percent in 1983–1985, a trend certainly reflective of the economic dislocations and uncertainty of the era. Stabilization did not produce any resurgence of goods production; the composition of goods versus services for the 1986–1989 period was virtually identical to that of 1982–1985 (averages calculated from figures in UDAPE 1990:1). The drift toward commercialization during the NEP is more evident in the "informalization" of the labor force. In 1980–1982, urban informals constituted 25.1 percent of employed labor; in 1983–1985, the figure had nudged upward

to 25.2 percent; and, in 1986–1989, urban informal employment, often centered around selling imported articles, had shot up to nearly 31 percent of total employment (UDAPE 1990:193–195).

35. The regressions covering the hyperinflationary and NEP periods use slightly different data: For the former, monthly data on the monetary base, prices, and the exchange rate was drawn from Morales (1987a) and Müller (1988a) while for the latter, data was taken from UDAPE (1990). The two sources have only slight differences for those observations that are covered by both sources; to be safe, however, each period was drawn consistently from one source.

36. The annual rates reported in the text are calculated using monthly real interest rates for lending to productive activities and fixed-term saving as reported in UDAPE (1990:176–178). The procedure involves annualizing the monthly rates and then taking a yearly average; the results are nearly identical if one instead derives the annual return by summing monthly returns over a year on a fixed initial amount.

37. Given these problems in the financial system, a 1987 U.S. Agency for International Development (AID) study of the financial system calculated that banks had to charge from 11 to 13 percent above their own cost of funds simply to break even. This partially explains the large spreads between savings and lending rates observed in 1987 and 1988.

38. Table 4.3 shows the sharp drop in public enterprise investment in both the hyperinflationary and NEP periods. Capital expenditures in this sector fell from an average of 4.1 percent of GDP in 1980–1982 to 1. 9 percent in 1983–1985, the years of the most severe inflation. The NEP brought only an anemic recovery (to 2.3 percent of GDP for 1986–1989) primarily because of the strain that transfers to the central government placed on public enterprise revenues.

39. Details on Fund-Bolivia negotiations and conflicts are offered in Müller (1988b).

40. Reported in "Bolivian 'Miracle' is at Risk," in *Latin American Weekly Report*, August 3, 1989.

41. See Griffin (1991) for an analysis of the role of coca in the Bolivian economy and a discussion of the economic contradictions and costs of an eradication strategy.

5

Peru: Stabilization and Hyperinflation

Introduction

In any comparison of orthodox and heterodox adjustment strategies, Peru stands out as an especially dramatic case. The country began the 1980s firmly committed to an orthodox liberalization of the economy, albeit one marked by a somewhat contradictory fiscal policy. As external shocks piled up in the first years of the decade, the conservative government of President Fernando Belaúnde Terry adopted a series of International Monetary Fund (IMF) programs and orthodox adjustment strategies with quite unfavorable results: rising inflation, stagnant output, and regressive redistribution. In 1985, the worsening economy persuaded voters to select a new president, Alan García, who promised to reverse this negative pattern with a set of so-called heterodox strategies. Debt service was restricted, price controls adopted, and demand expanded. A few spectacular years of fast growth and lower inflation seemed to initially confirm the heterodox rejection of orthodoxy and offer the possibility that a new era of macroeconomic management had arrived.

By 1988, however, the Peruvian economy was out of control. High inflation gave way to hyperinflation, GDP collapsed, and the government scrambled to find new ways to reverse the worsening scenario. As political support for the government evaporated, the leading candidate in the 1990 presidential elections promised to resolve the economic problems with a return to traditional austerity. At the last minute, voters shifted gears, partly because of the memories of the regressive policies of Belaúnde Terry, and elected a relatively unknown agronomist, Alberto Fujimori, who promised to combat inflation with a "gradual" approach. Upon taking power, Fujimori immediately abandoned his promises of gradualism and introduced an orthodox shock program to halt the hyperinflation. The policy-making cycle had swung full circle.

This chapter explores this policy cycle, focusing particularly on the passage from temporary stabilization to hyperinflation during the García era. The first section begins with a brief review of the Peruvian economic structure and recent political history, then turns to an examination of the "neoliberal," or orthodox, strategy attempted by the administration of President Belaúnde. I argue that Belaúnde's policies failed for several reasons. First, the economy was buffeted by a series of external shocks that would have presented difficulties for policy makers of whatever persuasion. Second, the generally orthodox package adopted to weather the shocks was inappropriate given the structural features of the Peruvian economy. Third, those policies that were arguably appropriate were poorly or inconsistently implemented, causing problems of credibility. Fourth, the distributionally harsh nature of the orthodox program aggravated social tension and helped to produce a rejection of traditional approaches (Dornbusch and Edwards 1989:6–7). With output falling and inflation accelerating, orthodox policy gave way to a new heterodox alternative.

The second section reviews the rise and fall of the heterodox program that was implemented by President Alan García and his American Popular Revolutionary Alliance (APRA) party in 1985. After briefly reviewing the logic of Peruvian heterodoxy (modeled in detail in Chapter 3), I argue that the García administration's program was marred by insufficient attention to the external sector, a confused approach to inflation control, severe class conflict, and administrative incapacity. I then examine the paralysis that prevented the government from shifting gears and devising a more viable set of policies to avoid the hyperinflation and recession that began in 1988. I close this section with an exercise similar to that in Chapter 4: causality tests and regression analysis to explore the dynamics of the hyperinflation. This empirical review sheds some light on the rationale and viability of the various anti-inflation proposals that surfaced in the 1990 presidential elections.

The final section offers a brief requiem for Peruvian heterodoxy, seeking to sort out why a program that seemed so suited to the Peruvian macroeconomy managed to fail so miserably. I discount the view that García's government represented a simple populist strategy and suggest that a more wisely implemented heterodoxy could have been successful.[1] In its failure, however, the García administration managed to substantially discredit any such interventionist program of macroeconomic management. Like the Siles Zuazo administration in Bolivia, García and his economic team weakened social democratic forces, reversed the fortunes of popular sectors, and paved the way for what will likely be a long bout of orthodox policy.

Orthodox Strategy in Peru, 1980–1985

Background

With a per capita GNP of around $1,300, Peru is relatively poor by world standards, but nearly twice as "well off" as its neighbor, Bolivia. Its economy, as can be noted from Table 5.1, is also more developed (i.e., industrialized) than Bolivia's: At the beginning of the 1980s, manufacturing accounted for around 24 percent of Peruvian GDP, commerce for 14.5 percent, mining for nearly 13 percent, and agriculture for less than 10 percent, with construction and other activities

Table 5.1
Sectoral Composition of the Peruvian Economy, 1980-1989
(as percentage of GDP)

	Agriculture	Mining	Manufacturing	Commerce	Construction	Other*
1980	9.9	12.9	23.8	14.5	5.5	33.4
1981	10.4	11.9	22.9	14.8	5.9	34.1
1982	10.6	12.0	22.6	14.6	6.0	34.1
1983	10.9	12.4	21.5	13.7	5.4	36.1
1984	11.5	12.4	21.6	13.3	5.2	36.0
1985	11.5	12.6	22.1	13.1	4.6	36.0
1986	11.0	11.0	23.6	13.8	5.1	35.5
1987	10.9	9.9	24.9	13.9	5.4	34.9
1988	12.6	9.0	23.5	13.7	5.6	35.6
1989	13.5	10.5	21.2	13.1	5.3	36.3

* Including fishing, electricity and water, transport, restaurants and hotels, government administration, and financial and personal services.

Sources: For 1980-1988 from Instituto Nacional de Estadística (INE), *Peru: Compendio Estadístico, 1988*. For 1989, from INE, *Informe Económico*, February 1990.

constituting the remainder. Peru does share with Bolivia a dependent structure of exports and imports: As noted in Chapter 3, mining and other traditional products accounted for nearly 80 percent of Peru's exports in 1980 and the manufacturing sector was quite reliant on intermediate and capital goods imports, which themselves composed around 72 percent of total imports (Cuánto 1990a:838, 845).

Despite the relatively higher level of development, Peru's sectoral composition suggests an economy much like that described in typical structuralist models. One might therefore expect that structuralist development and stabilization strategies would have long ago made significant inroads into Peruvian thinking and policy making. In fact, the country has a long history of coupling its export reliance with laissez-faire domestic policy. This dominance of free market thinking is evidenced by Peru's relatively late adoption of import substituting industrialization (ISI) in the early 1960s, long after many of its Latin American neighbors had already moved in that direction (Angell and Thorp 1980).

Marking the beginning of a pattern of extreme policy swings, Peru's shift toward import substitution occurred with a vengeance. After a brief dalliance with some elements of ISI under President Fernando Belaúnde (1961–1968), the new military government of General Juan Velasco Alvarado adopted a particularly strong version of state capitalism, combining investments in export production (by both multinationals and a growing state sector) with strict limits (and sometimes sectoral bans) on imports. The government also implemented some far-reaching social reforms, such as land reform and the guarantee of certain worker rights.[2]

Both the interventionist role of the state and the ongoing increase in state investment and enterprise necessitated borrowing. As a result, Peru's external debt rose from $2.7 billion in 1970 to $9.2 billion by 1977, with most of this increase occurring in the post-1973 years of easy international credit.[3] A series of balance of payments crises led to problems with creditors, foreshadowing the generalized Latin American debt crisis of the 1980s. Private banks and the IMF insisted on a turn toward monetarist-style stabilization and adjustment in return for debt rescheduling. A new set of generals acquiesced, radically altering the previous statist thrust of government policy. By the time the military finally stepped aside and Belaúnde returned to power through elections in 1980, orthodox macroeconomic strategies were clearly in favor; Belaúnde continued the trend with an even tighter embrace of neoliberal principles.

Although the swing back toward orthodoxy was originally prompted by international pressure, it also reflected an historic tendency to revert back to free market policies when direct state intervention began to falter (Thorp and Bertram 1978). This underlying tendency was fortified by certain conjunctural factors in the late 1970s and early 1980s. The first was the improvement in Peruvian mineral prices in 1979, a phenomenon that produced a brief economic reactivation and led domestic elites to believe that the orthodox remedy had been successful (Paredes and Pasco-Font 1987; Schydlowsky 1986). The second was the popularity among Peruvian elites and policy makers of the neoconservative experiments underway in the Southern Cone countries of Chile, Uruguay, and Argentina in the 1970s (Foxley 1983; Ramos 1986). Although the attraction to these experiments may seem surprising given the spectacular failures in Argentina and Uruguay, the Chilean economy in 1980 was still trumpeted by international bankers and agencies as a free market miracle (Stallings 1989:185); the disastrous Chilean performance in 1982, which revealed the vulnerability of the newly open economy, was still two years off. In addition, the economic team assembled by Belaúnde was composed of technocrats who had spent the military years working abroad in banks and multilaterals, institutions in which orthodoxy was the norm, and Chilean-style neoconservativism the fad (Webb 1987b:30).[4]

The orthodox program that emerged in Peru in mid-1980 seems quite textbook in retrospect. The Belaúnde administration promised to shrink state enterprise and stimulate private investment. The economy was opened both domestically and internationally: Government intervention in pricing, marketing, and the financial system was eliminated; tariffs and trade barriers were reduced; and the government employed crawling peg currency devaluations in order to maintain Peru's competitiveness on foreign export markets.[5]

The Belaúnde program rapidly collapsed. Its problems can be discerned by examining four broad lines of policy: the privatization drive, trade liberalization, state investment to support export-led growth in the raw material sectors, and the ongoing management of the macroeconomy.[6] Although it is difficult to attribute the eventual difficulties to policy alone, particularly in light of the international economic shocks that hit in late 1981, the overall strategy was contradictory, inappropriate, and inconsistent.[7] The political and economic failure of orthodox adjustment created fertile ground for the emergence of a heterodox alternative.

Orthodoxy in Action: Policy and Politics

Privatization and Private Investment. In accordance with general orthodox principles, the Belaúnde regime sought to shed public enterprises and encourage private investment. The government initially announced that over eighty such enterprises would be sold, converted to joint ventures, or liquidated.[8] These privatization aspirations, however, soon proved to be unrealistic. First, the ministers responsible for the privatization drive were reluctant to erode their base of power and hence moved slowly on the sales of their own firms (Branch 1982:4). Secondly, private sector resources were inadequate for any massive sell-off, particularly in light of falling private investment (see Table 5.2). Foreigners were also of little help; although various estimates of the value of the targeted state enterprises ranged from $200–400 million, total net foreign direct investment flows to Peru barely surpassed $200 million over the period 1981 to 1983, and actually fell to −$89 million by 1984 (Thorp 1986). The privatization that did occur mainly consisted of the sale of government assets to special interests, and essen-

Table 5.2
Investment in Peru, 1980-1989

	Gross Fixed Investment (as % of GDP)	Private Investment (as % of GDP)	Public Investment (as % of GDP)	Foreign Direct Investment (millions of US$)
1980	24.2	18.0	6.1	27
1981	26.9	20.4	6.5	125
1982	26.3	18.8	7.5	48
1983	21.3	14.2	7.1	38
1984	19.1	13.2	5.9	-89
1985	16.7	12.0	4.6	1
1986	18.2	13.8	4.4	22
1987	19.4	14.3	5.2	32
1988	18.5	14.5	4.0	44
1989	16.7	8.5	8.1	---

Sources: Data on real GDP from Instituto Nacional de Estadística (INE) (1989:195) and INE (1990: 11). Data on investment from INE (1989:202-3) and INE (1990:69). Data on foreign direct investment from the International Monetary Fund's *International Financial Statistics Yearbook 1990*. "---" indicates that data were unavailable.

tially amounted to political patronage (Saulniers 1988:36). The government did manage to weaken some state companies by slashing investment funds, allowing unrestricted imports, and promoting private sector rivals (Alvarez 1984). But in the end, the government fully liquidated only a few less significant firms, such as a supermarket chain, a machine tool factory, and a fish freezing and canning plant (Reid 1985:83-84).

The privatization program assumed that shrinking the state sector would cause an upsurge in private domestic and foreign investment. The results on the latter were disappointing. As Table 5.2 shows, private sector gross capital formation fell from 18 percent of GDP in 1980 to 12 percent of GDP in 1985, an especially poor showing when compared to historical trends (Thorp and Bertram 1978:288–291). Government incentives for local investment, it seems, were quickly offset by the trade liberalization policy (see "Trade Liberalization," below), the erratic disbursement of export subsidies, and the negative overall macroeconomic scenario, especially the fall in GDP and hence market size.[9]

Foreign direct investment, of course, was a special target of the new orthodox team, both because such investment would bring foreign exchange and because demonstrable confidence by transnationals was likely to calm the jittery nerves of local capital. Despite generous incentives, including substantial breaks on export and other taxes, the neoliberal program was not able to overcome the unfavorable conditions offered by a slowing economy. Although 1981 foreign investment did register a dramatic improvement over 1980, the level of investment inflows was

Peru: Stabilization and Hyperinflation

still less than a third of the 1975 peak. When the debt crisis broke out throughout the region, foreign direct investment actually became negative, hitting an all-time low in 1984 (see Table 5.2).

Trade Liberalization. The trade liberalization program, begun in 1978 under strong pressure from the IMF, received a boost with the change of administration in 1980. The Belaúnde team was harshly critical of the country's previous import substitution efforts and also opposed the various state interventions used to promote nontraditional exports. This latter critique did have some merit: Although nontraditional exports had risen to $845 million by 1980 (Banco Central de Reserva del Perú 1987a:167), many observers viewed the record as weak in light of the incentives offered industrialists, including abundant credit at subsidized interest rates and favorable access to cheap production inputs and capital goods imports.

The Belaúnde team argued that industrial exports could be effectively stimulated through trade liberalization and a more "neutral" set of trade policies. Liberalization, it was suggested, would introduce competition and force the industrial sector to become more efficient; neutrality would steer toward the external sector only those industries in which the market, and not the state, determined that Peru had a comparative advantage. The actual policy measures were straightforward. The average nominal tariff was brought down from 46 percent to 32 percent, and a wide range of duty exemptions and quantitative restrictions were removed; by the end of 1981, 98 percent of all registered items could be imported freely, compared to 38 percent in 1978 (World Bank 1985:48). Though maintained, a tax subsidy (CERTEX) for priority exports was reduced, and interest rates on credit available from the state industrial bank were no longer set to favor nontraditional exporters.

The effects of this liberalization policy were immediate, but unfortunate. The lower tariffs brought a flood of foreign products onto the domestic market. While some of the new imports were necessary industrial inputs, the import of luxury consumer goods also skyrocketed. As a result, local manufacturing output dropped nearly 20 percent between 1980 and 1983, a decline so sharp that industry was left operating at less than half of installed capacity (Reid 1985:85). Losses caused by the increased competition gave rise to a new level of demand for credit on the part of local industry; because domestic liberalization had driven up interest rates, many firms went deeply into the red as they borrowed to weather the adjustment period. Under strong pressure from domestic capitalists, the administration began backtracking on the early measures. The 1984 CERTEX tax subsidy rose above the amount that the government had spent in 1979, and nominal tariffs were brought back up to their pre-1978 levels (World Bank 1985:49).

The Public Investment Program. The third set of orthodox policy goals centered on steering state investments away from state enterprise expansion and toward economic infrastructure that would support private enterprise, particularly in the export sector. The 1981–1985 public investment plans included over eighty projects and budgeted an annual average expenditure of $2.3 billion. In the end, however, the government did not meet these optimistic spending targets. By 1982, many projects still lacked financing, resulting in a level of public investment 40 percent below the amount originally programmed (World Bank 1985:30). After 1983, some projects simply stood still as unpaid contractors and suppliers stopped work, while other projects moved along at a greatly reduced pace.

The public investment program, then, ultimately hurt the very private sector it was intended to benefit. With the state's energies absorbed by the tasks entailed in implementing the project portfolio, less attention was paid to the negative effects the worsening macroeconomic scenario was having on the private sector. Once the economic crisis set in, some private sector interests, particularly direct subcontractors, were hurt by the paralysis in state projects. Lastly, the sheer ambition of the program constrained future policy: The half-completed portfolio handed down from this period necessarily formed the core of the state investment program for years to come, tying the hands of the subsequent administration.

Macroeconomic Policy. In theory, the macroeconomic policies of the Belaúnde administration were traditional IMF orthodoxy: restraining monetary growth, devaluing local currency, encouraging private initiative, and lowering trade barriers in order to increase Peru's integration into the world economy. For reasons detailed in Chapter 3, structuralist economists generally argue that such a program may be inappropriate and unwise. But even structuralists would agree that orthodoxy, if it is to be adopted, should be implemented in a consistent, rather than a "stop-go" fashion. Continuity in policy, even if such policy is suboptimal, allows economic agents to form stable expectations about the future. Continually shifting policy makes planning difficult, erodes the credibility of the government, and usually causes capital to withhold investment.

The Belaúnde government's macroeconomic policy, however, was far from consistent. Faced with nationwide municipal elections early in the Belaúnde regime, the government "softened" policy: The public sector deficit was tolerated, the exchange rate was allowed to appreciate, and government-controlled prices were held down. Belaúnde's Popular Action (AP) party did score a victory in the general elections, but the shifting economic policy caused conflict between the AP and its ally, the Popular Christian Party (PPC), as well as between politicians from both parties and the president's technocratic economic team. The divisions quickly sharpened and policy decisions and program implementation became more difficult.

One area in which orthodox theory and policy seems to have been rigorously and consistently pursued was the management of domestic inflation. Belaúnde's technocrats were firm adherents of the sort of simple monetarist model presented in Chapter 2, and hence believed that reserve accumulation necessarily produced both monetary growth and inflation. Accordingly, they argued that the 1980 inflation rate of 61 percent stemmed from the 1979 balance of payments surplus; to counter this inflation, the government should combine fiscal and monetary restraint with a "burning off" of reserves (Schydlowsky 1986:230–231). The IMF, sharing a faith in the basic monetarist framework, blessed the macroeconomic prescription and Peru operated under a series of IMF programs until mid-1984.

Overall, the macroeconomic results of the Belaúnde program were disappointing: Between 1980 and 1985, GDP stagnated, inflation doubled, and external debt rose over 70 percent (see Tables 5.3 and 5.4). External or *exogenous* shocks did, of course, play a large role in this performance: The terms of trade shifted dramatically against Peru through the early 1980s (see Table 5.4), and Peru was simultaneously buffeted by the same high interest rates and private creditor reluctance affecting the rest of Latin America. In addition, agricultural production was severely weakened by the freak weather conditions caused by the El Niño ocean current inversion.[10] In this context, almost any set of policies would have faced serious problems.

But the orthodox macroeconomic program surely contributed to the poor economic results. Inflation-fighting was excessively focused on monetary or demand restraint, and there seemed to be little awareness of the cost pressures being exerted by the policies of currency depreciation and high interest rates. In general, liberalizing imports and "burning" reserves hardly seems the appropriate macroeconomic recipe for an economy historically constrained by foreign exchange. Moreover, government policy, particularly with respect to the budget, was sometimes inconsistent. The program, in short, must share some of the blame for Peru's poor performance in the first half of the 1980s.

Politics, Class, and Program Implementation. As noted above, the Belaúnde administration's unsuccessful effort to stabilize the economy was not simply due to exogenous shocks and inappropriate technical measures; inconsistency and poor implementation played a role. These factors were rooted in both the weakness and fragmentation of the Peruvian state and the difficulties involved in securing a stable political and class basis for adjustment measures.

The ability of the Peruvian bureaucracy to successfully execute state economic policy was quite limited. The public sector's administrative potential had already been shaken by the massive layoffs of top public personnel in 1978 (Vallenas and Bolaños 1985) and the Belaúnde government made no effort to reverse this trend. Given the weakness in the middle levels of the bureaucracy, policy making came to rely almost solely on executive decree.[11] Relations between state institutions responsible for economic management were marked by conflict, making coordination problematic. Tensions between the finance ministry and the central bank were especially severe. The National Institute Planning (INP) was relocated from downtown Lima to a remote suburban zone, which reduced its ability to communicate with other state agencies on daily policy matters, and physically symbolized its role as a policy "outsider" (Cornejo 1985:117). Peru thus suffered from both a "balkanization" of economic policy making (Webb 1987b:47) and a neglect of long-term planning.

Table 5.3
Macroeconomic Performance in Peru, 1980-1989

	Growth of Real GDP (% change)	Growth of Manu- facturing (% change)	CPI Inflation Rate (Dec.-Dec.)
1980	4.5	5.7	60.8
1981	4.4	0.7	72.7
1982	0.3	-1.0	72.9
1983	-12.3	-16.9	125.1
1984	4.8	5.5	111.4
1985	2.4	4.9	158.3
1986	9.5	16.8	62.9
1987	7.8	13.7	114.5
1988	-8.8	-13.9	1722.3
1989	-10.4	-19.2	2775.6

Sources: Growth of real GDP and real manufacturing based on data in Instituto Nacional de Estadística (INE) (1988:133), INE (1989:195), INE (1990:11), and Cuánto (1990a:268). Inflation rates calculated using the Lima consumer price index available in Cuánto (1990a:602).

This fragmentation of the state and its institutions was caused partly by the orthodox program itself. Having rejected state-led development in favor of a market strategy, the Belaúnde government tended to work around traditional bureaucratic and institutional structures. These institutions, however, were crucial for the effective implementation of any development program; even market policies are "interventions" that demand a basic level of capacity, coordination, and political support (Haggard and Kaufman 1989). Neoliberal policy makers discounted the very tools they needed for program implementation and downplayed the institution-building necessary to truly transform economic policy.

Program implementation was also constrained by the inability to forge a secure class or political basis for adjustment. Business was the principal *class* basis of the program, a role fitting in light of the drive to have the state reduce its own profile and thereby make room for the private sector. Capital was initially eager to cooperate and business viewed the Belaúnde regime as an opportunity to reverse the crisis of representation suffered during the nominally leftist regimes of the previous decade (Conaghan 1991). Organized labor was eager, on the other hand, to show that the government lacked support among workers and would therefore be unable to implement its proposed policies (Bollinger 1987). To bridge the gap and create a new set of relations between capital, labor, and the state, the administration formed a National Tripartite Commission composed of representatives from industry, government, and the four major labor confederations (Malloy 1982:8). The government, however, was unable to persuade business or workers

Table 5.4
Trade, Reserves, and Debt Service in Peru, 1980-1989

	Exports (US$ mil.)	Imports (US$ mil.)	Trade Balance (US$ mil.)	Terms of Trade (1978=100)
1980	3,916	3,090	826	152.5
1981	3,249	3,802	-553	124.9
1982	3,293	3,722	-429	103.0
1983	3,015	2,722	293	110.6
1984	3,147	2,140	1,007	100.9
1985	2,978	1,806	1,172	90.6
1986	2,531	2,596	-65	66.4
1987	2,661	3,182	-521	66.9
1988	2,695	2,750	-56	73.5
1989	3,540	2,141	1,399	76.7

	Net International Reserves (US$ mil.)	Long-term External Public Debt (US$ mil.)	Debt Service (as a % of exports of goods and services)	Accumulated Interest Arrears on Long-term Debt (US$ mil.)
1980	1,276	6,043	28.6	0
1981	772	6,127	45.8	0
1982	896	6,825	36.7	0
1983	856	8,256	20.1	0
1984	1,103	9,648	17.4	374
1985	1,383	10,462	16.3	703
1986	866	11,068	14.7	1319
1987	81	11,747	11.7	1904
1988	-317	12,465	4.3	2489
1989	546	---	---	---

Sources: Data on exports, imports, and the trade balance from Cuánto (1990a:827) and Cuánto (1990b:12). The terms of trade are calculated as the price of traditional exports relative to imports and are taken from Cuánto (1990a:84). Net international reserves taken from Cuánto (1990a:827) and Cuánto (1990b:12). Long-term external public debt from Cuánto (1990a:827). Debt service figures are for non-BCR (Central Bank) debt and taken from Banco Central de Reserva del Perú (BCRP) (1987:59) and Instituto Nacional de Estadística (INE) (1989:605); exports of goods and service calculated from data in Cuánto (1990a:827,831). Interest arrears are from World Bank (1989:306); arrears including principal are substantially higher. "---" indicates that data were unavailable.

to accept its income and price proposals and the commission soon unraveled as the government proved unable to meet designated inflation targets. The relationships between the government, business, and workers became more conflictual, which helped fuel inflation. With the economy shrinking and inflation heating up, even business became hostile to the government and its program.

As evident from the political description above, the working and popular classes were both most hostile to and most damaged by orthodoxy. Table 5.5 presents the data on real wages, informal income, wage share, and the agricultural-manufacturing terms of trade; all these variables moved in a regressive direction as the government tried to manage the crisis of the early 1980s. It is little wonder that the popular sectors began to look for new leadership and a new economic strategy.

This search for a new popular response took a variety of forms. On the one hand, *Sendero Luminoso* and other insurgent groups bypassed legal forms of political participation and argued for (and practiced) armed revolution.[12] As *Sendero* proceeded from low-level political agitation in 1981–1982 to violent assassinations of locally elected officials and destruction of state investment projects, the government declared much of the area of guerilla activities in the southern Andes an emergency zone. A full-scale military operation was deployed in 1983, and the government turned to U.S., Argentine, and Israeli advisers for counterinsurgency training (Reid 1985:114).[13]

Taking a different tack, many of Peru's poor employed the ballot box to register their discontent with hardships of orthodox austerity. In the 1983 nationwide municipal elections, Belaúnde's conservative alliance slipped, and there emerged a new hegemonic bloc consisting of the center-left sections of the APRA led by Alan García and a group of six left-wing parties that had organized into a United Left (IU) coalition. The APRA captured 33 percent of the vote, and the IU another 29 percent, with the latter winning the municipality of Lima.

By 1985, the political momentum had shifted enough for APRA's Alan García to win the presidency with a convincing majority. Taking power in July, García enjoyed enormous personal popularity and was able to secure a tacit alliance with much of the left opposition (IU) and even the support of certain business sectors frustrated with the shallow markets left by orthodox management. The new government promised not only to reduce inflation but also to spur economic growth and redistribute income. Unfortunately, the method for doing this—"heterodox" economic policy coupled with a social-democratic commitment to private investment—proved disastrous.

The Rise and Fall of Peruvian Heterodoxy

The era of Peruvian heterodoxy was heralded by the central economic policy announced in President García's inaugural address: the limitation of Peruvian debt service to no more than 10 percent of export earnings. Although the debt ser-

Table 5.5
Real Wages and Distribution in Peru, 1980-1989

	Index of Real Salaries (1980=100)	Index of Real Wages (1980=100)	Index of Informal Income (1980=100)
1980	100.0	100.0	100.0
1981	105.6	105.1	125.1
1982	109.7	105.1	131.1
1983	94.1	87.2	103.5
1984	86.7	74.4	102.6
1985	80.0	64.1	105.6
1986	99.8	87.2	151.9
1987	106.0	94.9	195.9
1988	70.0	61.5	75.8
1989	54.5	48.7	72.3

	Wage Share of National Income (percent)	Profit Share of National Income (percent)	Agricultural-Manufacturing Terms of Trade (1979=100)
1980	37.7	38.1	115.1
1981	38.0	38.3	117.5
1982	39.0	34.9	104.5
1983	40.9	32.4	106.2
1984	37.2	35.2	96.0
1985	34.4	38.4	66.9
1986	36.4	34.8	87.9
1987	36.5	36.3	92.9
1988	28.8	42.5	53.5
1989	---	---	---

Sources: Real salaries are for nonmanual workers and real wages for manual workers; both series taken from Cuánto (1990a:718). Index of informal income is for December of each year and is taken from Cuánto (1990a:730). Wage and profit shares taken from data in Cuánto (1990a:275). National income is national product minus net interest payments abroad; profit share includes rent, profits, and domestic net interest payments; the remainder of income accrues to independent producers in both agricultural and non-agricultural activities. The agricultural-manufacturing terms of trade taken from sectoral GDP deflators reported in Instituto Nacional de Estadística (INE) (1989:214). "---" indicates that data were unavailable.

vice policy drew immediate international attention, the domestic measures soon introduced were equally crucial to Peru's future and represented a sharp break with the previous administration (Wise 1986).

The economic team responsible for articulating and eventually implementing the new program emerged from a small group of economists that had long offered criticisms of IMF-style policy and suggestions of an alternative (Carbonetto 1987; Carbonetto et al. 1987; Dancourt 1986a, 1986b; and Ferrari 1986). As noted in Chapter 3, this group adhered to the Latin American structuralist tradition and argued that various rigidities present in the Peruvian economy made orthodox stabilization policy inappropriate. Prices in industry, it was suggested, were mostly set via a mark-up on costs (including wages, interest payments on working capital, imported capital goods, and intermediate goods provided by state-owned firms). Prices of exports and imports were set by the world markets and neither exports nor the import share of output were very responsive to devaluation-induced changes in their domestic value; exports were largely driven by supply (that is, previous investment in capacity) while import coefficients were mostly fixed by the technical requirements of production. Spending patterns were varied by socio-economic class: Workers and peasants spent virtually all their income while capitalists engaged in capital flight, consumed luxury imports, and occasionally invested. Finally, unlike industry, agricultural prices were flexibly determined by demand, but supply responses were slow and uncertain.

Taken together, these features implied that IMF-style policy was ineffective and, in fact, stagflationary.[14] While the Belaúnde team had seen inflation as a signal of excess demand and trade imbalance as the result of an "incorrect" exchange rate, the heterodox critics suggested that devaluation had barely budged exports, while leaving the import coefficient untouched; improvements in the trade balance had come from recessionary cutbacks in domestic absorption. Meanwhile, devaluation had contributed to inflation by raising import costs; other cost pressures resulted from increases in the prices of state-supplied inputs (due to deficit-cutting) and higher interest costs on working capital (due to monetary restraint). In such a context, it was little wonder that real wages had fallen and that the resulting decrease in urban demand had also produced a reduction in real agricultural prices and peasant income.

But if orthodox policies could not combat inflation, reactivate growth, and raise real wages in the Peruvian context, what could? Although this issue was central to the political forces aligned with García, it was a novel question for a structuralist vision in which inflation had generally been considered an acceptable outcome of growth and the pressure it placed on food prices. Now, however, was the time to move beyond critique.

The result was a heterodox economic policy that sought to contain inflation by directly controlling both prices and cost-push factors (Schuldt 1986). The APRA government began its domestic policy with a single sharp devaluation to gain competitiveness followed by an exchange rate freeze in order to control import costs. Interest rates were mandated downward to reduce working capital costs. The real price of government-supplied inputs was also reduced, producing a favorable impact on cost pressures. The effects on inflation were immediate and reassuring: within a year, the rate had been halved.

Although the attempt to reduce inflation by directly controlling costs was similar to the Argentine and Brazilian "heterodox" experiments of the same period (Arida 1986; Cardoso 1986; Dornbusch and Simonsen 1987), the Peruvian program differed in several key ways: (1) It made an explicit effort to relieve the external growth constraint through limitations on debt service; (2) it discounted the possibility of excess demand inflation and sought instead to pump up demand through real wage hikes and widening government deficits; (3) it explicitly sought to cement an alliance with private capital by holding ongoing talks about state economic policy with the country's most powerful capitalists; and (4) it included a medium-term objective (albeit an unfulfilled one) of restructuring the economy toward industrial exports and greater self-sufficiency.

Below, I focus on such key issues as debt service limits, inflation and demand management, relations with private capital and the state's administrative capacity. I argue that the debt strategy was incomplete and that inflation management was too little concerned with demand factors. I suggest that the social democratic coalition sought by García was wrecked by his own inconsistent attitude toward private capital, and that the overall program was constrained, as was Belaúnde's, by bureaucratic incapacity and fragmentation. I then examine the emergence of hyperinflation. I econometrically explore the relationships between monetary growth, the exchange rate, and prices, and use these results to evaluate the logic of the competing anti-inflation proposals that emerged in the 1990 elections. A postmortem on heterodoxy completes the chapter.

Heterodoxy in Action: Policy and Politics

Debt Service Limits. A limit on debt service was the announced cornerstone of the heterodox program. Reducing the outflow of dollars through restricting debt service was expected to stabilize the exchange rate (and hence prices) and allow an increase in the intermediate imports needed for economic reactivation.

The debt policy was neither as dramatic nor as ill considered as some observers seem to have thought. The Belaúnde government had already quietly stopped most payments to commercial creditors, reducing the ratio of debt service to exports from over 45 percent in 1982 to less than 20 percent in 1984. Moreover, APRA's stated policy through 1987 was to selectively honor obligations that would lead to trade and development financing; in this vein, Peru continued to service short-term trade finance and make payments to multilaterals such as the World Bank and the Inter-American Bank. The García strategy was, in fact, the first attempt at a coherent approach to the Peruvian debt problem since servicing difficulties emerged in the late 1970s and seemed sensible in light of the dim prospects of new voluntary lending by commercial creditors (Wise 1988).

There were, however, several problems with García's debt strategy. First, the Peruvian government found it difficult to make payments deemed important for maintaining trade and development finance *and* stay below the self-imposed limit of 10 percent. Not until 1988 did the debt service ratio dip below 10 percent and this mostly reflected incapacity to pay rather than any conscious strategy (see Table 5. 4).[15] Second, the public stance against the IMF and the anti-imperialist rhetoric that accompanied it was in distinct contrast to the quiet nonpayment of Belaúnde, and isolated Peru from the international financial institutions. The Fund declared Peru an "ineligible borrower" in August 1986 and flows from the other multilaterals fell steadily through the period of heterodoxy, reflecting both a lack of confidence in the APRA program and an irritation with the debt challenge being proffered by García.

The key problem with the debt stance was the lack of a clear strategy to create alternative sources of foreign exchange. The negative reactions from foreign creditors were to be expected and attention should have been immediately turned toward vigorous export promotion and more efficient import substitution. Unfortunately, this ran against the desire to import more in order to feed the reactivation. Even as export revenues fell over 10 percent between 1985 and 1987, imports rose from $1.8 billion to $3.2 billion. The result was a shift from a $1.2 billion trade surplus in 1985 to a more than half billion dollar trade deficit in 1987 (see Table 5.4). Reactivation was indeed fed—GDP grew nearly 16 percent in these two years—but net international reserves fell from $1.4 billion at the end of 1985 to a paltry $81 million at the end of 1987.

To be fair, some members of the economic team were conscious of the problems in the external sector by late 1986 but they proved unable to persuade García to slow the politically popular reactivation. With reserves in collapse through 1987, the government further antagonized official lending agencies by announcing a new "ability to pay" program that was supposed to further reduce outpayments until growth targets were met. Loan disbursements from the multilaterals turned negative and the last years of the García administration were marked by a tense stand-off between international creditors and the Peruvian government. The debt limits that had held so much promise had instead produced a brief party and then an incapacitating hangover.

Inflation and Demand Management. The heterodox program emphasized both inertial and cost-push inflation (see Chapter 3), contending that excess demand was an unlikely culprit when the country's productive capacity was half idle. Price controls (to break inflationary expectations) were coupled with attempts to force down costs by lowering interest rates, stabilizing the exchange rate, and reducing the relative price of parastatal inputs (such as electricity). Because reactivation and redistribution were also central goals, the government allowed the fiscal deficit to grow (mostly through reducing taxes and increasing subsidies) and mandated increases in the real wage.

The initial successes on the growth front have already been mentioned; equally impressive was the fall in inflation from 158 percent in 1985 to 63 percent a year later. By 1987, however, the inflation rate had nearly doubled and in 1988, Peruvian inflation hit 1,722 percent. What went wrong?

There were at least three reasons for the inflationary outburst. The first involved the external sector and the behavior of the exchange rate. As noted in Chapter 3, output in an economy like Peru's is constrained primarily by the capacity to import intermediates and not by the productive limits of existing plant and equipment. This implies that demand should be tailored to fit external and not internal constraints—and that long-run attention should be focused on export expansion and import substitution. The Peruvian team instead argued that inflation could not be triggered short of full employment and thus worried little about the massive growth spurt in 1986–1987. Growth, however, drained reserves and eventually reduced import capacity. This, in turn, constricted supply and allowed producers to increase mark-ups, a phenomenon that also redistributed income toward capital (see Table 5.5 for distributional patterns).[16] The shortage of foreign exchange also led worried investors to "dollarize" savings (even before García's attempt at bank nationalization accelerated this trend). As a result, the parallel market exchange rate rose, putting pressure on the official exchange rate, and inducing firms to anticipate devaluation and engage in "defensive" price hikes.

The second source of inflationary difficulties was the government deficit (see Table 5.6). APRA economists believed that deficits would have little inflationary impact as long as there was unemployment and idle productive capacity.[17] As a result, the government allowed the "economic deficit" of the public sector to rise from 2.4 percent of GDP to 6.5 percent.[18] This deficit expansion was not due to rising central government expenditures (which fell in real terms throughout the period) but rather to declining tax revenues. The tax take fell from 12.4 percent of GDP in 1985 to 8.2 percent in 1987 and slipped even further to 7.4 percent of GDP by 1988 (Cuánto 1990a:263, 758–759). The first phase of the decrease was mostly a result of conscious policy on the government's part while the second essentially reflected, as in Bolivia, a "Tanzi effect" in which, given fixed lags in tax collection, high inflation erodes the real value of tax revenues.[19]

Despite heterodox protestations, the deficit was inflationary for three reasons: (1) It added to demand when the economy had already spurted past the inflationary trigger of import capacity; (2) key economic actors in both business and labor associated deficits with inflation and hence tended to shift inflationary expectations upward; and (3) the deficits were accompanied by rapid growth in monetary measures, including a rise in M1 of nearly 150 percent in 1987. A particular culprit in the monetary expansion was the differential between export and import exchange rates, a feature that contributed to Central Bank losses on the order of 2.8 percent of GDP in 1987 and poured excess liquidity into the economy.[20]

Table 5.6
Public Sector Finances in Peru, 1980-1988

	Central Government Income (% of GDP)	Central Government Spending (% of GDP)	Public Sector Income (% of GDP)	Public Sector Spending (% of GDP)
1980	17.1	19.5	45.8	49.7
1981	14.3	18.2	39.2	45.9
1982	13.9	17.0	40.2	47.6
1983	11.5	18.7	43.8	53.6
1984	13.2	17.4	39.3	45.5
1985	14.1	16.2	43.2	45.6
1986	12.0	15.5	32.6	37.6
1987	8.7	14.3	26.1	32.6
1988	8.1	10.7	23.1	29.0
1989	---	---	---	---

	Deficit of Central Govt. (% of GDP)	Deficit of Public Sector (% of GDP)	Change in Real Tax Income	Change in Real Central Govt. Expenditures
1980	-2.4	-3.9	6.0	16.7
1981	-3.9	-6.7	-22.0	-6.9
1982	-3.1	-7.3	0.0	-8.1
1983	-7.2	-9.8	-24.1	-1.4
1984	-4.1	-6.1	13.2	-3.6
1985	-2.0	-2.4	16.9	-5.4
1986	-3.5	-4.9	-12.9	0.8
1987	-5.5	-6.5	-22.9	-3.7
1988	-2.6	-5.8	20.2	-9.9
1989	-2.7	---	---	---

Sources: Data on central government income and expenditures as a percentage of GDP taken from Cuánto (1990a:755-756); public sector income and expenditures from Cuánto (1990a:738-739); nominal GDP from Cuánto (1990a:263). Real tax income and central government expenditures calculated using the relevant expenditure deflator taken from Instituto Nacional de Estadística (INE) (1989:546, 548). The figures for the public sector include the central government as well as state enterprises, local governments, public institutions, and the social security system. The deficit figures are for the "economic" deficit (i.e., not including amortization). The central government deficit as a percentage of GDP for 1989 is figured as a simple average of the monthly series reported in Cuánto (1990b:11) and is quite preliminary. "---" indicates that data were unavailable.

A final inflationary impetus was the misalignment in relative prices that resulted from the combination of selective price controls and demand expansion.[21] While administered or controlled prices increased only 38.4 percent in the first seventeen months of the program (between July 1985 and December 1986), rising demand put pressure on flex-price markets in agricultural products and informal services, leading uncontrolled prices to rise 133.9 percent over the same period (Paus 1991:419). The spillover of demand into these markets did yield some positive distributional shifts: The rural-urban terms of trade increased (in favor of agriculture) by nearly 40 percent between 1985 and 1987 and real informal sector income rose over 80 percent in the same period (see Table 5.5). This, however, implied that inertial inflation had not been eliminated outside of formal industry and, once the controls were lifted, industrialists were sure to attempt an inflationary round of price hikes in order to restore the previous relative prices. The government appeared to have little coherent strategy to deal with this sequencing problem, preferring to believe that inflation was eliminated when in fact it had merely been bottled up.

Class Relations. One of the most crucial elements of the Peruvian heterodox program was its class character. As noted in the conclusion of Chapter 3, the structuralist theory that informed heterodox thinking generally recognizes the existence of social classes and sees distributional conflict between classes as an important motor of inflation. For the structuralists, this suggests that inflation can only be reduced via incomes policy; this, in turn, requires that the government seek a social consensus built on class conciliation.

Peru faced special tensions in arriving at such a consensus. Social demands were high, especially in light of the regressive effects of Belaúnde's orthodoxy. The APRA government needed to satisfy its political base in the working class and derail the increasingly popular revolutionary message of *Sendero Luminoso*. At the same time, it could not afford to alienate business, particularly because the state seemed to lack both the resources and the management skills to replace private capital as the investing agent. Indeed, the long-run future of the program hinged on a private investment boom that would expand capacity, especially in the export sector, in order to relieve foreign exchange constraints and inflationary pressures.

Against this backdrop, the APRA attempted a complicated social-democratic "dance" with both labor and capital. The government gave workers, campesinos, and the informal sector little voice in actual policy making, but the macroeconomic package did raise wages and farmer and informal income, providing a basis for support from these sectors (as well as providing the burst of aggregate demand needed for reactivation). To attract the support of business, the APRA government reduced its own investment, supposedly to create space for the private sector;[22] protected profit margins by counteracting real wage hikes with reductions in taxes, interest rates, and parastatal prices; and began a series of direct meetings between President García and representatives from the country's twelve largest business groups (the so-called "twelve apostles"). The intent of this latter process was to assure private capital that higher wages and enhanced government intervention were not real threats; business would still enjoy its crucial role as investor and would simultaneously benefit from the positive effect that macroeconomic expansion would have on aggregate profits.

The courting of capital, labeled *concertación*, did initially yield some positive results: Private investment rose from 12 percent of GDP in 1985 to over 14 percent of GDP in 1987. But the private sector generally remained wary, put off by an early government attempt to sop up profits with a mandatory bond-purchasing scheme (which was soon suspended) and concerned about the stability of the political climate and the continuity of government policies. García, frustrated with the slow progress in generating private investment, decided to nationalize the country's remaining private banks as a way of gaining leverage over the "twelve apostles"; a related purpose was to prevent (or at least slow) capital flight through the banking system. Designed in secret by a small group of advisors, the announcement of the measure in a July 1987 speech by the president—billed as part of a program to "democratize" credit—signaled the death of any semblance of *concertación* and the beginning of a war with private capital.

The struggle over the banks gained García few allies and instead produced a cohering of business forces around a resurgent rightist opposition.[23] Labor was already alienated from the president because of his efforts to attract the support of capital and his seeming disinterest in affording labor a role in the determination of policy. The left opposition, the IU, supported the attempted bank seizure but criticized virtually every other initiative of the APRA government. Meanwhile, Mario Vargas Llosa, a famed author and political novice, became the darling of the Peruvian right by forming a "Liberty Movement," which portrayed the nationalization as an arbitrary taking of private property that threatened the security of not just big business but also middle-class entrepreneurs and even informal street vendors. In the end, the banks remained private due to a combination of legal challenges and, in some banks, the transfer of majority ownership to employees (a category exempted from the nationalization decree). Unfortunately, the damage was already done: García was isolated politically, business was hostile, and the right, once marginalized by its poor showings in the 1985 elections, was reborn.

Far from accomplishing an inflation-dampening class conciliation, the heterodox team had provoked an increase in social conflict and, in its wake, spiraling inflation. Why did the García administration allow the politics of the program to go awry? The excessive concentration of power and decision making in the hands of the president was a contributing factor, because it allowed important decisions such as the banking nationalization to be made without careful consideration. The more fundamental reasons, however, lie in the sharp divisions preexisting in Peruvian society and in Peru's integration into international capital markets. García fancied himself a Rooseveltian figure in a Keynesian drama: He would redistribute to lower income groups, pursue rapid growth, and rescue capital from its own shortsightedness. But after Velasco's more threatening state capitalism, the private sector was hesitant about such government-driven experiments. And unlike capitalists in the Depression-era United States, the Peruvian elite could simply exit both themselves and their wealth to safer climes in, say, Miami, an exodus that exacerbated the foreign exchange problems created by the cut-off of external credit. Against this background, social democracy seemed sure to fail.

Administrative Capacity. Blame for the heterodox collapse has so far been placed on excessive consumption of reserves, scant attention to underlying inflationary dynamics, and an ill-considered attack on the same capitalist class that was supposed to invest and hence save the program. All these difficulties were sharpened by the administrative incapacity of the government. The historically weak Peruvian state had suffered a further gutting during the "free-market" era of the early 1980s. This slippage in state power was aggravated in the García period by rising interagency conflict, the isolation of key policy makers, and the president's tendency to dominate rather than delegate decisions on the economy (Wise 1989).

The interagency conflicts involved both politics and policy. The Ministry of Economics and Finance was controlled by Alva Castro, a potential challenger within the APRA to Alan García; although generally supportive of the heterodox growth model, Alva Castro resigned as soon as problems emerged, apparently to protect his political standing for the 1990 presidential elections. The Central Bank, although headed by a García supporter, retained its traditional support for more conservative policy, particularly in the ranks of middle management. The National Institute Planning did experience a revival, becoming home to many of the economists and technicians that made up the heterodox *equipo*. Its long-term plans were, however, generally ignored by the administration and the institute itself was torn by internal dissent.[24]

Economic policy making quickly became the domain of the president and a small group of advisors.[25] Like Belaúnde's technocratic group in the early 1980s, the heterodox *equipo* was highly insulated but extremely influential, a combination that created several problems for actually implementing policy. First, middle managers in the various ministries neither understood the program nor believed in it; as a result, they often carried out state directives with less than full enthusiasm. Second, the wide discretionary power of the team allowed it to engage in sharp policy shifts (for example, the mandatory profit bonds and the banking nationalization); had the team exercised less influence with García, policy change would have been moderated by the typical interministerial consultations and negotiations. Third, the smallness of the team and its reliance on executive mandate gave the president an extraordinary degree of control over economic policy. García sometimes took carefully crafted adjustment packages and arbitrarily changed policy measures in order to soften their political impact; the result was economic inconsistency.[26] By mid-1988, even the members of the small team were bickering among themselves, particularly over exchange rate policy.

The failure of the heterodox program and the eventual passage into hyperinflation brought additional difficulties. Tax revenues fell and forced a cut in government expenditures; both government salaries and the ability to effect change were reduced, diminishing the incentives for public service. Hyperinflation soon made planning as difficult for the state as it did for the private sector. Finally, the apparent collapse of heterodoxy in 1988 led the *equipo* to abandon their positions (and, in the case of presidential advisor Daniel Carbonetto, the country). This further isolated the president and left him with no economic advisor with which he was truly comfortable, a fact that posed severe problems for designing and implementing policy in the final year and a half of the García administration.

Hyperinflation

By mid-1988, the critical economic situation forced a major policy shift. In September, the government pushed through a new program that included a sharp devaluation, public sector price hikes, and several tax-raising measures (including a shortening of collection lags to combat the Tanzi effect and a 4 percent tax on exports, the latter measure seemingly in conflict with the need to induce export expansion). The government proposed an industrial price freeze but allowed adjustments prior to its imposition; the result was an extraordinary round of price hikes. In September alone, inflation hit 114 percent while GDP fell 10 percent. Hyperinflation had set in and monthly inflation averaged 35 percent from October 1988 through July 1990 when the new president took power (see Fig. 5.1).[27] Meanwhile, output continued to fall; although there was some recuperation in mid-1989, by April 1990, GDP was 15 percent below its level in the first month of the García administration and 30 percent below the December 1986 peak reached during the glory days of the heterodox experiment.[28]

The persistence of hyperinflation through 1989 and 1990 may be somewhat surprising given the general improvement in the fiscal deficit, the trade balance, and the level of reserves through this period.[29] Although the continuing price pressure was partly due to the government's strategy of reactivating the economy in time for the November 1989 municipal and March 1990 presidential elections, it may have also been a "normal" part of hyperinflationary dynamics. As noted in the review of the Bolivian experience, many economists have argued that hyperinflations are often accompanied by a reversal in the usual chains of causation: Rather than prices chasing money, monetary growth rises following inflation's negative effect on real tax payments and hence government deficits; rather than the exchange rate adjusting to inflation, prices instead follow the exchange rate as most prices become effectively "dollarized." Ending hyperinflation therefore requires exchange rate stabilization and may also require fiscal reform in order to reduce monetary emission (Pastor 1991a, Sachs 1986, and Sargent 1986).

Unfortunately for the Peruvian government, instilling private sector confidence in fiscal and exchange reforms usually requires a dramatic shift in political and policy regime. García, in short, probably had to go before any policy changes would stick. This point had been recognized in the Bolivian case. There, Siles

Peru: Stabilization and Hyperinflation 129

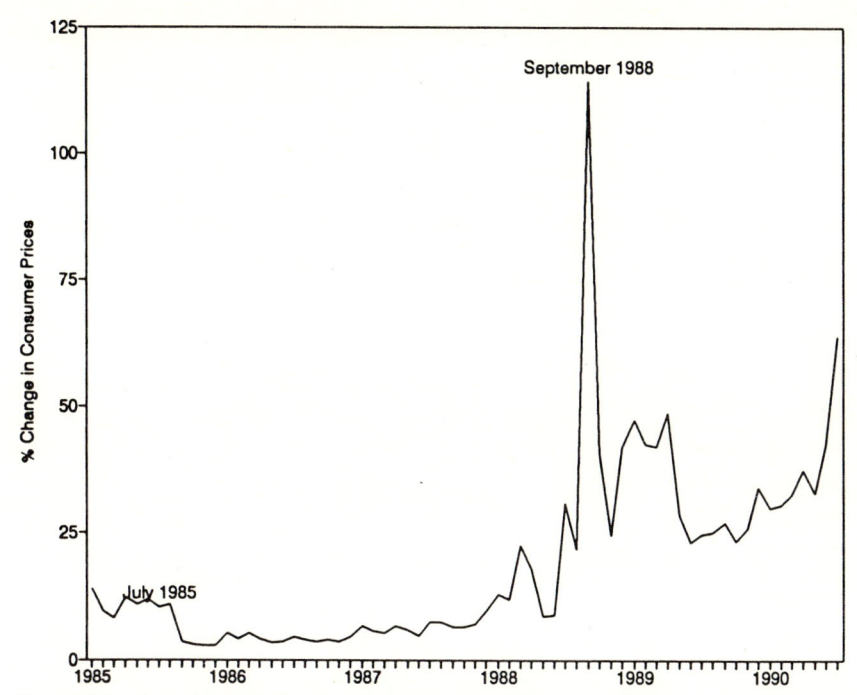

Figure 5.1 Monthly Inflation in Peru, January 1985 to July 1990

Source: Data on monthly inflation from the Instituto Nacional de Estadística (INE) as elaborated in the data base, *Banquito de Corto Plazo,* maintained by Coyuntura Económica, Centro de Investigación Universidad del Pacífico.

Zuazo failed to stop a hyperinflation despite eventually adopting some orthodox measures. As a result, he called elections early, allowing a new president to implement a similar set of macroeconomic reforms with much better results (Morales 1987 and Pastor 1991). President García instead held on until the designated transfer of power in July 1991, a positive turn for the emerging democratic tradition in Peru, but a negative turn for the economy.

Intermediate Causes: Prices, Money, and the Exchange Rate. As the electoral season began, both the right and left offered their own solutions to the hyperinflation. Before examining these in detail, it is useful to explore the intermediate determinants of inflation; although the fundamental problems, as in the Bolivian case, centered on external difficulties and social conflict, any coherent program also had to address the proximate causes, including monetary growth and exchange depreciation. As in the examination of the Bolivian inflation, the strategy here is to first determine the lines of causation using Granger-Sims tests and then to subject the relevant determinants of inflation to regression analysis.

Recall that the Granger-Sims procedure tests for causality by regressing one variable against the leads, current value, and lags of another variable; if the leads are jointly significant (as determined by an F-test), this suggests that causality is actually running from the independent variable to the dependent variables. The procedure, as noted in Chapter 4, is slightly more complicated. The regression must first be run and the autoregressive parameter extracted to "quasi-difference" both left- and right-hand variables. The predictive power of the leads is gauged from tests using this transformed data.

Table 5.7 reports on such causality tests for the relationship between prices, the monetary base, and the parallel market exchange rate, exactly the same variables tested in Chapter 4's consideration of the Bolivian hyperinflation. Two time periods are examined, with the longer beginning in January 1986 and the shorter in March 1988. The starting point of the longer period is chosen to cover the whole García period; given the use of four lags (and the additional use of a previous month to "quasi-difference" the data) the first observation included is from September 1985, a month after the heterodox program was launched. The second starting point, March 1988, is selected because this was the first month in which annualized monthly inflation exceeds 1,000 percent, a rate of price increase often taken to signal a passage to "true" hyperinflation (see the discussion in Note 27 of this chapter). Ending points for each set of variables were determined by the shortest of the two series being tested, with the "last" current observation set two months back to allow the use of two leads.

Although the results here are statistically insignificant, their directions do parallel those obtained in the Bolivian case. For example, the F-statistics for money "leading" prices are slightly higher than for prices leading money. Meanwhile, the F-statistics for the exchange rate leading the price index are much higher than for prices leading the exchange rate; the F-statistic for the longer period actually attains a significance level of .242 which, while not usually considered significant, does stand out in this rather inconclusive crowd. What may be of special interest for Peruvian policy debates (and for the regression analysis below) is the relationship between the *official* exchange rate and prices. Granger-Sims tests, the results of which are detailed in Note 26, indicate that apparently prices led the official exchange rate and not the other way around.[30] This suggests that official devaluation was a response to inflation and not a cause as many of the die-hard heterodox enthusiasts argued. Overall, the causality results seem to suggest that, much as in Bolivia, monetary growth was a problem, prices were dollarized (although less so than in Bolivia), and the official exchange rate eventually ceased to be a primary causal factor in the inflation.

This change in the causal role of the official exchange rate could easily be missed through a straightforward regression of inflation on suspected determinants of price. Because many Peruvian economists, including most members of the heterodox team, viewed depreciation in the official exchange rate as a primary cause of inflation, I initially ran a regression that included on the right-hand side the current and lagged values of this variable as well as the lagged value of inflation and the current and lagged values of growth in the monetary base and depreciation in the parallel market. Recall that this inclusion of the official rate is some-

Table 5.7
Results for Granger-Sims Causality Tests on Prices, Money, and the Exchange Rate (Peru)

	P "leads" M	M "leads" P
January 1986– March 1990 (2,42)	0.129	0.314
March 1988– March 1990 (2,16)	0.284	0.380
	P "leads" E	E "leads" P
January 1986– May 1990 (2,44)	0.049	1.466 @
March 1988– May 1990 (2,6)	0.289	0.739

```
***  Significant at 1%
**   Significant at 5%
*    Significant at 10%
#    Significant at 20%
@    Significant at 25%
```

All regressions include four lags, a current value, and two leads; the numbers in parantheses report the degrees of freedom used in calculating the significance of the reported F-values. The figures in the tables are F-values testing the explantory power of the leads; the significance of each value is indicated below the reported F-value. All variables (X) are calculated as rates of change using the formula $\{\log(X^t/X^{t-1})\}$. Regressions are first "quasi-differenced" and include a time trend. P is taken from the consumer price index, M from the monetary base (i.e., emission), and E from the parallel exchange rate.

Sources: All data from a data base maintained by Coyuntura Económica, Centro de Investigación de la Universidad del Pacífico; price information originally from the Instituto Nacional de Estadística (INE), monetary base from Banco Central de la Reserva del Perú (BCRP), and exchange rates from BCRP's *Nota Semanal*.

what inappropriate in view of the "causality" tests; nonetheless, it seemed to be an interesting exercise and was one that yielded a coefficient for the current official exchange rate that was positive and significant at the .01 level. Because this result was surprising in view of the Bolivian results and my own prior, I investigated the regression further, starting with an inspection of the residuals. The month of September 1988 turned out to be an exceptionally large outlier; dropping it caused the current official exchange rate to turn completely insignificant while the lagged official exchange became negative (and significant for a regression covering the whole period). In short, the "predictive power" of the official rate is driven almost entirely by the "Black September" adjustment in which a large devaluation of the official rate was accompanied by other measures and, as it turns out, a 114 percent inflation rate. This is hardly the stuff from which to build a general theory and, for that reason, the regressions below exclude the month of September 1988.[31]

Table 5.8 reports the results of the appropriate regressions covering, as before, two time periods: the overall García era and the period after the inception of hyperinflation in March 1988. For the longer period, the first observation is September 1985, a month after the beginning of the García program (and so we are *not* employing a lag from a previous policy regime). As with the Bolivian case, the strategy is to first run a full model, then rerun the regression for each period after dropping variables that do not achieve significance at any traditional level. The results obtained differ from the Bolivian case in three ways: (1) Although the parallel exchange rate is quite significant for both countries, the coefficient for the Peruvian secondary rate is much smaller than for the Bolivian rate; (2) although the Bolivian monetary growth measure loses any significance in the short period of "true" hyperinflation, Peruvian monetary growth remains significant in *both* the longer and shorter periods; and (3) although Bolivian lagged inflation is barely significant in the long period and is insignificant in the short period, Peruvian lagged inflation has a sizeable coefficient and is significant in all regressions.[32]

Politics and Policy. Although formal econometric tests of inflation were in short supply in hyperinflationary Peru, the programs of both right and left did seem to incorporate the insights that such tests yield. Orthodox economists and the right in general followed their traditional pattern and blamed inflation on excessive monetary growth and the government deficit (see, for example, Velarde [1988]). Mario Vargas Llosa, the presidential candidate of a rightist coalition labeled the Democratic Front (FREDEMO), promised that he would reduce inflation to 10 percent through a harsh program involving cuts in public spending, mass firings of state workers, privatization of public enterprises, liberalization of both imports and domestic markets, and a tightening of monetary policy. He also argued for devaluation, presumably to encourage exports and recover reserves; it was unclear, however, whether he would attempt the same inflation-inducing policy of continual devaluations carried out by Belaúnde, or would instead adopt the once-and-for-all sharp devaluation and subsequent defense of the currency pur-

Peru: Stabilization and Hyperinflation

sued in the Bolivian case. The regression analysis above suggests that only the latter would have been viable: The government, in short, needed to conduct a sharp devaluation in the official rate in order to get ahead of the deterioration in the parallel rate, and thus render the official rate "credible."[33]

Leftist and heterodox economists, meanwhile, paid less attention to monetary measures and instead concentrated on the problems of inertial inflation and "dollarization." What is striking about the Peruvian hyperinflation—revealed in the econometrics above and sensed by policy practitioners at the time—is the persistence of inertial inflation. In most hyperinflations, including the Bolivian case detailed in Chapter 4, past inflation rates cease to play much of a role as formal and informal indexing disappears, and prices instead become anchored to the exchange rate; in this context, a strong defense of the currency can bring a quick end to the inflationary pressures. Recognizing this historical pattern and perplexed by the persistence of inertial inflation, leftist economists Oscar Dancourt and Ivory Yong (1989) suggested that the government should "artificially" accelerate the process and dollarize all prices as soon as possible. Because of the shortage of dollars in government coffers, Dancourt and Yong also proposed the creation of a new currency, the *amaru*, which would be tied to the dollar but not convertible (Dancourt and Yong 1988). The idea was immediately picked up by the United Left (IU) and became its official anti-inflation program.

The proposals from left and right were both curious and inadequate. The left's call to tie the Peruvian currency, the inti, to the "imperialist" currency seemed particularly out of character. The program was defended on the grounds that the wage would be one of the prices dollarized; this, in turn, would prevent adjustment from having undue distributional burdens. The problem was with the half-hearted approach implicit in the discussion of an *"amaru"*; although this appealed to nationalist sensibilities, it left quite open the question of exactly why anyone would turn in dollars for yet another government-issued monetary unit. Assuming credibility is not the same thing as getting it; *"amaru*-ization" was not "dollarization."

The right, meanwhile, soon realized that it was proposing financial disaster. Given the domestic borrowing of the García era, any immediate cessation of inflation would leave a new government saddled with high interest payments and hence a large structural deficit; as Argentine President Carlos Menem discovered when he implemented his own anti-inflation program in 1989, such an internal debt burden can easily derail budget adjustments and bring a return of inflationary pressures. As a result of watching the Menem experience, Vargas Llosa backpedalled from his promise of a quick orthodox shock and instead suggested that orthodox adjustment be implemented only after a massive monetary emission designed to drive up prices and reduce the real value of government debt. This implicit attack on asset-holders was as surprising for the right as was the so-called leftist program of obliterating the national currency.

Against this backdrop, one rather obscure candidate, Alberto Fujimori, promised to lick inflation with "Honesty, Technology, and Work." Vagueness, in this

Table 5.8
The Determinants of Hyperinflation in Peru

	Dependent = inflation			
	September 1985 to May 1990		March 1988 to May 1990	
Variables	(1)	(2)	(3)	(4)
Growth of monetary base	0.482 (5.781)***	0.457 (6.052)***	0.457 (3.066)***	0.440 (3.252)***
Growth of lagged monetary base	0.161 (1.887)*	0.143 (1.740)*	0.086 (0.566)	
Change in parallel exchange rate	-0.022 (-0.827)		-0.015 (-3.363)	
Lagged change in parallel exchange rate	0.063 (2.155)**	0.071 (2.553)**	0.069 (1.492)#	0.081 (1.983)*
Lagged inflation	0.217 (3.275)***	0.228 (3.485)***	0.212 (1.994)*	0.235 (2.392)**

Constant	0.034	0.033	0.070	0.790
	(1.582)#	(1.573)#	(1.190)	(1.564)#
Degrees of Freedom	(48)	(49)	(18)	(20)
Adjusted R-squared	0.887	0.888	0.521	0.561
Durbin Watson	2.135	2.110	1.908	1.861
F-test	14.064***	18.381***	2.856**	5.246***

```
*** Significant at  1% (two-tail)
 ** Significant at  5% (two-tail)
  * Significant at 10% (two-tail)
  # Significant at 20% (two-tail)
```

Inflation is calculated as $\log(P^t/P^{t-1})$; the other variables (growth of monetary base and change in the parallel exchange rate) are calculated similarly. For each variable, the coefficient is reported; beneath it (in parentheses) is the t-statistic accompanied by a mark indicating the significance level.

Sources: All data from a data base maintained by Coyuntura Económica, Centro de Investigación de la Universidad del Pacífico; price information originally from the Instituto Nacional de Estadística (INE), monetary base from Banco Central de la Reserva del Perú (BCRP), and exchange rates from BCRP's *Nota Semanal*. Procedures are all autoregressive and exclude the month of September 1988.

case, won; fearful of austerity, suspicious of Vargas Llosa's ties with the business elite, and resentful of the Peruvian author's obvious preferences for things European, the Peruvian electorate forced Vargas Llosa into a runoff with Fujimori. In the second round, leftist forces and APRA remnants grouped around Fujimori and helped the former agronomist and son of Japanese immigrants achieve a resounding victory.

Upon taking power, the new president promptly went back on his promises of a gradualist approach to inflation-fighting. On August 8, 1990, Fujimori's prime minister, Juan Carlos Hurtado Miller, announced a program that included a 3,000 percent increase in gasoline prices (primarily in order to raise government revenues), sharp upward adjustments in food and public sector prices, elimination of the multiple exchange rate system and thus a large effective devaluation, and an unclear but generally unsupportive approach to wage compensation. In broad terms, the program resembled Bolivia's 1985 stabilization package. Orthodoxy was once again triumphant in Peruvian policy; whether it could do any better than in its first round under Belaúnde remained in doubt.

Conclusion: Requiem for Heterodoxy?

The Peruvian macroeconomic experience of the 1980s offers a sad example of the failures of both orthodox and heterodox adjustment. The decade began with a taste of neoliberalism under the administration of President Fernando Belaúnde Terry. The orthodox policies implemented, including privatization, liberalization, and devaluation, were consistent with Peru's historical tendency toward export orientation and unregulated domestic markets, but represented a dramatic change from the more interventionist era of the 1960s and 1970s. The Belaúnde program faltered for reasons not entirely of its own making; almost any set of policies would have enjoyed only limited success in light of declining terms of trade, slowing capital flows, and the natural disasters wrought by El Niño. But the poor performance of the first half of the decade is also attributable to the logic and implementation of the neoliberal strategy. Its analysis of inflation generally ignored cost-push factors and the resulting policy focus on demand restriction produced recession without cutting inflation. On the implementation side, policy measures were often reversed midstream because of economic and political pressures. Efforts to reduce the public sector severely limited the administrative capacity to conduct any sort of adjustment or development program. With GDP stagnant, inflation on the rise, and popular sector income squeezed, both the Peruvian electorate and government policy makers were ready for a change.

In the latter half of the 1980s, orthodoxy was dropped in favor of an untested heterodox program. Wage and price controls were combined with restrictions on debt service; the former was intended to dampen inflationary inertia while the latter was designed to create the "space" for economic growth. Demand was pumped up by increasing worker's real wages and consumption levels and by allowing a rise in the government deficit. Business, it was argued, would go along with this novel strategy partly because of the swelling domestic markets and partly because such redistributionist reactivation seemed the only way to quell social demands. To sweeten the deal for capital, the government lowered domestic interest rates, kept foreign currency cheap and available, and pledged to otherwise stay sensitive to business interests and profit margins.

The initial results were positive and confounded orthodox predictions that disaster lurked right around the corner. The early success, however, produced problems: Euphoric about rekindling growth, slowing inflation, and improving the lot of the poor, García and his economic advisors refused to make necessary midcourse corrections (Thorp 1987 and Mann and Pastor 1989). As the economy worsened, García provoked a war with domestic capital by attempting to nationalize the banking system. Labor, meanwhile, remained suspicious of a government that seemed uninterested in its advice or input. International creditors, irritated with Peru's bold stance on repayment, refused to extend any new credit. With his political base slipping as rapidly as the country's international reserves, García offered a series of one-shot adjustment packages that did little to slow Peru's passage into hyperinflation. By 1989, the economy had more or less collapsed and the political and economic system awaited a new approach that might restore credibility with domestic and international actors.

If the heterodox analysis of Peruvian economic structure and critique of orthodox measures seemed so compelling in 1985, what went so wrong in its actual implementation? Some have argued that Peruvian heterodoxy was merely a new form of traditional Latin American populism (Dornbusch and Edwards 1989). This characterization certainly contains an element of truth. The typical populist episode usually involves a government that attempts to create a multiclass coalition. The easiest way to appeal to both capital and labor is through rapid economic expansion. Growth brings swelling imports, inflationary pressures, fears of devaluation, and eventually capital flight. As the class alliance shatters, the program collapses and a new government arrives (sometimes through a military coup) to reverse both the macroeconomic policies and distributional concerns.[34]

But Peruvian heterodoxy and García's political project were surely more sophisticated and coherent than their populist cousins in Perón's Argentina and Allende's Chile. The limits on debt service were both necessary and initially well-designed; the program was shipwrecked primarily because the debt strategy was accompanied by inflammatory rhetoric and because, forgetting their structuralist roots, the heterodox team allowed the economy to expand beyond its external bottlenecks.[35] Controls on key prices to slow inertial inflation were also well considered and have been successfully used, for example, in Mexico since late 1987. The problem in Peru was coupling selective price controls with demand expansion, a combination that misaligned relative prices and only temporarily smothered inflationary pressures.

In the political arena, García sought to counter the challenge posed by long-standing inequities and the increasingly violent response by *Sendero Luminoso* and other insurgent groups. The social democratic project he attempted essentially involved redistributing resources downward while preserving the private sector's investment role. The problem with this "Rooseveltian" response to economic crisis was both structural and conjunctural: (1) The growth required to cement social democratic alliances is often difficult in the Third World due to external constraints and vulnerability to exogenous shocks; and (2) García's particular approach to capital was chaotic and confused and soon forced business into opposition.

It is difficult to construct a defense of Peruvian heterodoxy as practiced. Certain technical elements of the program—the lack of concern about fiscal deficits and monetary emission, the notion that real wage increases would spur demand without denting profitability, and the view that real interest rates on the order of -30 to -40 percent in 1987 were not a real problem—defied common sense as well as economic logic. But, as Eva Paus has cogently argued, "the failure of the PHP [Peruvian Heterodox Program] does not warrant the conclusion that a *well-conceived and well-implemented* heterodox program cannot work" (Paus 1991:427; emphasis added).

Such subtle distinctions found a limited audience in the electoral atmosphere of 1990. Heterodoxy was basically discredited: Inflation was raging; GDP falling; and real wages, wage share, and informal sector income had declined to levels lower than any experienced in the previous decade. The state had been dramatically weakened by the collapse in tax revenues and appeared unable to stop the inflationary spiral. International banks and agencies, holding more than $2 billion in Peruvian arrears, made it painfully clear that any mention of heterodox adjustment measures would fail to unlock required credit flows.

Orthodoxy seemed equally unpopular: When Vargas Llosa promised austerity and liberalization and offered little explanation of why this program would work better than in the Belaúnde period, Peruvian voters opted for the relatively unknown Alberto Fujimori. Fujimori, however, shifted sharply right and, upon taking power, immediately implemented a strong dose of orthodox austerity. As in Bolivia, there may have been little choice: Stopping hyperinflations seems to require a stern combination of currency defense and fiscal reform. The poor, betrayed by Fujimori and ravaged by hyperinflation, braced for yet another experiment in macroeconomic management.

Notes

1. This view is also expressed in Paus (1991).
2. For a review of both the Velasco experiment and the literature on this topic, see Jaquette and Lowenthal (1987); a good review is also available in Schydlowsky (1986). For a more detailed exposition on the economic policies of the era, see Fitzgerald (1976).
3. Debt figures are for total external debt and come from the World Bank's *World Debt Tables, 1988–1989*, Vol. 3.
4. Schydlowsky also suggests that the policy pendulum swung so dramatically precisely because the previous import substitution strategy had created such severe problems;

it was therefore perceived that "the orthodox IMF-type view had to be correct" (Schydlowsky 1986:229).

5. The initial program was sketched out in a lengthy presentation to the Peruvian Congress by Finance Minister Manuel Ulloa, "Mensaje al congreso del presidente del consejo de ministros," Lima, August 27, 1980.

6. The organization of this analysis of the Belaúnde period is derived from Wise (1990), which was also the source for that portion of our joint paper on Peruvian heterodoxy (Pastor and Wise 1992).

7. Other analyses of this period in Peruvian macroeconomic policy include Conaghan, Malloy, and Abugattas (1990), Reid (1985), Schydlowsky (1986), Thorp (1986), Webb (1987b), and Wise (1986). Webb's analysis is particularly interesting as he was Central Bank president during the Belaúnde administration.

8. "State Company Sell-off to Begin," *Andean Report*, February 1981, p. 21; "Mining and Oil Get Going While Government Streamlines State Companies," *Andean Report*, November 1981, p. 213; "State Companies for Sale," *Andean Report*, October 1982, p. 183.

9. "Funding Private Sector Growth," *Andean Report*, April 1981, p. 63.

10. By Webb's estimate, El Niño itself may have been responsible for as much as a 4 to 5 percent decline in GDP (between 30 and 40 percent of the total decrease in GDP registered in 1983); see Webb (1987b:14). This is, however, an outer-bound or maximum estimate of El Niño's impact and even Webb argues that the government's inappropriate macroeconomic response to this natural disaster and the concurrent external shocks were principally responsible for Peru's economic problems (see Webb 1987b:14).

11. During 1981, for example, major laws concerning agrarian reform, taxes, and the media were passed through a barrage of executive decrees, as was the entire economic program (Malloy 1982:7).

12. Out of the growing literature on Peru's *Sendero Luminoso*, good starting points are McClintock (1984), Reid (1985:Chapter 7), and Degregori (1986).

13. Raúl González, "Gonzalo's Thought, Belaúnde's Answer," *Report on the Americas*, June 1986, pp. 34–36.

14. For the formalization of these insights, see Chapter 3. I assume there, as in the text of this chapter, that heterodoxy postulated a *fixed* mark-up on costs. In fact, the heterodox team sometimes went so far as to assume that the mark-up varied *inversely* with the level of economic activities: capitalists raised prices as markets shrank in an attempt to maintain the same target rate of profit on capital stock. This view implies that orthodox contraction would be even more inflationary than depicted in Chapter 3 and helps to explain why the García administration was so confident that economic reactivation might even lower prices. This view, however, assumes extreme monopoly power and contradicts both common sense and the usual structuralist assumptions. For the Peruvian heterodox view, see Carbonetto et al. (1987); for a critique see Dornbusch (1988c), and Dornbusch and Edwards (1989).

15. The inability to stick within the "10 percent" led to a somewhat strained attempt by the Institute of National Statistics to classify debt service in terms of what was included in the 10 percent and what was not. Such sleight of hand did not replenish the reserves being drained by excess debt payments.

16. As noted in Table 5.5, the share of national income going to employers and owners rose over 20 percent (from 0.348 to 0.425), a trend that accords with such a mark-up adjustment to ration demand. Further evidence of a rise in mark-ups is indicated by the in-

crease in the ratio of consumer price inflation to wholesale price inflation from .95 in 1985 to 1.6 in 1987.

17. Indeed, the heterodox team argued that deficits were *not* inflationary because the expanded demand and output would allow producers to realize economies of scale and hence lower unit costs (Carbonetto et al. 1987:82). This was a rather heroic assumption and one that was quickly shattered by the reality of demand-side pressure and foreign exchange constraints.

18. The "economic deficit" does not include amortization of debt, little of which was actually done anyway. The "financial deficit" that included amortization (usually financed in the García period by arrears) was naturally much higher but is less important for determining demand pressure in the economy.

19. High inflation in Peru induced taxpayers to lengthen their usual delays in tax payments in order to reduce the real value of their obligations. The government, as noted later in the chapter, responded by attempting to shorten collection lags.

20. To see why a multiple exchange rate system can promote monetary expansion and inflation, consider the case of an exporter that receives 200 intis per dollar of exports from the Central Bank but only needs to expend 100 intis for a dollar's worth of imports. The result is an extra 100 intis that can be spent locally; because domestic production has not risen in the transaction, the exporter's expenditure will now drive prices up in order to ration others out of the market. In this sense, a traditional deficit is less damaging as it generally adds to output and therefore dampens some of the inflationary pressure; the *brecha cambiaria* that arose from the multiple exchange rate system was far more problematic. The figure for the effect of the *brecha* on Central Bank losses comes from Dornbusch and Edwards (1989:43).

21. This argument borrows heavily from the excellent analysis in Paus (1991).

22. This curtailment of public investment to "crowd in" private investment ran against evidence that public investment had actually been complementary to private investment in Peru's past (Pastor 1991b).

23. For an excellent analysis of how the attempted nationalization "galvanized the private sector into a cohesive political opposition," see Conaghan (1991:13).

24. I discovered this first-hand when I made a presentation on macroeconomic stabilization at the INP in mid-1988. Done at the invitation of a high-ranking member of the economic team, the presentation pointed out the limits to heterodox reactivation signaled in Chapter 3 and discussed in more detail in this chapter. Upon issuing my own prescription for a new economic program (see Pastor 1988a, 1988b), half the audience pronounced complete agreement with the articulated policies, while the other half denounced the recommendations as totally irrelevant. What is interesting here is the sharp disagreements among those jointly working on long-term development plans for the country. In this light, it is perhaps not surprising that no long-term strategies were actually adopted or implemented.

25. Prominent among the latter was Daniel Carbonetto, an Argentine who shared Alan García's social-democratic vision and took the lead in developing and implementing the heterodox model.

26. This active presidential interference with economic policy was widely rumored in the Peruvian press and was confirmed to the author by members of the economic team.

27. As noted in Note 1 of Chapter 4, the classic definition of hyperinflation is Cagan's (1956): It begins when monthly inflation exceeds 50 percent and ends when inflation dips below that level and remains so for a year. By this rather restrictive definition, Peru's price chaos was never officially "hyperinflation." However, an alternative and increasingly common threshold of 1,000 percent inflation on an annual basis (or 22 percent monthly; see Dornbusch and Fischer 1990:663) does qualify Peru as a hyperinflationary economy and gives us the starting point of March 1988 used in the regression analysis of this chapter. Recent work by Dornbusch, Sturzeneger, and Wolf (1990) even suggests a definition of *extreme* inflation as occurring when monthly price hikes exceed 10 percent, a figure that generates an annual percent inflation rate of just over 200 percent and seems by Latin American standards to be rather modest.

28. For a detailed history of the economic adjustment efforts of this period of the García government, see Lago (1990).

29. Webb, in commenting on Kuczynski's (1990) sharp attack on the García government, notes the contrast between raging inflation and the improvement in fiscal and external sector variables and suggests that "I have a sense that we do not know enough about what makes or breaks an adjustment program" (Webb 1990:104). Would that other key protagonists in the Peruvian drama were so modest.

30. The evidence for this comes from two different official rates, the Mercado Unico de Cambio (MUC) and the banking rate. The first is misnamed; it was only "único" for a brief time and soon became the bottom anchor of a multiple exchange rate system. The banking rate was an official rate that tracked the parallel rate and was set for legal exchanges of dollars in the Peruvian banking system, a clear attempt to rein in some of the action occurring in the unregulated parallel market. For MUC, prices led the exchange rate with an F-statistic of 11.4 for the long period and 5.6 for the short period; F-statistics for reverse causality were lower at 7.8 and 3.1. As for the banking rate, prices led the exchange rate at 8.6 for the long period and 3.1 for the short period with F-statistics for the reverse hypothesis coming in at an anemic .5 for both time periods.

31. This month is not excluded in the causality tests, which involve the official exchange rate (reported in Note 30), because the role of an observation in leads and lags would force the exclusion of a whole period, rather than a single month. Moreover, those results square with the notion, generally supported by the regression results here, that the official exchange rate was *not* a significant causal factor.

32. The results come from regressions in which I employed a Hilu procedure to correct for autocorrelation. In the Bolivian case, tests for the autocorrelation of residuals were inconclusive and no corrective action was warranted. In the Peruvian case, autocorrelation was more severe as evidenced by the Durbin's H, the appropriate test statistic when a lagged dependent is included on the right-hand side.

33. I argued for exactly this strategy in policy discussions and papers produced in 1988 (see Pastor 1988b), based mostly on a preliminary study of the Bolivian experience. The program I presented went beyond this seemingly "orthodox" exchange rate policy and included a number of measures to place the adjustment burden on higher income groups, including lump-sum nominal wage adjustments that would protect low-wage workers and "flatten" the wage distribution.

34. This populist "story" draws from Diaz-Alejandro (1981), Drake (1982), Sachs (1989), Dornbusch and Edwards (1989), and my own experience in Peru in the latter half

of the 1980s. Lago follows Dornbusch and Edwards (1989) in attributing the García macroeconomic disaster to the excesses of populism but roots both these excesses and the "stop-go" policy cycle in the structural inequalities of Peruvian society (Lago 1990).

35. Sachs (1989:30–31) also suggests that "many actions of the populist governments (such as the debt moratoria of Peru and Brazil in the 1980s . . .) may be meritorious even though they are . . . part of an otherwise ill-designed program."

6

Evaluating the Experiments

Introduction

The macroeconomic experiments in Peru and Bolivia seem to have run their course. The end of Peruvian heterodoxy is quite apparent: Standing in the ashes of a hyperinflation, the Peruvian government elected in 1990 has rejected the interventionist strategies associated with structuralism and is trying to tame inflationary pressures with the tools once employed in the Bolivian New Economic Policy (NEP). Yet the NEP itself is tattered. Inflation has been vanquished but growth remains low. Orthodoxy is dominant in Bolivian policy circles, partly because of the need to secure foreign finance, but social pressures could force the nominally leftist government to deviate from this course. For both countries, ends have been reached and new beginnings may be dawning.

What do the experiences of Peru and Bolivia indicate about the relative merits of orthodoxy and heterodoxy? What do these macroeconomic adjustment efforts illustrate about the constraints—imposed by external dependence, inequitable income distribution, and weak states—that face any stabilization program in the Third World? And what does stabilization along either orthodox or heterodox lines imply for the development of a new and viable structure of accumulation for the debt- and conflict-ridden nations of Latin America?

In this chapter, I return to the four foci that have been central throughout the previous analysis: the technical consistency and coherence of stabilization policies; the role of external resource flows, particularly those related to debt; class structure, distributional patterns, and political coalition-building; and the complex and sometimes contradictory relationship between short-run measures and longer-run restructuring. I begin with the technical issues, giving an overall evaluation of orthodox and heterodox analysis and policy. I argue that structuralist models seem to offer a better description of macroeconomic reality in Latin America, but criticize the implementation of heterodox policies in Peru and suggest that dramatic episodes of hyperinflation unfortunately require quite orthodox cures.

In the next section, I delineate the external constraints that are faced by any adjustment program. The need for capital flows often forces governments to adopt orthodox or "market-oriented" strategies; alternative measures such as the unilateral debt restrictions employed by Peru may be theoretically appropriate, but tend to provoke hostile responses by commercial and official creditors. Of course, debt flows and capital movements do not exhaust the range of external sector issues. Small Latin American countries face other important external constraints imposed by their reliance on traditional exports and imported intermediate and capital goods. To reduce this dependence, countries should promote nontraditional exports, a strategy that may unfortunately necessitate an exchange rate policy that contradicts the currency stability often necessary to tame inflation.

The next section examines the politics of stabilization. Any adjustment program has distributional effects that help to build or erode class alliances and political coalitions. In the Peruvian case, the political project was acknowledged, but turned out to be impossible: The social democratic consensus was forged upon an unsustainable growth boom. In Bolivia, the political project was implicit but evident: The government attempted a restoration of capital's power over labor in order to resolve the social tensions driving inflation. In both cases, the administrative capacity of the state also played a role: Peru's state proved too weak to implement an interventionist heterodoxy, while the narrow focus of the Bolivian program reflected an awareness of the state's limited capabilities.

The final section considers the relationship between short-run adjustment and the longer-term needs of accumulation. Growth, I argue, requires a reduction in external dependence, a more progressive distribution of income, and a leaner but more effective state. There are, however, important contradictions between the policies needed for stabilization and those required for medium-term restructuring: Stable exchange rates may dampen inflation, but the resulting overvaluation discourages exports; real wage cuts may curtail absorption, but they also erode social consensus; fiscal restraint may slow monetary growth, but it also constrains the requisite public investment in social and economic infrastructure. The experience of Bolivia illustrates these contradictions: It has conquered inflation, but seems unable to forge a new social contract or generate new growth. Structuralist analysis seems quite powerful at recognizing long-term considerations, but heterodox adjustment in Peru neglected these issues and sacrificed the country's future to the cause of a two-year growth program. The paradox posed by these contradictions leads into some final reflections on the Bolivian and Peruvian macroeconomic experiments.

Orthodoxy Versus Heterodoxy: Short-term Adjustment

The outcomes of the Bolivian and Peruvian experiments may tempt analysts to draw hasty but firm conclusions about orthodox and heterodox adjustment; after all, one country seems to have rescued itself from hyperinflation while another was driven to it. Nonetheless, a simple conclusion that orthodoxy is "better," however one may define that word, would mask some important issues and leave aside critical nuances. Below, I make the following points: First, despite the Peruvian debacle, the structuralist analysis upon which heterodox policy was based may be a more accurate description of Latin American economic reality; second, the application of orthodoxy in Latin America has often met with poor results; third, the stellar performance of orthodoxy in Bolivia may be because such a strategy is uniquely suited to ending hyperinflation; and, finally, both orthodox and heterodox strategies share certain problems, including a tendency for policy makers to be overwhelmed by initial successes, and then become reluctant to push through needed policy shifts.

Orthodoxy, of course, dominates the discourse of international agencies, the U.S. Treasury Department, and most graduate economics programs in the United States.[1] As noted in Chapter 2, this framework assumes an economy in which demand and supply interact to determine prices, producers change production technique or mix in response to those prices, and all such changes occur with sufficient rapidity to keep the economy near full employment. In this view, trade deficits and inflation are necessarily linked to excess demand, usually from fiscal expansion. The required corrections include monetary restraint, deficit reduction, and currency devaluation; the oft-required agent of change is the International Monetary Fund (IMF).

Latin American economies, however, hardly seem to fit the textbook models. High unemployment rates are the rule rather than the exception. Exports, particularly of the traditional sort, often have relatively low price elasticities while import coefficients are similarly rigid (Krugman and Taylor 1978; Taylor 1988:43). Not surprisingly, devaluation is generally ineffectual, doing little to stir growth and much to raise inflation.[2] And the record in Latin America since 1982, a period of intense intervention by the orthodox IMF, has been decidedly poor: Exports have stagnated, output has collapsed, and inflation has accelerated (see Table 6.1).[3]

The experience in Peru also casts doubt on the merits of orthodox adjustment. An IMF-sponsored trade liberalization in the early 1980s brought a devastating import flood. As unfavorable external shocks piled up, the government reacted with budget cutting and devaluation. Exports and growth fell, inflation rose, and income distribution became more unequal. Reserves were accumulated, but mostly because of the recession-induced cut in imports and the government's quiet (and seemingly unorthodox) decision to cease full debt service.

Although the Bolivian experience in the latter half of the 1980s yielded far more appealing results, the government's program diverged from traditional orthodox medicine in that it employed the exchange rate targeting typical of Argentina and Chile in the late 1970s; as in those earlier cases, Bolivia's reliance on exchange rate targeting eventually produced a serious overvaluation problem and financial fragility. The Bolivian program also included other elements usually anathema to orthodox institutions and thinking: a unilateral moratorium on debt service, significant levels of negotiated debt relief, and the able use of coca-dollars to stabilize the exchange rate and replenish domestic savings.

Table 6.1
Latin American Economic Performance, 1980-89

	1980	1981	1982	1983	1984	1985	1986	1987	1988	1989
Domestic Macro Variables										
GDP growth (annual change)	6.0	-0.2	-1.1	-2.8	3.6	3.4	4.1	3.0	0.5	1.6
Inflation (weighted average)	55.7	60.7	67.1	108.7	133.5	145.1	87.8	130.9	286.4	538.2
Fiscal surplus (as % of GDP, weighted average)	-0.7	-5.6	-5.8	-5.8	-5.3	-7.1	-9.2	-9.2	-9.4	-15.5
Gross capital formation (as % of GDP, weighted average)	23.4	23.3	21.2	17.4	16.9	17.5	18.0	19.8	19.8	18.2
Trade Variables										
Exports (FOB) (billions of US$)	94.4	100.6	91.1	91.9	101.5	96.5	81.1	91.5	105.5	115.4
Imports (FOB) (billions of US$)	96.4	103.5	83.7	62.6	63.8	63.3	64.2	71.8	81.6	86.3
Trade Balance (billions of US$)	-2.0	-2.9	7.4	29.2	37.7	33.2	16.9	19.7	23.9	29.1
Debt Stocks and Flows										
Net external borrowing (billions of US$)	38.6	56.1	40.0	19.4	12.9	5.7	7.5	11.3	2.4	7.8
Basic transfer (billions of US$)	12.2	17.7	-5.2	-20.8	-31.0	-35.6	-29.2	-22.6	-35.0	-33.0
Basic transfer (as % of GDP)	1.8	2.4	-0.7	-2.8	-4.0	-4.4	-3.4	-2.4	-3.4	-3.0
Total debt (as % of GDP)	34.5	39.8	43.0	46.8	46.4	45.2	43.9	44.0	39.4	37.6

All series are for the Western Hemisphere, which includes the Caribbean. The "basic" transfer is calculated as net external borrowing minus interest payments (Stewart 1985). Because the interest payments measure used here includes dividends and other investment income, the measure of basic transfer has a slight negative (downward) bias.

Sources: 1982-1989 figures from the IMF's *World Economic Outlook 1990*; 1981 figures taken from the IMF's *World Economic Outlook 1989*; 1980 figures taken from the IMF's *World Economic Outlook 1988*.

Structuralism seems to be a useful alternative to the orthodox analysis, particularly because of its explicit recognition of slow export responses, import and debt flow dependence, conflict-driven inflation, and other features typical of Latin American economies. Unfortunately, there are significant risks when one applies the structuralist/heterodox remedy of incomes policy. Prices may become misaligned if controls are selectively enforced. In Peru, this resulted in repressed inflation, which eroded the credibility of the program and gave rise to huge price increases each time controls were relaxed. The heterodox focus on cost-push inflation can also cause policy makers to ignore the demand side; in all the heterodox experiments of the mid-1980s, but especially in Peru, fiscal deficits were not restrained and excess demand persisted. It is also important to note that in a dependent economy like Peru's, the inflation-triggering level of output is set not by capacity constraints but rather by the availability of foreign exchange and hence critical imports. Demand-induced inflation can surge with plants and labor still idle; with foreign reserves in short supply no amount of heavy-handed price controls can effectively stop the mark-up increases that accelerate inflation, ration demand down to fit supply, and redistribute income to the rich.

These likely problems are often discounted due to "policy euphoria." The initial success of a heterodox strategy can unfortunately lead decision makers to postpone necessary but painful measures to correct fiscal deficits and foreign exchange shortages. Part of this reluctance in Peru, Argentina, Brazil, and elsewhere may have been historically rooted. As the first heterodox experiments in Latin America, these countries were greeted with dire warnings about the immediate disasters that would greet those daring to depart from traditional free market tactics. When instead growth rose and inflation fell, policy makers became deaf to orthodox concerns, much to the undoing of the experiments themselves.

In the current era, sharp critiques of heterodoxy find an audience that is perhaps too receptive. Incomes policies remain exceptionally useful for both economic reactivation and macroeconomic management. Mexico lowered inflation from over 150 percent in 1987 to around 20 percent in 1989 using a "quasi-heterodox" approach that combined wage, price, and exchange rate controls with fiscal restraint, import liberalization, and privatization. A crucial role for interventionist strategies remains; however, those employing such strategies must be cautious, willing to change direction, and always conscious of such orthodox concerns as realistic exchange rates.[4]

Policy flexibility is crucial. In Peru, economic policy makers stuck with fixed exchange rates, low nominal interest charges, and fiscal and wage expansion long after reserves had drained and inflation had returned. In Bolivia, the government's persistent exchange rate targeting, despite evidence that the relationship between the exchange rate and prices had weakened, contributed to currency overvaluation and excessive domestic interest rates.

Too much flexibility, however, can signal policy incoherence. The experience of Hernán Siles Zuazo, president during Bolivia's hyperinflationary years, is a clear example. After his first program (a primitive version of the future Peruvian heterodoxy) faltered, Zuazo switched to traditional austerity and prompt debt payments, then shifted to a strategy based mostly on compensatory wage hikes, then rejected this in favor of a program with the IMF, and finally rejected Fund advice and finance, ceased payments on the debt, and allowed unsustainable increases in the real wage. Not surprisingly, economic agents stopped paying attention to government pronouncements and instead set prices according to the behavior of the parallel market in foreign exchange. In Peru, policy was also erratic, although here what was perhaps most volatile was the government's treatment of private capital: from active courting, to compulsory "bonds," to large investment subsidies, to strict capital controls and the attempted nationalization of the financial system. The eventual collapse of private investment certainly indicated displeasure with the nature of state policy, but it also simply reflected capital's growing frustration with the constantly changing rules.

The experience of hyperinflation and stabilization in Bolivia illustrates a final important point: Although orthodoxy seems to be a costly way to slow a high inflation, it does appear uniquely suited for ending a hyperinflation. As accelerating inflation makes past price hikes an increasingly unreliable guide to the future, the inertial inflation central to heterodox theory and policy ceases to play much of a role.[5] The econometric analysis of both Chapters 4 and 5 confirms this process, showing that past inflation diminishes in explanatory power as inflation speeds up, nearly completely so in the Bolivian case. The results further point to the leading role of the exchange rate, implying that currency stabilization is crucial to ending hyperinflation; monetary restraint is also important given both the causal role of money and the credibility signal that such new-found restraint will emit.

Orthodox theory, of course, focuses directly on these exchange rate and monetary variables. The simple remedies that emerge from this limited analysis—slowing currency depreciation and fiscal expansion—are also probably all that is within the reach of a state severely weakened by hyperinflation. Moreover, orthodoxy is popular with international institutions and can, as in Bolivia, attract the sort of financial support necessary to defend the exchange rate. Finally, the social exhaustion produced by a hyperinflation may cause the populace to accept austerity, as long as it is perceived to be working successfully against price pressures.

This does not necessarily imply that the postheterodox program adopted by Peru will ultimately be successful. Newly elected President Alberto Fujimori did decide to employ the sort of exchange rate defense and gasoline "tax" that were important initial elements in the Bolivian stabilization plan. But while the "Fujishock" of August 1990 received quiet words of approval from international agencies, arrears on past loans tended to impede the resumption of capital flows from the multilaterals and official lenders. Bolivia survived the period between stabilization and the reopening of official lending by legalizing the deposit of dollars without proof of origin, an obvious gambit to attract coca-dollars. However, coca-dollars were already circulating in Peru's formal and informal financial system, implying that this avenue of dollar inflows may have been mostly tapped. Social tensions in Peru are sharp and guerilla violence has escalated since Fujimori took office. In addition, the government began its new reign by promptly reversing campaign promises and shattering Fujimori's original political coalition, a strategy seemingly inconsistent with garnering credibility or achieving social consensus. Against this backdrop, even orthodox nostrums may be of little help.

The jury remains out on the heterodox-orthodox debate. The Peruvian case establishes that any poorly implemented framework will fail, although poor implementation is arguably more probable when one attempts the extensive interventions associated with heterodoxy. Peru also offers some crucial lessons for any strategy of macroeconomic management, particularly the need to restrain demand, conserve foreign exchange, and utilize initial political support to push through longer-term changes. Orthodoxy seems somewhat ineffective at stopping moderate inflations in Latin America but is well-suited to stopping a hyperinflation. Nonetheless, orthodoxy remains the remedy of choice at international financial institutions, which given the crucial role of external support in the adjustment process, gives this view an eminently practical edge.

External Constraints and Debt

The era of macroeconomic experimentation in Latin America was provoked by the debt crisis of the early 1980s and the resultant need to create sizeable trade surpluses even as slow worldwide growth limited export markets (see Table 6.1). Debt and other external factors remain crucial variables and must be considered in any evaluation of a stabilization program.

Both countries examined in this book have external sectors characterized by the dominance of traditional exports and a reliance on imported intermediate and capital goods. With trade an unreliable engine of growth, both Peru and Bolivia borrowed heavily through the 1970s and both encountered servicing problems in the latter part of that decade, years before the rest of Latin America. The regional crisis, which effectively shut down the flows of resources to most of Latin America, exacerbated these countries' problems and required the development of a new approach to both debt and the external sector.

Bolivia's response (after the chaos of the hyperinflationary years) involved unilateral restrictions on debt service, an opening of the capital account, and a strenuous effort to attract new funds. The debt service limits initially emerged because of union pressure on the leftist government of Hernán Siles Zuazo. The 1985 New Economic Policy (NEP) maintained these restrictions, a strategy that "amounted to a self-administered external loan" (Dornbusch 1988b:8). Although this position was seemingly at odds with the NEP's generally conservative agenda, it failed to tarnish Bolivia's reputation as an orthodox adjuster.

This reputation was instrumental to a second method of obtaining external resources: the courting of official international lenders, who were simultaneously eager to bless one small (and relatively inexpensive) experiment in Washington-style macroeconomic adjustment. Timing here was crucial: Bolivia was lucky enough to be drifting toward freer markets just as Peru, Argentina, and Brazil were charging toward interventionism. Official lenders were hopeful that the "miracle of La Paz" would serve as an example to other, more wayward debtors.

While waiting for new resources, Bolivia implemented a quicker set of measures to replenish reserves. As noted in the previous sections, rules were liberalized to allow private agents to deposit foreign currency without proof of origin, bringing into the banking system coca-dollars previously circulating in the informal economy. Remonetization was pursued slowly; the resulting high interest rates in the context of a liberalized capital account helped induce a repatriation of flight capital. For the longer run, the external sector needed to be restructured in the direction of nontraditional exports. The NEP unfortunately accomplished little on this front. In 1986, the first year of stabilization, nontraditional exports recovered to $111 million, the best performance since 1981, but still short of the 1980 dollar level of $170 million. Nontraditionals declined through 1987 and 1988 but finally rose to $202 million (25 percent of total exports) in 1989; however, the leading products (accounting for half of total nontraditionals) were soya and wood, hardly the stuff of an East Asian-style export drive.[6]

The centerpiece of Peru's heterodox approach to the external sector was an explicit restriction on debt service. The now-famous "10 percent" limit was designed to create the space for noninflationary growth; the redistribution from foreign creditors was also supposed to help cement the worker-capitalist alliance implicit in President Alan García's social democratic vision. Like the rest of the program, this was far less successful in practice than in theory. For the first two years, debt service ratios did not actually fall below those achieved in the last year and a half of the previous administration. Meanwhile, official and commercial creditors were dismayed by Peru's changing rules with regard to which debts would be serviced under the 10 percent rule. When the debt service ratio finally declined dramatically in 1988, this reflected not conscious policy, but empty Central Bank coffers.

The Peruvian debt strategy was also plagued by its high visibility. García chose a very public forum, his inauguration, to announce the limits on debt service and continued to press other countries to follow Peru's lead. Bankers naturally responded by cutting off Peru's access to long-term official or commercial credit, and no other countries chose to follow García's vainglorious charge. A quieter strategy would surely have been preferable, particularly given the previous difficulties at forming a regional debtor's cartel and Peru's limited influence over other Latin American states.

The hostile reaction from international capital could have and should have been anticipated. Policy attention should have immediately been devoted to reducing the country's reliance on traditional exports and imported intermediates. But long-term thinking was in short supply, and the development of import substitutes and nontraditional exports lagged severely. This could have been anticipated as well: Structural transformations, unlike price controls, take a long time to enact.

What common external sector lessons emerge from the Bolivian and Peruvian experiences? The first is the crucial role of the exchange rate as an inflation-fighting tool. In both cases, congealing the exchange rate was a key element of the stabilization program; the difference was in how this was done and how sustainable it proved to be. In Bolivia, a sharp devaluation brought the official rate up to the parallel rate. The government then dumped scarce reserves in an attempt to stop depreciation and lower inflationary expectations, supporting this approach with tight money, high interest rates, and a new openness to foreign currency deposits. The Peruvian program fixed the currency by fiat, then swelled demand, printed money, lowered interest rates, and drained international reserves. With credibility understandably low, the parallel and official rates diverged and capital fled. The government responded by nationalizing the banking system and the parallel rate rose higher as private agents quickly sought to exit from an unsupportive regime. With reserves low due to the growth-induced import boom, Peru was eventually forced into a series of inflation-inducing maxi-devaluations. Exchange rate fixing, in short, is a useful way to temporarily quell inflation but it can also be a recipe for economic destabilization when no new resources are in sight.

The second lesson is—perhaps surprisingly—the useful role of debt service restrictions. Both cases illustrate the importance of limits on debt service in providing space for growth and exchange rate support. Such a policy can, however, represent a fundamental challenge to the power and prerogatives of international capital; restricting service, after all, essentially implies that the welfare of the nation should take precedence over the property rights of creditors. García relished the challenge to "imperialist bankers"; the quieter approach of Bolivia, particularly because it also included a loyal implementation of orthodox domestic policy, was perceived as less threatening, and was generally accepted by official lenders.

The final lesson is that dependence on external credit severely limits domestic policy options: Those holding the foreign exchange are likely to dominate decision making. In Bolivia, the first post-NEP government found its hands tied: The openness of the capital accounts and the dependence on foreign credit gave both domestic capital and international lenders veto power over economic policy. As a result, the Paz Zamora government has postponed its promise of social justice and offered little deviation from orthodox policy. In the Peruvian case, newly elected President Alberto Fujimori was forced to implement orthodox policy when he quickly realized that his own gradualist program would neither curtail hyperinflation nor attract the required support of foreign bankers and governments. External dependence, in short, can dictate economic policy as well as economic structure: As noted earlier, the appeal of structuralist theory, so useful at analyzing real world constraints, may diminish when one recognizes the advantage that orthodoxy enjoys in securing the support of foreign financiers and domestic investors.

Politics and Stabilization

As much ink as blood has been shed about the distributional character of stabilization policies. Much of the literature centers on the "social costs of adjustment" (see Cardoso and Helwege 1992, and Cornia, Jolly, and Stewart 1987) and includes both vigorous critiques of IMF-style programs (see Pastor 1987a and

Pastor and Dymski 1990) and equally strong defenses of orthodox adjustment (see Sisson 1986 and Heller et al. 1988). For macroeconomic adjustment, however, the issue is not simply distributional consequences, but rather how these consequences help to create or destroy the political basis for stabilization.

In Bolivia, distributional conflict played a crucial role in triggering and sustaining the hyperinflation of the first half of the 1980s. Responding to the sharp decline in real wages in 1980–1982, the new government of Hernán Siles Zuazo tried to protect workers' income through indexation. This fed into an inflationary spiral, which was also exacerbated by the refusal of either capital or labor to shoulder the burden of government expenditures. With external finance in short supply, the government resorted to monetary emission and inflation skyrocketed. Any government seeking to end the inflation had to break the class stalemate and force one group to accept both lower incomes *and* higher taxes.

The architects of the 1985 Bolivian stabilization program did just that. Real wages were depressed and labor union leaders were arrested and exiled. A new regressive value-added tax was announced and then implemented. Controls on prices and productive activity were lifted and the government dramatically reduced the size of public enterprise. This procapitalist character of the program played a crucial role in establishing "credibility."

The Peruvian attempt at class conciliation was considerably more complicated—and much less successful. Peru's heterodox program followed a period in which income disparities had worsened and insurgent activity had escalated. Incoming President Alan García promised to forge a new social compact between workers, peasants, and capitalists: Price controls would be used to tame inflation; real wages would be increased to provide new demand; peasant income would be enhanced by economic growth and low-interest loans; and capitalists would be given government support in return for new investment. This was social democracy in the European tradition—but without a European-style economy or political history.[7]

The economic and political contradictions quickly became apparent. The only way to finance higher real wages *and* protect capitalist profits was to strip resources from foreign creditors, the financial system, and the state. Debt service limits produced a strongly negative reaction by international bankers and agencies. Suppressed interest rates temporarily protected mark-ups but also provoked capital flight. Fiscal revenues declined even as government decisions to postpone adjustments in the exchange rate and public sector prices provided higher effective subsidies to private capital. By mid-1987, the effective "taxes" on international creditors and domestic finance had run out, and the government was faced with the need to tame its own deficit as well as restrain growth in labor and capital incomes.

The government instead nationalized the financial system, hoping to curtail capital flight and reestablish control over the exchange rate. The act provoked the hostility of financial and productive capital and essentially destroyed the government's project of *concertación* with the country's largest capitalists. Labor, always a junior partner in García's social pact, failed to rally behind the government, and popular resentment became widespread as hyperinflation returned real wages to their pre-García levels. The politically isolated government never again found the social consensus necessary for stabilization. Against this backdrop, the rural insurgencies and urban political violence escalated.

The failure of the Peruvian program also points to the crucial role of administrative capacity. Heterodox theories of inertial inflation and the concomitant recommendations of wage and price controls *assume* a state that can in fact constrain the important social actors. Peru's heterodoxy was even more ambitious: It sought to challenge international financial institutions, redirect domestic investment, and implement a complicated system of subsidies and multiple exchange rates. Unfortunately, the government was desperately weak, in part due to the previous administration's attempt to shrink the state in the name of neoliberalism. President García exacerbated matters with a highly centralized style, vesting power over economic policy in himself and a small group of advisors. This allowed the executive to make dramatic shifts in economic policy, including the ill-advised nationalization attempt, and made it difficult to secure the support of those midlevel bureaucrats that were supposed to actually implement the program. As hyperinflation set in, tax revenues and government salaries were eroded. A project critically reliant on intelligent intervention by state managers had instead shattered the capability of the government to design and enact new macroeconomic policy.

State capacity was equally important in the Bolivian economic program. Here, however, the policy makers responsible for the 1985 New Economic Policy recognized the ravages wrought to government power by the previous period of hyperinflation. They immediately sought to replenish revenues, partly by raising gasoline prices and then raiding the coffers of the state oil company, and later by implementing a new regressive tax system. Policy attention was limited to very few variables: Rather than directing prices or production, the government closed the fiscal deficit, supported the exchange rate, and persecuted labor. The limited focus proved appropriate—hyperinflation was tamed. But the continued weakness of the state meant that Bolivia was poorly equipped to tackle the subsequent and perhaps more important task of reactivating economic growth.

Politics and state capacity remain crucial to any program of macroeconomic stabilization. Policy makers must consider whether economic measures are consistent with the creation and maintenance of class and sectoral coalitions. Any existing or newly acquired political support must be used to push through difficult medium-term changes. The state's ability to implement policy must also be taken into account before deciding on the policy itself. In these respects, heterodoxy falls short: Although its distributional intentions are to be applauded, its tendency to avoid real macroeconomic adjustment is too great and its demands on state capacity are too high. Orthodoxy's vision of a limited state seems more consistent with Third World realities, but its class biases and consequences tend to sharpen social divisions. The choices facing Latin American adjusters are therefore difficult and unappealing.

Toward the Long Run

Stabilization and adjustment have naturally been the focus of macroeconomic thinking and policy in Latin America in the 1980s. This "tyranny of the short run" has been understandable in light of both significant external pressures and accelerating domestic inflation. But if there is a reason to stabilize, it must be the hope that this will pave the way for another round of long-term growth. And stabilization efforts themselves must be politically and economically consistent with medium-term strategies for accumulation.

The road from stabilization to growth is the subject of much new research. As usual, orthodox adherents celebrate private investment as the motor and the market mechanism as the regulator of accumulation (Balassa et al. 1986; Khan and Reinhart 1990). Liberal and radical analysts disagree, often stressing the need for effective state intervention and improvement in the distribution of income (Amsden 1990; Berg and Sachs 1988; Pastor and Dymski 1990; Pastor 1990b; Pollin and Alarcon 1988; and Sachs 1987). In what follows, I focus on several policies that are essential for long-term growth, but tend to conflict with the requirements of short-run stabilization.

First and foremost is the need for lifting the external limits on domestic growth. In an immediate sense, this involves debt relief, particularly because many authors have now argued and demonstrated that the looming stream of future debt payments discourages both investment and output growth (Green and Villanueva 1990; Krugman 1988; Pastor 1991b; Sachs 1986). In the longer run, countries must develop more permanent sources of the foreign exchange necessary to import growth-enhancing capital and intermediate goods. Although some analysts remain fond of import substitution strategies (albeit amplified with new regional trading systems; see Pollin and Alarcon 1988 and Taylor 1986), most economists have become convinced that the best path lies in the promotion of exports (Edwards 1989; Sachs 1987).[8]

Orthodox economists, of course, see a direct link between exports and economic growth (see Balassa 1978; Krueger 1985). Other analysts, including Fishlow (1985), take a more structuralist view of the role of exports, suggesting that they are mostly important because they finance the critical imports needed for output expansion.[9] There is, moreover, sharp disagreement over the proper nature of export promotion policies. On one side, IMF-style economists suggest market liberalization—"getting the prices right"—as a way to remove distortions and allow private exporters to flourish. Others convincingly argue that "several of the most outward-oriented economies (such as Korea and Taiwan) have highly *dirigiste* governments, with highly regulated trade" (Berg and Sachs 1988:278). Despite these divergences in reasons and method, the general conclusion—striking in light of the previous dominance of inward-oriented analysis and policy—is that export growth will be crucial to resuscitating economic development in Latin America.

A new body of evidence also suggests that improvements in income distribution are a necessary component of medium-term restructuring. Older theories, both from the right and the left, had linked regressive distribution with relatively faster growth (see Ahlusalia 1976; Bowles 1987; Gurley 1984; Lecaillon et al. 1984; and Paukert 1973). A highly unequal distribution of income, however, can lead to strong pressures on government spending from poorer groups and thereby trigger macroeconomic instability (Sachs 1987). Inequitable rewards can also directly dampen output via negative effects on worker morale and effort (Dymski and Pastor 1990).[10] Equality, in short, may be central to forging the social accommodations necessary for longer-run productivity growth and accumulation.

A more effective state is also essential for growth. While an antigovernment attitude remains popular in Washington circles (see Balassa et al. 1986, and the discussion in Williamson 1990), most analysts agree that the East Asian "success story" is "not one of an unfettered market economy, but rather one of enlightened policy activism of national governments" (Sachs 1985:545). South Korea, for example, regulated private accumulation via a nationalized banking system and explicit export targets for private producers; the government also maintained strict controls on capital flight, effectively cutting off one avenue for capital to express its short-run displeasure with domestic policies (Amsden 1990:22). In Latin America, economic elites have dominated decision making with disastrous consequences for distribution, as well as for growth (see Pastor 1990b and Pollin and Alarcon 1988). In contrast, the East Asian state "had the power to *discipline big business,* and thereby to dispense subsidies to big business according to a more effective set of allocative principles" (Amsden 1990:16; emphasis in original).

Shrinking the state may, of course, be an important part of increasing government effectiveness, particularly if such downsizing allows the government to focus more effectively on critical policies and sectors. Privatization and other such measures need not work in a regressive direction; peripheral state enterprises could be devolved to workers, for example, stemming the drain on government coffers even as it spreads the ownership of assets. Government deficit-cutting is also consistent with a stronger state; revenue shortfalls, after all, essentially tell us that the government has proved unable to tax and redistribute surplus in socially desirable ways. Tax reform is also required, particularly measures (such as taxes on domestic wealth and earnings on flight capital; see Pastor 1990a) that challenge the traditional elite reluctance to contribute to national coffers. The bottom line is that the state's power should grow, not diminish, and that state administrative capacity, a weak link in Peru's heterodox strategy, should be a special object of attention.

These key components for long-run growth—a reduction in external dependence, a better distribution of income, and a stronger state—contradict many of the policies and consequences of short-run stabilization. The exchange rate freeze crucial to dampening inflation in Bolivia runs against the need for shifting resources to the tradeable sector. Adjustment often involves cuts in real wages, particularly if depreciation has been foregone as an export-enhancing tool. And stabilization's usual sharp reduction in government expenditures and salaries tends to weaken state power and capacity.[11]

The path from stabilization to accumulation is therefore fraught with problems and pitfalls. Policy change is necessary, but may be constrained by the need to maintain "credibility." In Bolivia, the government's fears of inflation kept the exchange rate overvalued and remonetization low. Public investment was constrained by concerns about the deficit and IMF insistence on expenditure-slashing. Sticking with stabilization priorities, however, impeded investment; business did not believe that the government would really pursue reactivation and therefore remained reluctant to stake its own capital (Morales 1990:9).[12]

The Peruvian heterodox model did attempt to blend the short and long term: Distribution was to be improved, social compacts forged, and state intervention increased. The García administration revived the Peruvian National Institute Planning and the Institute solemnly designed and issued a long-range strategy to promote nontraditional exports, develop agricultural self-sufficiency, decentralize production, and widen the domestic market (Instituto Nacional de Planificación 1986). Unfortunately, heterodoxy quickly unraveled due to exchange shortages, accelerating inflation, and increased social conflict. With double-digit inflation on a monthly basis, economic thinking and policy acquired a distinctly short-term focus. The paradox is that a program rooted in long-term structuralist insights had instead left the country with little future at all.

Conclusion

It has been a long and difficult decade for Latin America. Pressed by stagnant exports and rising debt service, growth has fallen and inflation has risen. Peru and Bolivia, early casualties in the "lost decade," took strikingly different directions in macroeconomic adjustment. Bolivia's orthodox approach quelled a hyperinflation but failed to restore significant economic growth. Peru experimented with debt service limits and price controls, managing in the process to widen social divisions and trigger an uncontrollable inflation.

In a simple balance, orthodoxy appears the victor: Bolivia's scenario, however dismal, seems superior to the chaos and poverty that now characterize Peru. In a deeper sense, however, each country's experience indicates the limits to adjustment posed by external dependence, rigid and unequal class structures, and ineffective states. In analyzing these factors and their contribution to inflation, structuralism seems quite appropriate. Unfortunately, the results of the heterodox application in Peru has discredited such thinking. Structuralism has become like Marxism: Abused by politicians claiming its mantle, it is now rejected despite the pressing need for its analytical power. And like Marxism, there may be quite a lengthy road to recovery.

The economy does not wait for ideological battles to be settled. In Peru and Bolivia, the poor still scramble for survival. International financiers continue to demand their share of a shrunken pie. Domestic capitalists are pleased about wage-cutting but remain reluctant to step up investment. Inflation may soon be tamed in Peru as well as in Bolivia, but for both countries, the long-term outlook is quite uncertain.

Notes

1. John Williamson (1990) refers to the near unanimity of opinion in these institutions as the "Washington Consensus." He includes in this policy consensus both the aforementioned policies of fiscal retrenchment and devaluation and longer-term measures such as liberalization and privatization.

2. For example, in the period prior to the debt crisis, IMF programs in Latin America (which often included devaluation measures) had mixed effects on growth and were generally associated with *higher*, not lower inflation (see Pastor 1987a, 1987b).

3. In Pastor (1989), I examine Latin American performance from 1982–1987 and argue that orthodox policies, particularly those implemented by the IMF, share a significant portion of the blame for the deteriorating regional economy.

4. This general embrace of heterodoxy coupled with an attention to seemingly orthodox concerns is also advocated in Taylor (1988).

5. The rational expectations view of this diminishing importance of past inflation is nicely discussed in Sargent (1986). He demonstrates that hyperinflations have sometimes been ended with relatively low output costs, a result that suggests to him that inertial inflation is not an important factor in hyperinflation. Whether this also suggests the irrelevance of inertial inflation—and, by extension, incomes policy—for more moderate inflations is the subject of debate; the rational expectations school argues that it does while most other economists are hesitant to apply the lessons learned from ending hyperinflations to more normal economic situations.

6. The data on nontraditional exports comes from Unidad de Análisis de Políticas Económicas (UDAPE) (1990:60). The figures given for export values differ slightly with the F.O.B. figures given in Table 4.1 but trends are quite similar.

7. Conaghan echoes this notion of economic limits on Peruvian social democracy when she completes her own review of the Peruvian and Bolivian experiences by suggesting that "the essential 'hegemonic' problem for Bolivian and Peruvian capitalists is that they are part of incompetent capitalist systems—economies that have failed persistently to produce the material base of a sustainable class compromise" (Conaghan 1991:19).

8. The argument for outward orientation has emerged, in part, from comparisons of East Asian economic performance with the Latin American record. Sachs argues, for example, that East Asia's relatively higher export-to-GDP ratios made those economies

more capable of absorbing the capital and interest rate shocks of the early 1980s (Sachs 1985). Berg and Sachs (1988) offer more direct econometric evidence that trade openness helped diminish the probability of debt difficulties, an outcome that also emerges from the empirical exercise in Dymski and Pastor (1990).

9. Fishlow backs up his assertion by regressing the growth rate of output in thirty-one developing countries on the growth rates of import and export volume; import volume turns out to be more statistically significant and has a coefficient value nearly three times that of export volume (Fishlow 1985:140). For a similar set of regressions involving just a Latin American country set, see Pastor (1990a).

10. Both Berg and Sachs (1988) and Dymski and Pastor (1990) econometrically associate more regressive income distributions with a *higher* probability of debt problems, a result consistent with this new argument that challenges the traditional growth-equity tradeoff. More direct tests on growth as a function of income equality also suggest a complementary relationship; see Berg and Sachs (1988:283) and Pyo (1987).

11. The conflict between short-term tools and long-term transformation is detailed in Mann and Pastor (1989) and Sachs (1987).

12. Dornbusch is likewise pessimistic that orthodox stabilization will produce the required "growth optimism" in either Bolivia or elsewhere (Dornbusch 1990:25–26).

Bibliography

Ahlusalia, Montek S. 1976. "Income Distribution and Development: Some Stylized Facts." *American Economic Review*, 66, 2.
Alvarez, Augusto. 1984. "Estado, Gestión y Objectivos de las Empresas Estatales: El Caso de la Empresa Siderurgica del Perú (SIDERPERU)." Bachelor's thesis. Lima, Peru: Universidad del Pacífico.
Amsden, Alice H. 1990. "Third World Industrialization: 'Global Fordism' or a New Model?" *New Left Review*, 182 (July–August).
Angell, Alan, and Thorp, Rosemary. 1980. "Inflation, Stabilization and Attempted Redemocratization in Peru, 1975–1979." *World Development*, 8, 11.
Arida, Persio, ed. 1986. *Inflación Cero*. Bogota, Colombia: Editorial Oveja Negra.
Balassa, Bela. 1978. "Exports and Economic Growth: Further Evidence." *Journal of Development Economics*, 5, 2.
Balassa, Bela; Bueno, Gerardo M.; Kuczynski, Pedro-Pablo; and Simonsen, Mario Henrique. 1986. *Toward Renewed Economic Growth in Latin America*. Washington, D.C.: Institute for International Economics.
Banco Central de Reserva del Perú. 1987a. *Memoria 1986*. Lima, Peru: Banco Central de Reserva del Perú.
———. 1987b. *Análisis de Largo Plazo del Sector Externo de la Economía Peruana, 1975–1986*. Lima, Peru: Banco Central de Reserva del Perú.
Berg, Andrew, and Sachs, Jeffrey. 1988. "The Debt Crisis: Structural Explanations of Country Performance." *Journal of Development Economics*, 29.
Beveridge, W. A., and Kelly, Margaret R. 1980. "Fiscal Content of Financial Programs Supported by Stand-by Arrangements in the Upper Credit Tranches, 1969–1978." *IMF Staff Papers*, 27.
Bollinger, William. 1987. "Organized Labor in Peru: A Historical Overview." *Occasional Paper Series*, No. 10. Los Angeles, Calif.: Interamerican Research Center.
Bowles, Samuel. 1987. "Profits and Wages in an Open Economy," in Mangum, Garch, and Philips, Peter, eds. *Three Worlds of Labor Economics*. Armonk, N.Y.: M. E. Sharpe.
Branch, Brian. 1982. "Public Enterprises in Peru: The Perspectives for Reform." *Technical Papers Series*, No. 37. Austin: Institute of Latin American Studies, University of Texas.
Bresser Pereira, Luiz, and Nakano, Yoshiaki. 1987. *The Theory of Inertial Inflation*. Boulder, Colo.: Lynne Rienner Publishers.
Bruno, Michael. 1989. "Opening Up: Liberalization with Stabilization," in Dornbusch, Rudiger, and Helmers, F. Leslie C.H., eds. *The Open Economy*. New York: Oxford University Press.

Burke, Melvin. 1979. "The Stabilization Programs of the IMF: The Case of Bolivia." *Marxist Perspectives,* 2, 2.
Cagan, Phillip. 1956. "The Monetary Dynamics of Hyperinflation," in Friedman, Milton, ed. *Studies in the Quantity Theory of Money.* Chicago, Ill.: University of Chicago Press.
Carbonetto, Daniel. 1987. "Marco Teórico de un Modelo de Consistencía Macroeconómica de Corto Plazo," in Carbonetto, Daniel, and Carazo de Cabellos, M. Inés, et al., eds. *El Perú Heterodoxo: Un Modelo Económico.* Lima, Peru: Instituto Nacional de Planificación.
Carbonetto, Daniel, and Carazo de Cabellos, M. Inés, et al., eds. 1987. *El Perú Heterodoxo: Un Modelo Económico.* Lima, Peru: Instituto Nacional de Planificatión.
Cardoso, Eliana. 1986. "What Policy Makers Can Learn From Brazil and Argentina." *Challenge,* 29, 4.
Cardoso, Eliana, and Dantas, Daniel. 1990. "Brazil," in Williamson, John, ed. *Latin American Adjustment: How Much has Happened?* Washington, D.C.: Institute for International Economics.
Cardoso, Eliana, and Helwege, Ann. 1992. "Below the Line: Poverty in Latin America." *World Development,* 20, 1.
_____. 1990. "Populism, Profligacy and Redistribution." Mimeograph. Medford, Mass.: Tufts University.
Carriaga, Juan. 1989. "Bolivia," in Williamson, John, ed. *Latin American Adjustment: How Much Has Happened?* Washington, D.C.: Institute for International Economics.
Cline, William R. 1983. "Economic Stabilization in Developing Countries: Theory and Stylized Facts," in Williamson, John, ed. *IMF Conditionality.* Washington, D.C.: Institute for International Economics.
_____. 1984. *International Debt: Systemic Risk and Policy Response.* Washington, D.C.: Institute for International Economics.
Conaghan, Catherine M. 1991. "Hot Money and Hegemony: Andean Capitalists in the 1990s." Mimeograph. Department of Political Studies, Queen's University at Kingston, Ontario, Canada. Presented at the Latin American Studies Association XVI International Congress, Washington, D.C.
Conaghan, Catherine; Malloy, James M.; and Abugattas, Luis A. 1990. "Business and the 'Boys': The Politics of Neoliberalism in the Central Andes." *Latin American Research Review,* 25, 2.
Corden, Warner Max. 1986. *Inflation, Exchange Rates, and the World Economy.* Chicago, Ill.: University of Chicago Press.
Cornejo, Roberto. 1985. "La Planificación y el Presupuesto en el Perú." Mimeograph. Lima, Peru: Proyecto de Gestión Pública, Universidad del Pacífico.
Cornia, Giovanni Andrea. 1987. "Adjustment Policies 1980–1985: Effects on Child Welfare," in Cornia, Giovanni; Jolly, Richard; and Stewart, Frances, eds. *Adjustment With a Human Face.* Oxford: Clarendon Press.
Cornia, Giovanni Andrea; Jolly, Richard; and Stewart, Frances, eds. 1987. *Adjustment With a Human Face.* Oxford: Clarendon Press.
Cuánto. 1990a. Webb, Richard, and Fernández Baca de Valdez, Graciela, eds. *Perú en Números 1990.* Lima, Peru: Cuánto, S.A.
_____. 1990b. *Suplemento Para el Ejecutivo,* No. 2. Lima, Peru: Cuánto S.A.

Bibliography

Dancourt, Oscar. 1986a. "Sobre las Políticas Macroeconómicas en el Perú, 1970–1984," *Documentos de Trabajo*, No. 12. Lima, Peru: Instituto de Estudios Peruanos.

———. 1986b. *Deuda vs. Crecimiento: Un Dilema Político.* Lima, Peru: Centro de Investigaciones Sociales, Económicas, Políticas, y Antropologicas, Universidad Católica.

———. 1986c. "Restricción Externa, Economía de Mercado y Economía de Guerra." *Economía,* 9, 17–18.

———. 1987. "Cuando se Abandonan las Políticas Fondomonetaristas," in *Reactivación y Política Económica Heterodoxa 1985–1986.* Lima, Peru: Taller de Investigación, Fundación Friedrich Ebert.

Dancourt, Oscar, and Yong, Ivory. 1989. "Sobre la Hiperinflación Peruana," *Economía* 12, 23.

Davila, Sonia. 1991. "In Another Vein." *NACLA Report on the Americas,* 25, 1.

Degregori, Carlos Ivan. 1986. "Sendero Luminoso: Los Hondos y Mortales Desencuentros." *Documentos de Trabajo,* No. 4. Lima: Instituto de Estudios Peruanos.

Delons, Jacques R., and Bour, Juan Luis. 1988. *Empleo, Recursos Humanos e Ingresos en Bolivia Una Propuesta Para la Acción.* La Paz, Bolivia: Unidad de Análisis de Políticas Económicas.

De Soto, Hernando. 1989. *The Other Path: The Invisible Revolution in the Third World.* New York: Harper and Row.

Diaz-Alejandro, Carlos. 1981. "Southern Cone Stabilization Plans," in Cline, William R., and Weintraub, Sydney, eds. *Economic Stabilization in Developing Countries.* Washington, D.C.: Brookings Institution.

Doria Medina, Samuel. 1987. *1987: La Quimera de la Reactivación.* La Paz, Bolivia: EDOBOL.

Dornbusch, Rudiger. 1980. *Open Economy Macroeconomics.* New York: Basic Books.

———. 1988a. "Mexico: Stabilization, Debt and Growth." *Economic Policy,* 3, 2.

———. 1988b. "Notes on Credibility and Stabilization." *National Bureau of Economic Research Working Papers,* No. 2790. Cambridge, Mass.: National Bureau of Economic Research.

———. 1988c. "Peru on the Brink." *Challenge,* 31, 6.

———. 1990. "From Stabilization to Growth." *National Bureau of Economic Research Working Papers,* No. 3302. Cambridge, Mass.: National Bureau of Economics Research.

Dornbusch, Rudiger, and Edwards, Sebastian. 1989. "Macroeconomic Populism in Latin America." *National Bureau of Economic Research Working Papers,* No. 2896. Cambridge, Mass.: National Bureau of Economic Research.

Dornbusch, Rudiger, and Fischer, Stanley. 1990. *Macroeconomics.* New York: McGraw-Hill.

Dornbusch, Rudiger, and Reynoso, Alejandro. 1988. "Financial Factors in Economic Development." Paper presented to the American Economics Association, New York, December.

Dornbusch, Rudiger, and Simonsen, Mario Henrique. 1987. "Inflation Stabilization with Incomes Policy Supports: A Review of the Experience in Argentina, Brazil, and Israel," *National Bureau of Economic Research Working Papers,* No. 2153. Cambridge, Mass.: National Bureau of Economic Research.

Dornbusch, Rudiger; Sturzenegger, Federico; and Wolf, Holger. 1990. "Extreme Inflation: Dynamics and Stabilization." *Brookings Papers on Economic Activity,* 2.
Drake, Paul W. 1982. "Conclusion: Requiem for Populism?" in Connift, Michael L., ed. *Latin American Populism in Comparative Perspective.* Albuquerque: University of New Mexico Press.
Dunkerley, James, and Morales, Rolando. 1986. "The Crisis in Bolivia." *New Left Review,* 155 (January–February).
Dymski, Gary, and Pastor, Manuel, Jr. 1990. "Bank Lending, Misleading Signals, and the Latin American Debt Crisis." *International Trade Journal,* 6, 2.
Edwards, Sebastian. 1984. "The Order of Liberalization of the External Sector in Developing Countries." *Princeton Essays in International Finance,* No. 156. Princeton, N.J.: Princeton University Press.
———. 1985. "Stabilization with Liberalization: An Evaluation of Ten Years of Chile's Experiment with Free-Market Policies, 1973–1983." *Economic Development and Cultural Change,* 33, 2.
———. 1989. "The International Monetary Fund and the Developing Countries: A Critical Evaluation." *National Bureau of Economic Research Working Papers,* No. 2909. Cambridge, Mass.: National Bureau of Economic Research.
Edwards, Sebastian, and Edwards, Alejandra Cox. 1987. *Monetarism and Liberalization: The Chilean Experiment.* Cambridge, Mass.: Ballinger Pub. Co.
Evans, Peter B., and Rueschemeyer, Dietrich. 1985. "The State and Economic Transformation: Toward an Analysis of the Conditions Underlying Effective Intervention," in Evans, Peter B.; Rueschemeyer, Dietrich; and Skocpol, Theda, eds. *Bringing the State Back In.* New York: Cambridge University Press.
Ferrand, Alfredo, and Salazar, Arturo. 1980. *La Década Perdida.* Lima, Peru: Sociedad de Industrias.
Ferrari, Cesar. 1986. "De la Teoría Económica a la Política Económica: Reflexiones en Torno a la Economía Peruana." *Socialismo y Participación,* 33 (March).
Fishlow, Albert. 1985. "The State of Latin American Economics," in Inter-American Development Bank. *Economic and Social Progress in Latin America; External Debt: Crisis and Adjustment.* Washington, D.C.: Inter-American Development Bank.
Fitzgerald, E.V.K. 1976. *The State and Economic Development: Peru Since 1968.* Cambridge, Eng.: Cambridge University Press.
———. 1979. *The Political Economy of Peru, 1956–1978: Economic Development and the Restructuring of Capital.* Cambridge, Eng.: Cambridge University Press.
Foxley, Alejandro. 1981. "Stabilization Policies and Their Effects on Employment and Income Distribution: A Latin American Perspective," in Cline, William R., and Weintraub, Sidney, eds. *Economic Stabilization in Developing Countries.* Washington, D.C.: Brookings Institution.
———. 1983. *Latin American Experiments in Neoconservative Economics.* Berkeley: University of California Press.
Gold, Joseph. 1970. *The Stand-By Arrangements of the International Monetary Fund.* Washington, D.C.: International Monetary Fund.
Green, Joshua, and Villanueva, Delano. 1990. "Private Investment in Developing Countries: An Empirical Analysis." Mimeograph. Washington, D.C.: International Monetary Fund.

Griffin, Keith. 1991. "The State, Human Development, and the Economics of Cocaine: The Case of Bolivia." Mimeograph. Department of Economics, University of California, Riverside.

Gurley, John G. 1984. "Some Elements of Marxist Theory of Socialist Economic Development," in Syrquin, Moshe; Taylor, Lance; and Westphal, Larry E., eds. *Economic Structure and Performance: Essays in Honor of Hollis B. Chenery.* London: Academic Press.

Haggard, Stephan, and Kaufman, Robert. 1989. "The Politics of Stabilization and Structural Adjustment," in Sachs, Jeffrey, ed. *Debt and Economic Performance: Selected Issues.* Chicago, Ill.: University of Chicago Press.

Hazleton, William A., and Woy-Hazleton, Sandra. 1987. "Sustaining Democracy in Peru: Dealing with Parliamentary and Revolutionary Changes," in Lopez, George A., and Stohl, Michael, eds. *Liberalization and Redemocratization in Latin America.* Westport, Conn.: Greenwood Press.

Heller, Peter S.; Bovenberg, A. Lans; Catsambas, Thanos; Chu, Ke-Young; and Shome, Parthasarthi. 1988. "The Implications of Fund-supported Adjustment Programs for Poverty: Experiences in Selected Countries." *IMF Occasional Papers,* No. 58.

Herrera, César. 1985. "Inflación, Política Devaluatoria y Apertura Externa en el Perú: 1978–1984." *Documentos de Trabajo,* No. 7. Lima, Peru: Instituto de Estudios Peruanos.

——————. 1987. "Política Antiinflacionaria, Desinflación y Reactivación," in *Reactivación y Política Económica Heterodoxa 1985–1986.* Lima, Peru: Taller de Investigación, Fundación Friedrich Ebert.

Horton, Susan. 1991. "Labour Markets and the Shock Treatment in Bolivia." Mimeograph. Presented at the Latin American Studies Association meetings, April, Washington, D.C.

Hunt, Shane. 1975. "Foreign Direct Investment in Peru: New Rules for an Old Game," in Lowenthal, Abraham F., ed. *The Peruvian Experiment: Continuity and Change Under Military Rule.* Princeton, N.J.: Princeton UniversityPress.

Instituto Nacional de Planificación. 1986. *Plan Nacional de Desarrollo, 1986–1990.* Lima, Peru: Instituto Nacional de Planificación (draft).

Instituto Nacional Estadística. 1988a. *Perú: Compendio Estadístico, 1987.* Lima, Peru: Instituto Nacional Estadística.

——————. 1988b. *Informe Económico, Marzo 1988.* Lima, Peru: Instituto Nacional Estadística.

——————. 1989. *Perú: Compendio Estadístico, 1988.* Lima, Peru: Instituto Nacional Estadística.

——————. 1990. *Informe Económico: February 1990.* Lima, Peru: Instituto Nacional Estadística.

International Monetary Fund. Various years. *International Financial Statistics.* Washington, D.C.: International Monetary Fund.

Jaquette, Jane, and Lowenthal, Abraham F. 1987. "The Peruvian Experiment in Retrospect." *World Politics,* 39, 2.

Jiménez, Felix. 1986. "El Significado Económico del Antimonetarismo o del Enfoque Heterodoxo No-Neoclassico." *Socialismo y Participación,* 35 (September).

_____. 1988. "Los Limites Internos y Externos al Crecimento Económico en el Perú, 1960–1984." Mimeograph. Lima, Peru: Fundación Friedrich Ebert.

Kaufman, Robert R. 1987. "Politics and Inflation in Argentina and Brazil: The Austral and Cruzado Packages in Historical Perspective." Paper presented to the annual conference of the American Political Science Association.

Khan, Mohsin; Montiel, Peter; and Haque, N. 1986. "Adjustment with Growth: Relating the Analytical Approaches of the World Bank and the IMF." Development Policy Issues Discussion Paper. Washington, D.C.: World Bank.

_____. 1988. "The Macroeconomic Effects of IMF-Supported Adjustment Programs: An Empirical Assessment." Mimeograph. Washington, D.C.: International Monetary Fund.

Khan, Mohsin S., and Reinhart, Carmen M. 1990. "Private Investment and Economic Growth in Developing Countries." *World Development*, 18, 1.

Klamer, Arjo. 1983. *Conversations with Economists*. Totowa, N.J.: Rowman & Allanheld.

Krueger, Anne. 1985. "Import Substitution Versus Export Production." *Finance and Development*, 2, 2.

Krugman, Paul. 1988. "Financing vs. Forgiving a Debt Overhang." *Journal of Development Economics*, 29, 3.

Krueger, Paul, and Taylor, Lance. 1978. "Contractionary Effects of Devaluation." *Journal of International Economics*, 8, 3.

Kuczynski, Pedro-Pablo. 1990. "Peru," in Williamson, John, ed. *Latin American Adjustment: How Much Has Happened?* Washington, D.C.: Institute for International Economics.

Lago, Ricardo. 1990. "The Illusion of Pursuing Redistribution Through Macropolicy: Peru's Heterodox Experience (1985–1990)." Mimeograph. Washington, D.C.: World Bank.

Lecaillon, Jacques; Paukert, Felix; Morrisson, Christian; and Germidis, Dimitri. 1984. *Income Distribution and Economic Development: An Analytical Survey*. Geneva, Switzerland: International Labour Office.

Leibenstein, Harvey. 1986. "The Theory of Underemployment in Densely Populated Backward Areas," in Akerlof, George A. and Yellen, Janet L. *Efficiency Wage Models of the Labor Market*. New York: Cambridge University Press.

Lessard, Donald R., and Williamson, John. 1987. "The Problem and Policy Responses," in Lessard, Donald R., and Williamson, John, eds. *Capital Flight and Third World Debt*. Washington, D.C.: Institute for International Economics.

Lupo, Jose Luis, and Larrazabal, Erik. 1986. "Una Medición Funcional de la Distribución del Ingreso en Bolivia: 1970–1985." *Análisis Económico*, 2 (December). La Paz, Bolivia: Unidad de Análisis de Políticas Económicas.

Malloy, James M. 1982. "Peru's Troubled Return to Democratic Government." Mimeograph. Hanover, N.H.: Universities Field Staff International.

Mann, Arthur J. 1988. "The Role of Tax Reform in Bolivia Under Economic Liberalization and Stabilization." Paper presented to the Harvard Institute for International Development (HIID) Conference on Development Reforms, Marrakech, Morocco.

Mann, Arthur J., and Pastor, Manuel, Jr. 1989. "Orthodox and Heterodox Stabilization Policies in Bolivia and Peru, 1985–1988." *Journal of InterAmerican Studies and World Affairs*, 31, 4.

Mayorga, Rene Antonio. 1978. "National-Popular State, State Capitalism and Military Dictatorship in Bolivia: 1952–1975." *Latin American Perspectives*, 5, 2.
McClintock, Cynthia. 1984. "Why Peasants Rebel." *World Politics*, 37, 1.
McClintock, Cynthia, and Lowenthal, Abraham F., eds. 1983. *The Peruvian Experiment Reconsidered*. Princeton, N.J.: Princeton University Press.
McKinnon, Ronald I. 1973. *Money and Capital in Economic Development*. Washington, D.C.: Brookings Institution.
_____. 1982. "The Order of Economic Liberalization: Lessons from Chile and Argentina," in Brunner, K., and Meltzer, A., eds. *Economic Policy in a World of Change*. Amsterdam: North-Holland.
Mercado, Rolando. 1988. "El Sistema Bancario y el Proceso de Reactivación Económica en Bolivia," in Toranzo Roca, C., ed. *La Reactivación Económica (Aspectos Financieros)*. La Paz, Bolivia: Taller de Investigaciones Socio-Económicas, Instituto Latinoamericano de Investigaciones Sociales.
Morales, Juan Antonio. 1987a. *Precios, Salarios, y Politica Económica Durante la Alta Inflación Boliviana de 1982 a 1985*. La Paz, Bolivia: Instituto Latinoamericano de Investigaciones Sociales.
_____. 1987b. "Money Creation and the Demand for Money During the Bolivian High Inflation of 1982–1985." Mimeograph. La Paz, Bolivia: Universidad Católica Boliviana.
_____. 1990. "Bolivia's Post-stabilization Problems." Mimeograph. La Paz, Bolivia: Universidad Católica Boliviana.
Morales, Juan Antonio, and Sachs, Jeffrey. 1988. "Bolivia's Economic Crisis," *National Bureau of Economic Research Working Papers*, No. 2620. Cambridge, Mass.: National Bureau of Economic Research.
Müller, Herbert and Associates. 1988a. *Estadísticas Económicas 1988*. La Paz, Bolivia: Instituto Latinoamericano de Investigaciones Sociales.
_____. 1988b. "El Comportamiento Económico del Primer Cuatrimestre." *Informe Confidencial Boletín*, No. 33. La Paz, Bolivia: Müller & Associados.
Paredes, Carlos Eduardo, and Pasco-Font, Alberto. 1987. "The Behavior of the Public Sector in Peru 1970–1985: A Macroeconomic Approach." Mimeograph. Washington, D.C.: The World Bank, Trade and Adjustment Policy Division.
Pastor, Manuel, Jr. 1987a. *The International Monetary Fund and Latin America: Economic Stabilization and Class Conflict*. Boulder, Colo.: Westview Press.
_____. 1987b. "The Effects of IMF Programs in the Third World: Debate and Evidence from Latin America." *World Development*, 15, 2.
_____. 1988a. "Ascenso y Caída de la Heterodoxia Peruana: Un Modelo Simple del Nuevo Estructuralismo." *Apuntes*, 23, 2.
_____. 1988b. "Hacia Dónde va la Política Económica?" in Augusto Alvarez Rodrich et al. *La Urgencia de Cambio: Propuestas de Política Económica*. Lima, Peru: Universidad del Pacífico.
_____. 1989. "Latin America, the Debt Crisis, and the International Monetary Fund." *Latin American Perspectives*, 16, 1.
_____. 1990a. "Capital Flight from Latin America." *World Development*, 18, 1.
_____. 1990b. "Debt, Stabilization, and Distribution in Latin America." Mimeograph. Los Angeles, Calif.: Economics Department, Occidental College.

———. 1991a. "Bolivia: Hyperinflation, Stabilization, and Beyond." *Journal of Development Studies,* 27, 2.
———. 1991b. "Private Investment and Debt Overhang in Latin America." Mimeograph. Los Angeles, Calif.: Economics Department, Occidental College. Presented at the XVI Congress of the Latin American Studies Association, Washington, D.C.
Pastor, Manuel, Jr., and Dymski, Gary. 1990. "Debt Crisis and Class Conflict in Latin America." *Review of Radical Political Economics,* 22,1.
Pastor, Manuel, Jr., and Wise, Carol. 1992. "Peruvian Economic Policy in the 1980s: From Orthodoxy to Heterodoxy and Back." *Latin American Research Review,* 27, 2.
Paukert, Felix. 1973. "Income Distribution at Different Levels of Development: A Survey of Evidence." *International Labor Review,* 108.
Paus, Eva. 1991. "Adjustment and Development in Latin America: The Failure of Peruvian Heterodoxy, 1985–1988." *World Development,* 19, 5.
Pollin, Robert, and Alarcon, Diana. 1988. "Debt Crisis, Accumulation Crisis, and Economic Restructuring in Latin America." *International Review of Applied Economics,* 2, 2.
Pyo, Hak-Kil. 1987. "External Dependence and Economic Growth: An Empirical Inquiry," in Kim, K. D., ed. *Dependency Issues in Korean Development.* Seoul: Seoul National University.
Ramos, Joseph. 1986. *Neoconservative Economics in the Southern Cone of Latin America, 1973–1983.* Baltimore, Md.: Johns Hopkins University Press.
Reid, Michael. 1985. *Peru: Paths to Poverty.* London: Latin AmericanBureau (Research and Action) Limited.
Rodriguez, Carlos A. 1983. "Políticas de Estabilización en la Economía Argentina, 1978–1982." *Cuadernos de Economía,* 19, 59.
Rowthorn, Bob. 1980. *Capitalism, Conflict, and Inflation.* London: Lawrence and Wishart.
Sachs, Jeffrey D. 1985. "External Debt and Macroeconomic Performance in Latin America and East Asia." *Brookings Papers on Economic Activity,* No. 2.
———. 1986. "The Bolivian Hyperinflation and Stabilization." *National Bureau of Economic Research Working Papers,* No. 2073. Cambridge, Mass.: National Bureau of Economic Research.
———. 1987. "Trade and Exchange Rate Policies in Growth-Oriented Adjustment Programs," in Corbo, Vittorio; Goldstein, Morris; and Khan, Mohsin, eds. *Growth-Oriented Adjustment Programs.* Washington, D.C.: World Bank.
———. 1989. "Social Conflict and Populist Policies in Latin America." *National Bureau of Economic Research Working Papers,* No. 2897. Cambridge, Mass.: National Bureau of Economic Research.
Sargent, Thomas J. 1986. "The Ends of Four Big Inflations," in Sargent, Thomas J., ed. *Rational Expectations and Inflation.* New York: Harper & Row.
Sargent, Thomas J., and Wallace, Neil. 1981. "Rational Expectations and the Dynamics of Hyperinflation," in Lucas, Robert E., Jr., and Sargent, Thomas J., eds. *Rational Expectations and Econometric Practice.* Minneapolis: University of Minnesota Press.
Saulniers, Alfred H. 1988. *Public Enterprises in Peru: Public Sector Growth and Reform.* Boulder, Colo.: Westview Press.

Schuldt, Jurgen. 1986. "Desinflación y Reestructuración Económica en el Perú, 1985–1986: Modelo para Armar," in Persio Arida, ed. *Inflación Cero*. Bogota, Colombia: Editorial La Oveja Negra Ltda.
———. 1987. "Desinflación Selectiva y Reactivación Generalizada en el Peru, 1985–1986." *El Trimestre Económico*, 54, 215.
———. 1988. "Hacia la Hyperinflación en el Perú?" in *Cuadernos de Investigación*. Lima, Peru: Centro de Investigación, Universidad del Pacífico.
Schydlowsky, Daniel M. 1986. "The Tragedy of Lost Opportunity in Peru," in Hartlyn, Jonathan, and Morley, Samuel A., eds. *Latin American Political Economy: Financial Crisis and Political Change*. Boulder, Colo.: Westview Press.
Sheahan, John. 1989. "Review Essay: Economic Adjustment Programs and the Prospects for Renewed Growth in Latin America." *Latin American Research Review*, 14, 3.
Sisson, Charles A. 1986. "Fund-Supported Programs and Income Distribution in LDC's." *Finance and Development*, 23, 1.
Stallings, Barbara. 1979. "Peru and the US Banks: Privatization of Financial Relations," in Fagen, Richard R., and Arnson, Cynthia, eds. *Capitalism and the State in US-Latin American Relations*. Stanford, Calif.: Stanford University Press.
———. 1989. "Political Economy of Democratic Transition: Chile in the 1980s," in Kaufman, Robert, and Stallings, Barbara, eds. *Debt and Democracy in Latin America*. Boulder, Colo.: Westview Press.
Stewart, Frances. 1985. "The International Debt Situation and North-South Relations." *World Development*, 13, 2.
Taylor, Lance. 1981. "IS/LM in the Tropics: Diagrammatics of the New Structuralist Macro Critique," in Cline, William R., and Weintraub, Sidney, eds. *Economic Stabilization in Development Countries*. Washington, D.C.: Brookings Institution.
———. 1983. *Structuralist Macroeconomics*. New York: Basic Books.
———. 1988. *Varieties of Stabilization Experience*. Oxford: Clarendon Press.
Thorp, Rosemary. 1986. "Políticas de Ajuste en el Perú 1978–1985: Efectos de una Crisis Prolongada," in Thorp, Rosemary, and Whitehead, Laurence, eds. *La Crisis de la Deuda en America Latina*. Bogotá, Colombia: Siglo Veintiuno Editores.
———. 1987. "The APRA Alternative in Peru." Mimeograph. Lima, Peru: Instituto de Estudios Peruanos.
Thorp, Rosemary, and Bertram, Geoffrey. 1978. *Peru, 1890–1977: Growth and Policy in an Open Economy*. New York: Columbia University Press.
Ugarteche, Oscar. 1986. *El Estado Deudor Económica Política de la Deuda: Perú y Bolivia: 1968–1984*. Lima, Peru: Instituto Estudios Peruanos.
Unidad de Análisis de Políticas Económicas (UDAPE). 1986. "Anexo Estadístico," in *Análisis Económico*. La Paz, Bolivia: Unidad de Análisis de Políticas Económicas.
———. 1987. *La Economía Boliviana Durante El Año 1986*. La Paz, Bolivia: Unidad de Análisis de Políticas Económicas.
———. 1990. *Estadísticas Económicas de Bolivia*. La Paz, Bolivia: Unidad de Análisis de Políticas Económicas.
Vallenas, Silvia, and Bolaños, María Emma. 1985. "Empleo Estatal y Perfíl de los Renunciantes de la Administración Pública 1978–1979," in Giesecke, Alberto, ed. *Reporte de Investigación: La Organización del Sector Público Peruano*. Lima, Peru: Proyecto de Gestión Pública, Escuela de Administración de Negocios para Graduados.

Webb, Richard. 1987a. *Perú: La Distribución del Ingreso en 1986*. Lima, Peru: Instituto de Planificación Nacional.
———. 1987b. "Country Study: Peru." Mimeograph. *Stabilization and Adjustment Programmes and Policies*. Helsinki, Finland: World Institute for Development Economics Research of the United Nations University.
———. 1990. "Comment on 'Peru' by Pedro-Pablo Kuczynski," in Williamson, John, ed. *Latin American Adjustment: How Much Has Happened?* Washington, D.C.: Institute for International Economics.
Weisner, Eduardo. 1985. "Latin American Debt: Lessons and Pending Issues." *American Economic Review*, 75, 2.
Wilkie, James W. 1987. "Bolivia: Ironies in the National Revolutionary Process, 1952–1986," in Lorey, D., and Wilkie, James W., eds. *Statistical Abstract of Latin America*, Vol. 25. Los Angeles: UCLA Latin American Center Publications, University of California.
Williamson, John. 1990. "What Washington Means by Policy Reform," in Williamson, John, ed. *Latin American Development: How Much has Happened?* Washington, D.C.: Institute for International Economics.
Wise, Carol. 1986. "Economía Política del Perú: Rechazo a la Receta Ortodoxa." *Documentos de Trabajo*, No. 15. Lima, Peru: Instituto de Estudios Peruanos.
———. 1988. "Peru in the 1980s: Political Responses to the Debt Crisis." *Papers on Latin America*, No. 2. New York: Institute of Latin American and Iberian Studies, Columbia University.
———. 1989. "Democratization, Crisis, and the APRA's Modernization Project in Peru," in Kaufman, Robert, and Stallings, Barbara, eds. *Debt and Democracy in Latin America*. Boulder, Colo.: Westview Press.
———. 1990. *Peru Post-1968: The Political Limits to State-led Economic Development*. Ph.D. Dissertation. Columbia University.
World Bank. 1985. *Peru: Country Economic Memorandum*. Washington, D.C.: World Bank.
———. 1989. *Peru: Policies to Stop Hyperinflation and Initiate Economic Recovery*. Washington, D.C.: World Bank.
———. Various Years. *World Debt Tables*. Washington, D.C.: World Bank.

Index

Agricultural sector
  and flexible prices, 64(n12), 101(n5)
  and income distribution, 64(n19)
  in Peru, 48, 50, 63(n8), 115
  and structural adjustment, 53
American Popular Revolutionary Alliance (APRA), 108, 118, 136
AP. See Popular Action party
APRA. See American Popular Revolutionary Alliance
Argentina
  and credibility, 37(n15)
  exchange rate targeting in, 30(table)
  heterodoxy in, 67, 91
  macroeconomic performance in, 3(table)
  macroeconomic policy in, 1–2, 27, 29–33, 111
  politics in, 61
Austral program, 2

Balance of payments
  and Bolivian economic structure, 69–75, 73(figure), 91–92
  and heterodox models, 41–42, 43(fig.), 44(fig.), 47(fig.), 52, 55(fig.), 63(n6)
  monetary model of, 17–20, 34, 36(nn 2, 3, 5, 6)
  and Peru, 122
  See also Exchange rate; Trade
Banks
  Bolivian, 98, 106(n37)
  and heterodoxy, 49
  nationalization of Peruvian, 8, 12, 62, 126, 151, 152–153

and Peruvian debt, 110
  See also International agencies
Banzer, Hugo, 76, 86
Belaúnde Terry, Fernando, 7, 107, 110, 136
Berg, Andrew, 157(n8)
Beveridge, W. A., 36(n5)
Black market, 83. See also Exchange rate
"Black September," 132
Bolivia
  analyzing orthodoxy in, 144–149, 156–157
  causes of inflation in, 82–87, 85(table), 86(table), 94–96, 95(table), 96(table)
  and credibility, 26, 128–129
  and exchange rate targeting, 33, 92–94, 93(table)
  and external sector, 149–150
  liberalization in, 28
  and long-term growth, 156
  macroeconomic policy in, 5, 7–8, 10, 11, 75–79, 143
  macroeconomics of, 68–75, 70–71(table), 73(fig.), 74(figs.), 76(table), 78(table), 81(fig.)
  New Economic Policy, 67–68, 87–101
  political and class issues in, 79–82, 103(nn 10, 14), 104–105(n26), 152, 153
Brazil
  heterodoxy in, 59, 67, 91
  macroeconomic performance in, 3(table)
  politics in, 62
  stabilization programs in, 1–2
Bruno, Michael, 27

169

Business
  and Peruvian heterodoxy, 125–127, 136–137
  and Peruvian orthodoxy, 116–118
  See also Capital; Investment

Capital
  Bolivian capital shock, 74–75, 74(Fig. 4.3), 76(table), 77
  and Bolivian orthodoxy, 90–91, 98
  and heterodoxy, 56, 62
  liberalization and capital flight, 33, 37(n17)
  orthodoxy and liberalizing the capital account, 27
  and Peruvian heterodoxy, 127, 147–148, 151, 152–153
  and stabilization programs, 143–144
  See also Credit; Investment
Carbonetto, Daniel, 128, 140(n25)
Carter administration, 76
Castro, Alva, 127
Causality tests, 82–87, 94–96, 129–132
  Granger-Sims, 84, 85(table), 95, 95(table), 129, 130, 131(table)
  and Peru, 141(nn 31, 32)
Central Bank (Peru), 123, 127
Central Obrero Boliviano (COB), 81
Chile
  adjustment program in, 27, 29–33, 37(n16), 111
  exchange rate targeting in, 31(table)
Class
  and Bolivian macroeconomics, 68, 75–77, 79–82, 89–90, 99
  heterodoxy and, 61–62
  heterodoxy versus orthodoxy on, 15–16, 34–35
  inflation and, 40
  and Peruvian heterodoxy, 125–127, 137
  and Peruvian orthodoxy, 116–118
  and stabilization programs, 7–8, 12, 100, 152–153
  See also Income distribution; Labor
Club of Paris, 90–91
COB. *See* Central Obrero Boliviano
Coca. *See* Drug trade

COMIBOL, 75, 89
Conaghan, Catherine, 157(n7)
Concertación, 8
Credibility
  Bolivian repression of labor and, 68
  and change in leadership, 128–129
  and heterodoxy, 59, 60
  and orthodoxy, 24, 26, 28–29, 37(n15), 148
  and policy consistency, 114
  and stabilization programs, 156
Credit
  availability and debt service reduction, 56
  and Bolivia, 5, 79, 90–91
  ceilings, 36(n5)
  Latin American dependence on, 151
  and orthodox policies, 35, 149
  and Peruvian heterodoxy, 7, 122, 137, 150
  See also Debt; External sector
Cruzado program, 2
Currency, heterodoxy and new, 2. *See also* Exchange rate; Monetary policy

Dancourt, Oscar, 65(n23)
Debt
  Bolivian external, 75
  Bolivian hyperinflation and debt servicing, 69, 79, 82, 99
  Bolivian moratorium on payments, 81, 91, 104(n20), 145, 149
  limiting, service, 46–48, 54–56, 60, 61, 144, 151
  and long-term growth, 154
  Peruvian external, 110
  Peruvian servicing of, 117(table), 118–120, 121–122, 136, 137, 139(n15), 150
  stabilization programs and servicing, 1, 7, 149–151
  See also External sector
Demand
  determining export, 63(n4)
  and heterodoxy, 48, 59, 61, 121, 146–147

orthodoxy and excess, 15, 16, 22, 23(fig.), 58
and Peruvian heterodoxy, 122–125, 137, 139(n16)
Democratic Front (FREDEMO), 132
Devaluation
 and Bolivia, 88, 150
 in economic models, 102(nn 7, 8)
 in heterodox models, 42, 44(fig.)
 and income distribution, 72–73
 and orthodoxy, 16, 17, 20, 24, 132, 145
 and parastatals, 64(n16)
 and Peru, 128, 130, 132, 136, 141(n33)
 and stagflation, 52–53
Dollarization
 Bolivia and de-, 77–79
 and Peruvian hyperinflation, 133
Dornbusch, Rudiger, 28, 59, 65(n26)
Drug trade, and Bolivia, 76–77, 101, 145, 148, 149–150
Dymski, Gary, 35

East Asia, 28, 37(n14), 100, 155, 157(n8)
Edwards, Sebastian, 27, 35, 36(n1)
El Niño, 115, 139(n10)
Emergency Social Fund, 105(n30)
Employment
 Bolivian decline in public, 105(n28)
 and Bolivian informal sector, 105(n34)
 and orthodox theory, 145
 See also Unemployment
Exchange rate
 and Bolivian inflation, 84–87, 94–96, 95(table), 96(table), 104(n23)
 Bolivian stabilization and overvaluation of, 68, 92–94, 93(table), 99
 freezing, 54, 56
 and orthodoxy, 20, 22
 and Peruvian heterodoxy, 123
 and Peruvian hyperinflation, 128, 129–132, 131(table), 140(n20), 141(n31)
 Peruvian official rates, 141(n30)
 and promoting nontraditional exports, 144
 role in inflation of, 148, 150

targeting, 29–33, 30(table), 31(table), 32(table), 37(n13), 145
See also Devaluation
Expectations
 and heterodoxy, 57
 and inflation, 56, 157(n5)
 orthodoxy and, 25–26, 36(n11)
 and Peruvian heterodoxy, 123
Export(s)
 Bolivian collapse in, 73, 74(Fig. 4.2), 99, 102(n9)
 Bolivian growth in nontraditional, 105(n34), 150
 demand, 40, 63(n4)
 and long-term growth, 154–155, 157(n8), 158(n9)
 Peruvian promotion of nontraditional, 113, 150
 promoting nontraditional, 60, 144
 See also Trade
Extended Fund Facility, 45
External sector
 and Bolivian hyperinflation, 67, 80
 and Bolivian orthodoxy, 90–91
 Bolivian overreliance on, 75, 77
 effect on Peruvian orthodoxy of, 115
 and long-term growth, 154
 Peruvian heterodoxy and, 62, 65(n23), 123
 stabilization programs and, 6, 7, 143–144, 149–151
 See also Credit; International agencies; Investment

Financial sector. *See* Banks
Fishlow, Albert, 154, 158(n9)
Food. *See* Agricultural sector
Foxley, Alejandro, 28, 35
FREDEMO. *See* Democratic Front
Fujimori, Alberto, 107, 133–136, 138, 148, 151

García, Alan
 class issues and, 8, 152
 and heterodoxy, 5, 10, 53, 60, 107, 108
 inconsistency and autocracy of, 121, 127–128, 137–138, 140(n26), 153

and inflation, 48
nationalization of banks by, 126
and politics, 118, 128–129
and servicing debt, 7, 150
GDP. *See* Gross domestic product
GNP. *See* Gross national product
Government
   state strength and policy
     implementation, 115–118, 127–128, 153–154, 155–156
   and trade problems, 36
   See also Credibility; Government deficits; Macroeconomic policy
Government deficits
   and Bolivia, 5, 7–8, 75, 77, 80, 82, 89, 98–99
   and heterodox models, 42, 54, 57, 65(n22)
   and Mexico, 2
   and orthodoxy, 16, 18–20, 24
   and Peruvian heterodoxy, 123, 124(table), 140(nn 17, 18)
   and Peruvian hyperinflation, 128, 132
   and state strength, 155
   See also Debt; Social programs
Granger-Sims causality test, 84, 85(table), 95, 95(table), 129, 130, 131(table)
Gross domestic product (GDP)
   Bolivian, 75, 77, 81(fig.), 91, 92
   Peruvian, 122, 128, 139(n10)
Gross national product (GNP)
   Bolivian, 69
   Peruvian, 108

Heterodoxy
   assumptions and theory, 8–9, 15–16, 39–62, 63(nn 3, 4, 5)
   and Bolivia, 77–79, 100
   evaluating, 143–144, 144–149, 156–157
   and external sector, 150–151
   in Latin America, 1–5, 67
   models for, 40–57, 43(fig.), 44(fig.), 47(fig.), 50(table), 51(table), 55(fig.), 62(n1), 63(nn 6, 7), 65(n20)
   and Peru, 108, 118–138, 139(n14). *See also* Peru

See also Macroeconomic policy; Stabilization programs
Horton, Susan, 90
Hurtado Miller, Juan Carlos, 136
Hyperinflation
   Bolivian, 67, 68–69, 87(table), 92, 101(n1), 145, 148
   in Brazil and Argentina, 2
   definition of, 101(n1), 141(n27)
   and inertial inflation, 157(n5)
   in Latin America, 12
   and Peru, 128–136, 134–135(table)
   See also Inflation

IMF. *See* International Monetary Fund
Imports
   Bolivian surge in, 92
   heterodox model and food, 48
   lowering, 56
   Peruvian, 110, 113
Import substitution, 60, 110, 154
Income distribution
   in agricultural sector, 64(n19)
   and devaluation, 72–73
   and heterodoxy, 56–57, 61–62
   and long-term growth, 154, 155, 158(n10)
   and orthodoxy, 24, 37(n18), 53
   and Peru, 119(table), 139(n16)
   and stabilization programs, 6–8, 16, 34–35, 37(n18), 100, 152–153
   See also Labor; Wage-price controls; Wages
Incomes policy. *See* Wage-price controls
Inflation
   and Bolivia, 67, 69–75, 79–87, 94–96, 95(table), 96(table), 103(n15)
   causes of, 2, 82–87, 85(table), 86(table), 94–96, 104(nn 18, 21, 22, 23), 129–132, 134–135(table), 157(n5)
   and class conflict, 40
   and exchange rate targeting, 29–33. *See also* Exchange rate
   and heterodoxy, 15, 34, 42, 46–48, 56–57, 57–60, 63(nn 5, 9), 65(n24), 146–147

Index

and orthodoxy, 15, 16, 19, 58, 145, 157(n2)
and Peru, 120–121, 129(fig.), 141(n27)
and Peruvian heterodoxy, 122–125, 128–136, 139(n14), 139–140(n16), 140(n17)
and Peruvian orthodoxy, 114–115, 136
sequencing liberalization and stabilization of, 27–28
Informal sector
and Bolivian orthodoxy, 90, 105(n34)
and Peruvian heterodoxy, 125
INP. *See* National Planning Institute
Institute of National Statistics, 139(n15)
Inter-American Bank, 121
Interest rates
and Bolivia, 97–98, 105(n31), 106(n36)
and heterodoxy, 50, 54
orthodoxy on, 27, 37(n13), 52
International agencies
and Bolivia, 76–77, 90–91, 149
and heterodox policies, 60, 61, 62
lending policies, 1, 7. *See also* Credit
and orthodoxy, 145, 149, 157(n1)
and Peru, 122
See also External sector; International Monetary Fund
International Monetary Fund (IMF)
balance of payments model, 17
and Bolivia, 67, 76–77, 88, 90, 98–99, 103(n15)
and credit ceilings, 36(n5)
on devaluation and inflation, 20, 157(n2)
and income distribution, 34–35
and orthodoxy, 1, 22, 52, 145, 157(n3)
and Peru, 110, 115, 122
International relations, 35. *See also* Credit
Investment
and Bolivia, 82, 91, 98, 106(n38)
and devaluation, 53
and heterodox model, 49, 54, 56, 64(n17)
and long-term growth, 154
and Peruvian heterodoxy, 125–126, 140(n22), 148

and Peruvian orthodoxy, 111–113, 112(table), 113–114
ISI. *See* Import substitution
IU. *See* United Left coalition

Kelly, Margaret, 36(n5)

Labor
and Bolivian heterodoxy, 80–82
and Bolivian politics, 100, 103(nn 10, 14)
Bolivian repression of, 68, 69, 76, 89–90, 104(n26), 152
orthodoxy and repression of, 28, 35
and Peruvian heterodoxy, 126, 137, 153
and Peruvian orthodoxy, 116–118
See also Class; Income distribution
Latin America
heterodoxy in, 67
macroeconomic policy in, 1–2, 12, 156–157, 157(n3)
macroeconomics of, 145, 146(table), 157(n2)
stabilization programs and income distribution, 34
state strength in, 155
Liberalization
Bolivia and trade, 89
and orthodoxy, 16, 20, 154–155
Peru and trade, 113, 132, 145
sequencing, 27–29, 37(n14)
"Liberty Movement," 126

Macroeconomic policy
analyzing, 5–13, 15–16, 39–40, 143–149
Bolivian, 75–79, 87–101
and external sector, 149–151
flexibility versus inconsistency in, 147
heterodox model, 40–62
importance of consistency in, 114, 115, 127–128, 140(n24)
in Latin America, 1–5
and long-term growth, 6–7, 9–10, 154–156
orthodox model, 16–35
Peruvian heterodoxy, 118–132, 136–138

Peruvian orthodoxy, 108–118, 136, 138(n4)
and political issues, 86–87, 132–136, 151–154. *See also* Politics
See also Heterodoxy; Orthodoxy
Menem, Carlos, 133
Mercado Unico de Cambio (MUC), 141(n30)
Mexico, 2–5, 4(table), 61, 137, 147
Mining
  Bolivian, 75, 101(n3)
  and Peru, 110
  See also Tin
Ministry of Economics and Finance (Peru), 127
Monetarism, 15, 16. *See also* Orthodoxy
Monetary policy
  and Bolivian capital shock, 75
  and Bolivian inflation, 82–87, 83(table), 94–98, 95(table), 96(table), 97(table), 99–100, 104(n21)
  and financing Bolivian social programs, 80
  and heterodoxy, 60, 61
  and Peruvian heterodoxy, 123
  and Peruvian hyperinflation, 128, 129–132, 131(table)
  and pricing behavior, 63(n3)
  role in inflation of, 148
  See also Inflation
Morales, Juan Antonio, 84, 85, 89, 104(nn 22, 23)
MUC. *See* Mercado Unico de Cambio

Nationalization
  of Bolivian mines and industries, 75, 76
  of Peruvian banks, 8, 12, 62, 126, 151, 152–153
National Planning Institute (INP; Peru), 115, 127, 140(n24), 156
National Tripartite Commission, 116
Neoclassicism, 16, 25
Neoliberalism, 136
NEP. *See* New Economic Policy
New Economic Policy (NEP; Bolivia), 87–91
  and limiting debt service, 149
  outcomes of, 11, 67–68, 91–101, 143
  and promoting nontraditional exports, 150

Orthodoxy
  assumptions and theory, 8, 15, 16–35, 39, 58
  and Bolivia, 67–68, 87–101
  evaluating, 143–144, 144–149, 156–157
  and external sector, 149–150, 157(n1)
  and Latin American policy, 1–5
  and long-term growth, 154–155, 158(n12)
  models, 17–24, 22(fig.), 23(fig.), 29, 36(nn 2, 3, 5, 6, 9, 10, 11), 37(n12)
  and Peru, 45, 107–108, 108–118, 120, 132–133, 136
  and stagflation, 52–53
  See also Macroeconomic policy; Stabilization programs

Parastatal sector
  orthodoxy on losses in, 52, 64(n16)
  role in heterodox model of, 48, 52
Pastor, Manuel, 35
Paus, Eva, 138
Paz Estenssoro, Víctor, 5, 75, 86–88, 100
Paz Zamora, Jaime, 99, 100, 151
Peru
  analyzing heterodoxy in, 145–149, 156–157
  exchange rates in, 93
  and external sector, 150–151
  heterodoxy in, 39, 48, 54, 57, 60, 63(n2), 67, 91, 108, 118–138, 139(n14)
  and hyperinflation, 128–136, 129(fig.), 134–135(table), 141(n27)
  and long-term growth, 156
  macroeconomic policy in, 5, 7, 8, 9, 10, 11–12, 107–108, 132–138, 138(n4), 143
  macroeconomics of, 46(table), 109(table), 116(table), 117(table), 119(table), 124(table)
  orthodoxy in, 45, 53, 107–108, 108–118, 120, 136

policy implementation in, 115–118, 127–128
and political issues, 62, 152–153
trade structure of, 45(table), 110, 117(table)
and wage-price controls, 59, 63(n8). *See also* Wage-price controls
Policy. *See* Government; Macroeconomic policy; Monetary policy
Politics
  Bolivian, 68, 75–77, 80, 94, 99
  and heterodox policies, 60, 61–62
  and liberalization, 28–29
  and Peruvian macroeconomic policy, 114, 118, 126, 132–136, 137–138
  and stabilization programs, 6, 7–8, 100, 144, 151–154
Popular Action (AP) party, 114
Popular Christian Party (PPC), 114
Populism, 137, 141(n34), 142(n35)
PPC. *See* Popular Christian Party
Prices
  controls and misalignment of relative, 61, 125
  elasticity of, 145
  flexible food, 64(n12)
  and heterodoxy, 9
  orthodoxy and indexing, 21–24, 36(n8)
  in Peru, 45, 63(n8), 110
  and Peruvian hyperinflation, 128, 129–132, 131(table), 136
  role in Bolivian inflation of, 83–87, 94–96, 95(table)
  See also Inflation; Wage-price controls
Privatization
  and Peru, 111–113, 132
  and state strength, 155
Production possibilities frontier, 21, 22, 22(fig.), 36(n9)
Protectionism, 19. *See also* Liberalization; Tariffs

Reagan, Ronald, 89
Reforms, Peruvian social, 110, 139(n11)
Reserve loss
  and crisis in Bolivia, 77, 149–150
  and heterodoxy, 56
  orthodoxy on, 19
  and Peru, 116(table), 117(table), 122
  See also Capital; Exchange rate
Reynoso, Alejandro, 28

Sachs, Jeffrey, 28, 69, 84, 85, 88, 89, 100, 142(n35), 157(n8)
Sánchez de Losada, Gonzalo, 94, 99
Sargent, Thomas, 84
Savings, heterodoxy and private, 60. *See also* Investment
Sendero Luminoso, 118, 125, 137
Sequencing
  and heterodox model, 59–60, 65(n26)
  and orthodox adjustment, 27–29, 37(n14)
Siles Zuazo, Hernán
  inconsistency of, 147
  and limiting debt service, 81, 149
  politics and class conflict, 75, 76, 77, 80–82, 128–129, 152
Simonsen, Mario Henrique, 59
Social democracy, 61, 152, 157(n7)
Social indifference curve, 21, 22, 22(fig.), 37(n12)
Social programs, Bolivian, 80, 105(n30). *See also* Income distribution
Southern Cone countries, 27, 28, 29–33, 34–35, 37(n13), 111
South Korea, 155
Stabilization programs
  analyzing, 5–13, 143–149
  in Argentina and Brazil, 1–2
  Bolivian heterodox, 77–79
  Bolivian orthodox, 76, 87–101. *See also* New Economic Policy
  and external sector, 149–151
  and long-term growth, 6–7, 9–10, 154–156
  Peruvian heterodoxy, 118–132, 136–138
  Peruvian orthodoxy, 108–118, 136, 138(n4)
  and politics, 86–87, 132–136, 151–154
  sequencing, 27–28
  See also Macroeconomic policy

Stagflation
  and heterodox models, 48
  and orthodoxy, 52, 120
Structural adjustment. *See* Orthodoxy
Structuralism, 8–9, 15, 120, 125, 146, 157.
  See also Heterodoxy
Subsidies
  and heterodoxy, 54
  orthodoxy on, 52
  and Peruvian export promotion, 113

"Tanzi effect," 123, 128
Tariffs
  Bolivian, 104(n24)
  and Peruvian trade liberalization, 113
Taxation
  and adjustment programs, 64(n14)
  and Bolivia, 82, 89–90, 99, 104(n25)
  and Peru, 123, 128, 140(n19)
  reform and long-term growth, 155
Taylor, Lance, 39
Technical issues, 6–7, 8–9, 143
Thorp, Rosemary, 65(n23)
Tin, 75, 76(table)
Trade
  and Bolivia, 69–75, 89, 105(n33)
  and external dependence, 144
  heterodox model, 41–42, 43(fig.), 44(fig.), 47(fig.), 52, 55(fig.), 63(n6)
  monetary model, 17–20, 34, 36(nn 2, 3, 5, 6)
  Peruvian structure of, 45(table), 110, 116(table), 117(table)
  problems and orthodoxy, 16, 21–24, 23(fig.), 36(n3)
  See also Balance of payments; Exchange rate; Export(s); Imports

Unemployment
  and Bolivian heterodoxy, 89–90
  and orthodoxy, 24
  See also Employment
United Left (IU) coalition, 118, 126
United States, 101, 105(n33)
  Treasury Department, 145
Unrest
  Bolivian, 76
  in Peru, 118, 148, 153
Uruguay, 27, 29–33, 32(table), 111

Vargas Llosa, Mario, 126, 132, 133, 136, 138
Velasco Alvarado, Juan, 10, 110

Wage-price controls
  and heterodoxy, 2, 46, 54, 58–60, 61, 146–147
  and Peruvian heterodoxy, 5, 122, 125, 128, 136, 137
  removing, 65(n26)
  and state strength, 153
Wages
  and Bolivian heterodoxy, 77, 80–82, 81(fig.)
  and Bolivian orthodoxy, 90
  Bolivian real, 103(n16), 103(n17), 104(n19), 105(nn 27, 28, 29)
  and orthodoxy, 24, 36(n10), 58
  in Peru, 61, 119(table)
  See also Wage-price controls
Wallace, Neil, 84
Webb, Richard, 45, 141(n29)
Williamson, John, 157(n1)
World Bank, 22, 90, 121